RELATIONS OF LANGUAGE AND THOUGHT

COUNTERPOINTS: *Cognition, Memory, and Language*
SERIES EDITOR: Marc Marschark

Rochester Institute of Technology
National Technical Institute for the Deaf

STRETCHING THE IMAGINATION
Representation and Transformation in Mental Imagery
C. Cornoldi, R. Logie, M. Brandimonte, G. Kaufmann, D. Reisberg

MODELS OF VISUOSPATIAL COGNITION
M. de Vega, M. J. Intons-Peterson, P. N. Johnson-Laird,
M. Denis, M. Marschark

WORKING MEMORY AND HUMAN COGNITION
J. T. E. Richardson, R. Engle, L. Hasher,
R. Logie, E. Stoltzfus, R. Zacks

RELATIONS OF LANGUAGE AND THOUGHT
The View from Sign Language and Deaf Children
M. Marschark, P. Siple, D. Lillo-Martin,
R. Campbell, V. Everhart

RELATIONS OF LANGUAGE AND THOUGHT

The View from Sign Language and Deaf Children

MARC MARSCHARK
PATRICIA SIPLE
DIANE LILLO-MARTIN
RUTH CAMPBELL
VICTORIA S. EVERHART

New York   Oxford
OXFORD UNIVERSITY PRESS
1997

Oxford University Press

Oxford   New York
Athens   Auckland   Bangkok   Bogota   Bombay   Buenos Aires
Calcutta   Cape Town   Dar es Salaam   Delhi   Florence   Hong Kong
Istanbul   Karachi   Kuala Lumpur   Madras   Madrid   Melbourne
Mexico City   Nairobi   Paris   Singapore   Taipei   Tokyo   Toronto   Warsaw

and associated companies in
Berlin   Ibadan

Copyright © 1997 by Oxford University Press, Inc.

Published by Oxford University Press, Inc.
198 Madison Avenue, New York, New York 10016

Oxford is a registered trademark of Oxford University Press

Library of Congress Cataloging-in-Publication Data
Relations of language and thought : the view from sign language and
deaf children / Marc Marschark . . . [et al.].
p.   cm. — (Counterpoints)
Includes bibliographical references and index.
ISBN 0-19-510057-3; ISBN 0-19-510058-1 (pbk.)
1. Children, Deaf—Means of communication.   2. Children, Deaf—
Language.   3. Sign language.   4. Cognition in children.
I. Marschark, Marc.   II. Series: Counterpoints (Oxford University
Press)
HV2391.R45   1997
306.4'4'0871—dc20   96-33363

1 3 5 7 9 8 6 4 2

Printed in the United States of America
on acid-free paper

For deaf children everywhere—
and the parents who love them

Preface

For as long as we have known each other, we have been interested in the relations of language and cognitive development in deaf children. Both literally and metaphorically, this discussion started when we were in a different place; and we have since gone our separate ways only to end up together again. Throughout this period of almost 10 years, we both have struggled with the questions of how deaf children's early experiences might differ from the experiences of hearing children and how variable early communication between deaf children and hearing parents might influence both language and cognitive development. Pervading all of our arguments and our research together has been the overriding agreement that researchers, teachers, and parents often underestimate the abilities of deaf children.

Through our work together on creative language abilities of deaf children, for example, we have demonstrated that many earlier conclusions about deaf children's cognitive flexibility, based on findings concerning their comprehension of nonliteral English, were biased and overly simplistic. True, deaf children often do not understand figurative expressions in English, and they use them only rarely in their writing. Within sign language, however, they produce metaphors and other nonliteral devices just as frequently as their hearing age-mates, and in some domains, their apparent creativity and flexibility are greater than hearing peers. Still to be resolved, both between us and in the field at large, are the extent to which such flexibility is a reflection of underlying cognitive flexibility as opposed to a purely linguistic flexibility "provided by" sign language and how we identify valid predictors of which deaf children will show linguistic and cognitive adaptability and which will not. The results of these inquiries will have implications far beyond our original domain of investigation.

When we first started discussing the possibility of putting together a Counterpoints project on language and cognitive development of deaf children, we thought it would be an excellent way to answer some of these continuing questions and resolve our own disagreements and problems. This attempt at group therapy proved to be far more than we bargained for, and in hindsight, we should have expected that to happen. Ruth Campbell, Diane Lillo-Martin, and Pat Siple are all acknowledged experts in their fields. While we knew their work and saw it as dovetailing well on this topic, we never imagined the depth and breadth of their insights into the language and cognition of deaf children. The discussion became one not only of interactions of these domains during development but also of the contributions of human cognition to language, of human language to cognition, and of early social and perceptual experience to growth in all domains.

The result was a group dynamic that went far beyond what we had hoped in several respects. First, the amount of historical and theoretical background that each contributor provided in her own area of expertise made for a much clearer and cogent discussion (even if it meant rewriting our introductory chapter twice). Second, the way in which all three were able to cross over into the others' areas of expertise made the project more enlightening—and enjoyable. Third, our collaborators became so caught up in the issues that they offered to write mini-chapters for the concluding discussion, which was supposed to be our responsibility. These commentaries resulted in a more pointed and direct discussion of the issues than we could have provided (or had the nerve to provide) and truly brought the various threads of the multi-layered arguments together into whole cloth.

Taken together, the following chapters provide one of those rare events in which important investigators in a field are able to square off against each other in a context that promotes the seeking of common understanding rather than the defending of intellectual turf. Such opportunities are the raison d'être of the Counterpoints series, but this project was special. Not only did the contributors, rather than the organizers, take control of the format of the book, but also they took control of the discussion and circumscribed a larger and more complete area than we had envisioned.

At the outset of our collaboration, the single question submitted to the three contributors was: Does growing up deaf or having sign language as a first language affect children's cognitive development? From there, the journey ranged from theoretical linguistics to neuropsychology, from parent-child interactions to reading. As it turns out, the resulting volume presents a unique exploration of what has historically been one of the most central and difficult questions in philosophy and psychology: the linkage between what happens in the mind of the individual and what is communicated with others. Much of the discussion revolves around deaf children and sign language, as originally planned, but the applied and theoretical implications go to the roots of the study of language and thought and force us to challenge our belief systems as educators and scholars. For us, the experience has been as educational as it has been demanding; that makes it well worthwhile. There is nothing more that we can say other than to thank our contributors for a wonderful ride and let the reader take over from here.

We wish to thank Diane Clark, Harry Lang, and John Albertini for their comments on earlier versions of some of the chapters, Poorna Kushalnagar for indexing help, and Gus Kovalik for his assistance in the literature searches. We also express our appreciation to the many colleagues with whom we have discussed the issues raised in this volume. Their perspectives have helped to sharpen our focus and have made this possible.

Finally, a sad postscript. At the outset of this project, our group included Avraham Zweibel of the Bar-Ilan University, in Israel, then on leave in Toronto, Canada. Although we had never met Professor Zweibel, we had read his pioneering work on the contributions of heredity, early environment, and language to the development of deaf children. His work on deaf children's cognitive development was excellent. His argument about the influences of early environments and exposure to sign language within the family was superb. Known as a dedicated and delightful man, Avraham was excited about the project and looked forward to this discussion. Soon after beginning his chapter, however, he became seriously ill. Despite receiving medical attention in Canada, Israel, and the United States, Avraham Zweibel died in October 1994. With his passing, many people lost a trusted friend and valued colleague. All of us have lost the insight and inspiration of his work. He has been missed, and he will always be remembered.

Rochester, New York   M. M.
May 1996   V. S. E.

Contents

Contributors

Ruth Campbell, University College London, Chandler House, Wakefield Street, London, WC1N 1PG, England

Victoria S. Everhart, National Technical Institute for the Deaf, Rochester Institute of Technology, 52 Lomb Memorial Drive, Rochester, NY 14623 USA

Diane Lillo-Martin, Haskins Laboratory and University of Connecticut, Linguistics Department, 341 Mansfield Road, Room 230, Storrs, CT 06269-1145 USA

Marc Marschark, National Technical Institute for the Deaf, Rochester Institute of Technology, 52 Lomb Memorial Drive, Rochester, NY 14623 USA

Patricia Siple, Department of Psychology, Wayne State University, 71 West Warren, Detroit, MI 48202 USA

RELATIONS OF LANGUAGE AND THOUGHT

CHAPTER 1

Relations of Language and Cognition: What Do Deaf Children Tell Us?

Marc Marschark and Victoria S. Everhart

The issue of the relation (or relations) between language and thought is one of the oldest in philosophy, and in many ways, it was the issue that led to the emergence of psychology as a separate discipline. In Aristotle's time, the debate was about *analogy* versus *anomaly*. From his perspective, language development depended on analogy: that is, the assignment of words to meanings on the basis of their rational linkage—even if the details of that analogy had been lost over time due to changes in the language. The anomalists, in contrast, saw language as given by nature and the relations between words and their meanings as entirely arbitrary (see Bates, Bretherton, & Snyder, 1988; Vygotsky, 1934/1986, chap. 1, for discussion). In many ways, this contrast parallels the "nature-nurture" controversy and dovetails well with the more recent "modularity-interactionist" debate. Indeed, the language-thought issue and its corollaries emerge in every generation of psychological theory, even if the level of the arguments changes as a function of paradigm shifts and related advances in other fields.

In this and the following chapters, we hope to bring the language-thought discussion into clearer focus, both theoretically and practically, by placing it in the context of children who grow up deaf and by considering the influences of having sign language as the primary form of communication (regardless of whether one is deaf or hearing). The discussion is sharpened by the fact that it is carried on by contributors with specialties in different areas, all converging on a common interest on which each has conducted empirical research. It is further advanced by the fact that we are dealing with a natural situation that illuminates the essential linkages between language and cognition. Together, the process and content of this effort allow us to clarify (and challenge) some of the theoretical assumptions that have driven arguments on the matter for centuries.

Throughout the educational literature, and especially in the subfield that relates to children who are deaf, one can find a variety of attempts to integrate theory involving language-cognition relations with pedagogic concerns. Such aspirations are laudable, but many potential advancements have been hindered by the lack of empirical evidence and theoretical soundness that can withstand the tests of time and laboratory. In part, the problem (such as it is) has been that many investigators have sought *the* relation of language and cognition, whereas there are probably many such relations. As Karmiloff-Smith (1989) and Bates, Bretherton, and Snyder (1988) have suggested, it is likely that some language-cognition relations are specific to particular constructions or categories of language and to particular domains of cognition. Other relations are more general and apply broadly within and across languages and developmental environments. Bates et al. refer to this situation as *local homology* and argue that language-cognition relations vary over the course of development as well as across different content domains. As we will describe below, assumptions of this sort may prove more useful than views that envision a single direction of influence between language and cognition. In the meantime, one thing we can be sure of is that the historical lack of resolution of this issue does not make it uninteresting or unworthy of discussion. Although those who are on the front lines of providing services for deaf children may not always see the need for the theoretical grounding of educational methodologies, the kinds of work presented in the following pages hold important implications for practitioners as well as researchers across a variety of fields.

The story begins during the 1960s and 1970s, when researchers like William Stokoe, Ursula Bellugi, and Susan Fischer demonstrated that American Sign Language (ASL) and other signed languages have all of the characteristics of "true" languages (see Chapter 2). As the linguistic history books will show, those studies of ASL in the United States resulted in nothing short of a revolution in the education of deaf children.[1] With this now-obvious but then-astonishing discovery, educators were forced to confront the issue of whether or not they could adequately evaluate or understand the cognitive status of a deaf child (or anyone else for that matter) solely on the basis of the child's ability to function in a spoken and written language. Similar upheavals followed within the fields of linguistics and cognitive psychology as researchers struggled to determine whether their theories were general enough to account for language that was not spoken and for cognition that proceeded from different kinds of everyday experience. Interestingly, although the Piagetian tenor of the times proclaimed that language follows from cognitive development, the major thrust of developmental research on deaf children during that period focused on the ways in which early language experience affected early cognitive growth, not the other way around. Indeed, the blossoming recognition of sign language notwithstanding, many investigators continued to look to cognitive development in deaf children as a way to examine cognitive growth in the absence of language.

In this chapter, we will examine the primary issues that are raised by this historical and theoretical situation. First, we will consider alternative ways in which cognition and language may be related. Then, we will consider a sampling of empirical findings that have been offered in response to questions about language-thought relations in deaf children and the extent to which cognitive development of deaf children should be "the same" as that of hearing children. This chapter sets the stage for the following three chapters, written by individuals who have particular theoretical perspectives on the issues raised here. Each in her own area, Pat Siple, Diane Lillo-Martin, and Ruth Campbell articulate the evidence and arguments they find compelling in understanding the relations between language and cognition when viewed from the perspective of deafness and use of sign language. Experts all, their points of agreement and disagreement will highlight both what we know and what we do not know about these complex issues and point out the future directions for research that will clarify them. Consistent with the model of this series, the authors will then consider each other's perspectives in Chapters 5–8 and seek points of convergence—or at least consensus on where and why we do not converge.

Prior to our moving into these deeper waters, it is worthwhile to acknowledge that some of the topics we are confronting here touch on political issues as well as having psychological, linguistic, and educational implications. Although we do not shy away from the political issues, they are not the focus of our concern. We leave such topics to other commentators and emphasize that our agenda is the pursuit of scientific evidence that contributes to our understanding of language and cognition, particularly as they relate to the development of children who are deaf.

RELATIONS BETWEEN LANGUAGE DEVELOPMENT AND COGNITIVE DEVELOPMENT

Although the psychological processes of interest here transcend any particular age range, there is no doubt that the primary linkages between language and cognitive processes begin at birth, if not before (see Marschark, 1993, chap. 3). At least in the case of hearing children, early exposure to language in the context of socially, perceptually, and cognitively relevant experiences means that these domains necessarily will be interrelated from a young age. For deaf children, there also will be an early intertwining of social and cognitive development, but with a more diverse set of communication skills, the interactions will include different means as well as different ends. The inability of deaf children with hearing parents (the vast majority of all deaf children) to benefit substantially from exposure to spoken language likely will affect the course of development, varying in both magnitude and duration across domains. As a result, the natural interactions of language and cognition will differ in deaf as compared to hearing children and will vary more widely among deaf children than within a similar population of hearing peers.

Traditionally, hypotheses concerning the relation between language and thought have been driven more by theoretical concerns than by either educational or observational data. Several of these theoretical views are described below, all of which should be understood to be convenient simplifications. As the following chapters make clear, such theories serve as analytic tools, aiding us in describing various aspects of development; it should not be assumed that they will reveal any ultimate, unitary answers to the larger questions at issue here. Most of the following perspectives on language and cognitive growth have been around for some time in one form or another and have been described as parts of particular theories as well as by other reviewers (e.g., Bates, Benigni, Bretherton, Camaioni, & Volterra, 1977; Jenkins, 1969; Nelson, 1996; Piatelli-Palmarini, 1994; Tager-Flusberg, 1994). Some of these views also are described by Pat Siple and Diane Lillo-Martin in their chapters, and we will endeavor not to overlap too much with those discussions.

Language equals thought.   Perhaps the simplest view of language and thought is that they are essentially the same thing. This position is most frequently ascribed to American behaviorists, and especially to John Watson, who argued that thought is just subvocal speech. (The philosopher Herbert Feigl once remarked that Watson had made up his windpipe that he had no mind.) Although consistent with the observation of minute movements in the oral and manual articulators of hearing and deaf language users, respectively, during problem solving, the thought-as-language position usually has been ignored. This rejection follows primarily from the observation that an individual without language is nonetheless capable of thought. The related issue of whether or not an individual without language (a very rare event) has the same kinds of cognition as an individual who does have language will be considered in a later section.

Language and thought are independent. This view, most often attributed to theorists like Noam Chomsky and Jerry Fodor, suggests that the development of language and the development of cognition are distinct, depending on different underlying processes and experiences. Chomsky's early writings (e.g., Chomsky, 1965) provided clear direction in this regard, as he was the first to demonstrate that the relations (i.e., rules and derivations) within language were sufficient to account for many developmental and psycholinguistic phenomena that previously had been attributed to language users themselves. For Chomsky, language was "learned" by filtering out irrelevant and erroneous language examples from the larger corpus of correct language and determining which rules were the right ones for a particular language environment. The question then becomes: How much of that filtering depends on an innate or user-independent set of linguistic rules, and how much depends on experience and related cognitive functioning?

In support of this language-and-thought-as-independent position, now termed the *modularity hypothesis,* Diane Lillo-Martin makes a strong case for cognitive development being independent of any particular language or language modality. She argues that the language module is largely amodal and that differences between sign language and spoken language are largely superficial, "relying on the surface characteristics of the input." Lillo-Martin uses modularity theory as a way to deal with the apparent autonomy of grammar across languages (see also Bates et al., 1988). When we move into the realm of connections between a language module (and possible submodules) and a cognitive module (and possible submodules), the case becomes more complex—and more interesting. We then have to contrast the autonomous functioning of modules with the possibility of their interaction. The latter, *interactionist view* (discussed in depth by Siple in Chapter 2) could include a variety of possible relations between language and thought, some of which will be considered below. Nonetheless, the interactionist perspective is usually discussed in terms of the way language acquisition is shaped by cognitive development, not the other way around. In addition to that macro-level distinction, the following chapters consider whether the relations between language and thought in mature language users are necessarily the same as those found in children. Modules and submodules that can interact with each other in adults may be "delicate" enough in children that they can either develop or break down independently. There also may be domains even in adults where language and cognitive modules are more or less interactive (see Cromer, 1994, for arguments based on clinical cases).

Language determines thought. In Chapter 2, Pat Siple suggests that this position "has had perhaps the most profound influence on educational and social decisions concerning deaf individuals." In the form usually identified with the *linguistic determinism* and *linguistic relativity* theories of Sapir and Whorf, this perspective directly entails a correlation between language skill and cognitive skill (see Chapter 3 for discussion). One implication of this view is that individuals who have "inferior" (or superlative) language are expected to have "inferior" (or superlative) thought. Implicitly or explicitly, such a perspective has been used as a rationale for an emphasis on spoken language for deaf children by those who have seen sign language as little more than a set of pragmatic gestures. Even if the proponents of spoken language have changed the basis for that advocacy in the United States (toward advocating assimilation and English literacy), arguments of this sort continue to be used in countries of Western Europe and throughout the world. We suspect that they also still pervade the thinking of parents and professionals in this country who continue to have trouble accepting a visual-spatial language as functionally equivalent to a spoken-written one.

Diane Lillo-Martin writes that "despite their popular appeal, the two hypotheses, Linguistic Determinism and Linguistic Relativity, have been largely discredited through cross-linguistic study." She argues, instead, that differences in language that relate to differences in culture may be entirely accidental or "they may *reflect*—not determine—speakers' worldviews." The more interesting question for her is whether growing up with exposure to a signed language affects cognition in a way different from growing up with a spoken language. Indeed, that is one of the fundamental questions of this volume. While we fully agree with Lillo-Martin that any strong form of the Sapir-Whorf position appears untenable, it also seems clear that language can affect and guide cognition in a variety of ways. Much of what a child knows about the world, from religion to the habitats of penguins, is acquired through language. Children need never have encountered a unicorn, the Easter Bunny, or a member of a particular ethnic group to have confidence that they know all about them. The language in which information is expressed also can influence perception, memory, and cognition beyond the objective information itself (see, e.g., Carmichael, Hogan, & Walters, 1932; Intons-Peterson, 1996). The extent to which such effects prove to be of theoretical significance or end up as only interesting footnotes remains to be determined in coming chapters.

We would like to suggest that the reader entertain, for the moment at least, the possibility that a "weak" form of linguistic determinism is not so outlandish after all. It would stretch any theoretical view to suggest that language does not have a significant role in complex cognitive functioning. At minimum, therefore, we can acknowledge that individuals who truly lack coherent, rule-governed language would have cognitive processes somewhat different from those who "have" language. This suggestion need not imply that such a language has to be one that we would classify as a "formal" language. That is, we can imagine an internal or idiosyncratic communication system that nonetheless entails an arbitrary symbol system, internal coding, and manipulation and that permits an individual a full range of mental life (cf. Goldin-Meadow & Mylander, 1984). This suggestion also is not intended to imply that such an individual would lack thought or the potential for cognition in any absolute sense. We simply would like to leave open the possibility that, without a symbolic language of some sort, the nature of cognition will be lacking in some of its subtle or not-so-subtle aspects. Developmentally, this would mean that the cognition that occurs prior to the emergence of language or that occurs in a profoundly deaf child exposed only to spoken language (i.e., who may be "language deprived") would necessarily be of a different sort and in some ways perhaps less complex than that which is the case in normal development. For this position to be clear, we need to consider some alternatives.

Consistent with this view, Gopnik and Meltzoff (1993) noted at least three areas in which semantic development affects cognitive development. From general to specific levels of analysis, they suggested that (1) general language constraints can restrict or influence the decisions about which concepts are referred to by particular words; (2) specific linguistic structures can influence conceptual development; and (3) specific language patterns used by adults in interactions with children can affect conceptual development. All three of these dimensions can be observed in the prosodic, lexical, and grammatical features of language that parents use in communicating with young children and in the way that they label objects according to their assumptions about their children's cognitive abilities. This appears to be a clear case of language influencing cognitive development, even if it is *parental* language affecting *children's* cognition; and for Gopnik and Meltzoff, observations of this sort give strong support for an interactionist view of language and cognitive development. "What children hear apparently influences what they say. But, more significantly, it also influences what they do and perhaps how they think" (Gopnik & Meltzoff, 1993, p. 245).

Thought determines language. Most frequently, this position is identified with the views of Jean Piaget, whose writings suggest that cognitive development should be primary for the young child. From this view, shared by Pat Siple (see Chapter 2), the child brings to development a set of cognitive, not language, universals, and so it is cognition that drives or structures language. Similarly, Macnamara (1972), Slobin (1973), and many others have suggested that language maps onto the world, and thus correct language (grammar) develops through the co-occurrence of language with events rather than depending on feedback through language correction (cf. Brown, 1973). If this view is valid, then the ease of mapping what is being said onto what is being referenced should play a prominent role in determining what is talked about by young children, a point that figures prominently in Chapter 4 as it relates to language comprehension by eye and by ear. Marschark (1997) makes similar points with regard to the acquisition of metaphoric competence in young deaf and hearing children and the failure of sign iconicity to predict the rate of vocabulary development in children, even while it predicts learning in adults. In the latter case, Marschark points out that what appears to be iconic to an adult can be quite irrelevant to a child for whom the "correlation" may not be apparent for some number of years. Similar, unnoticed relations can be found in mature language users of English who have never taken the time to parse words like *antiseptic* or *submarine* that were learned holistically.

At this juncture, it is important to note that we can hypothesize cognitive prerequisites to language development without assuming a direct causal role (e.g., Gopnik & Meltzoff, 1993; Harris, 1982; Nelson, 1996). Thus, one does not need to find a strong correlation between language and sensorimotor development (from which all things Piagetian spring) to conclude that cognitive development drives language development in some ways, even if it does not determine it in any specific sense. That brings us to another possible alternative relation of language and thought.

Some other factor determines both language and thought.   Bates et al. (1977) pointed out that the observed correlation between cognitive and language development need not imply that one or the other was in the driver's seat. One possibility is that there is some other factor that influences or promotes development in both and thus may result in the observed relations between two domains that may be largely independent. It might be worthwhile to view Piaget's writings as coming from this perspective rather than the cognition-determines-language perspective. In Piagetian theory, the determinants of cognitive growth at any particular age are the result of children attempting to assimilate information they encounter and to accommodate their existing cognitive (and language?) structures to it. Indeed, it is the mismatch between new information and what is already known *(equilibration)* that stimulates active problem solving in infants as well as adults.

Early in development, according to Piaget, both cognition and language are promoted by a child's sensorimotor experiences. If we view such experience as influencing the development of both cognitive structures and language structures, we can explain similarities in complexity and reference in children's early vocabularies, as well as their growing problem-solving skills. At later points in development, however, both cognitive and language growth could be driven by qualitatively different kinds of experience. During the period of concrete operations and then the period of formal operations, there would be an epigenetic interaction between the child and the environment, such that their development both requires and reflects experience of differing levels of complexity. It is not essential that there be any simple one-to-one development between cognitive and linguistic domains in this view, but a common origin and interactions between them help to explain linkage between observations (e.g., in early expressive and referential vocabularies observed by Nelson, 1973).

Another possible common origin for both language and cognitive development could be the amount of processing capacity available to children. According to Pascual-Leone, many of the changes observed in development can be linked more closely to changes in processing mechanisms than to knowledge per se. As children develop greater mental and attentional capacity, they are better able to assimilate and accommodate (our words, not his) to information that is of cognitive and linguistic importance. There is certainly a connection between cognitive growth and language growth, and experience drives development in both domains. However, the primary changes that occur in children, and those that can give the appearance of qualitative, Piagetian-like stages, are of quantitative changes in information-processing capabilities and not anything inherent in the content of what is processed (e.g., Johnson, Fabian, & Pascual-Leone, 1989; see also Case, 1992). Ceci (1990) has made a similar argument involving central processing skill and the speed of encoding, which can be influenced by factors like practice, stimulus familiarity, and motivation.

At a more global level, the common root of cognitive and linguistic growth might not be in the child at all but may be inherent in the structure of the world and/or the phylogeny of human beings. Let us therefore expand the scope of the discussion one last time.

Language and thought are similar either due to the nature of their internal structures or the structure of the external world. If language and higher thought are both largely limited to humans who are raised in similar social and physical worlds (we leave tangential arguments about possible exceptions to other commentators), it does not seem so surprising that our perceptual, conceptual, and communication mechanisms are much the same, even if they differ in superficial ways. The essence of the following chapters thus can be seen as seeking to evaluate which ways are superficial and which are more central. Astronomers even appear to have made some related assumptions about the perceptual, conceptual, and communication mechanisms of nonterrans by choosing particular information and particular means of communicating that information from spacecraft sent to the stars.[2] At a more mundane level, the fact that human language and human cognition have developed in tandem phylogenetically lends some credibility to the expectation that they may have natural interconnections and interactions that are distinct from either of them and are perhaps synergistic in their effects. Once again, the nature of these relations may change over the course of development as the complexity of the user-thinker and the domain changes. Whether spoken language has any evolutionary primacy here as "human language" is a question addressed in the following chapters.

Although the changing nature of language-cognition relations is at the core of recent local homology models, the concept is traceable at least as far back as Vygotsky (1934/1986, chap. 4). For Vygotsky, the "genetic" origins of language and thought are initially independent, but the nature of development changes from being driven by biological factors initially to being driven by social-cultural factors later in development. Through this changing nature of ontogenesis, language and thought are mutually influential in different directions at various points in development.

> The "greatest discovery of the child" becomes possible only when a certain relatively high level of thought and speech development has been reached. In other words, speech cannot be discovered without thinking.
>
>   In brief, we must conclude that
>   1. In their ontogenetic development, thought and speech have different roots.
>   2. In the speech development of the child, we can with certainty establish a preintellectual stage, and in this thought development, a prelinguistic stage.
>   3. Up to a certain point in time, the two follow different lines, independently of each other.
>   4. At a certain point these lines meet, whereupon thought becomes verbal, and speech rational. . . .
>
> Schematically, we may imagine thought and speech as two intersecting circles. In their overlapping parts, thought and speech coincide to produce what is called verbal thought. Verbal thought, however, does not by any means include all forms of thought or all forms of speech. . . . We are therefore forced to conclude that the fusion of thought and speech, in adults as well as in children, is a phenomenon limited to a circumscribed area. Nonverbal thought and nonintellectual speech do not participate in the fusion and are affected only indirectly by the processes of verbal thought. (Vygotsky, 1934/1986, pp. 83, 86–88)

Bates et al. (1988) approach the concept of local homology more precisely, as a series of skill-specific relations that hold only for certain aspects of language and cognition and at certain points in development. Of primary interest to Bates and her colleagues is the point at which gestures give way to the first words and the ways in which early gestures might create cognitive and linguistic opportunities for language both within the child and within those around the child (see also Marschark, 1993, chap. 5). Thal (1991) has applied this view to clinical decision making with regard to atypical language development, and others have tied cognitive and language growth to each other in several specific domains relevant to normal development in deaf children (e.g., Dunlea & Andersen, 1992; Meier & Newport, 1990). Most important, such a view can accommodate both situations where there are strong relations between cognitive and language development (e.g., Slobin, 1973) and situations where there are not (e.g., Curtiss, 1981). Clearly there are constraints on cognition and language, both internal and external, that influence the course and timing of development at various points. To what extent are those constraints innate, determined by the "hardware" with which the child has to work and hence largely impervious to experience? Are those points crucial, and if so, to what extent might they be sensitive to signed versus spoken language and to the different experiences of deaf and hearing children during sensitive periods of language development (Clark, 1993)? These are key issues discussed in Chapters 3 and 4.

One element frequently left out of the cognition-versus-language-as-primary debate is the importance of environment, or experiential factors, independent of children's endowed "hardware" and "software." These factors might include individual-psychological variables, such as the emotions of hearing parents who want their deaf children to be able to "speak normally," as well as sociocultural-historical variables, like the cultural values of a newborn's family. In fact, many of the "observed" differences in thought ascribed to language by investigators like Whorf and Luria turn out to be culturally determined. Clark (1993), for example, draws on psychobiological theory in emphasizing the role of "the goodness of fit between the organism and its context" in interactions that affect development. In her view, like that of Bates, the timing of events is crucial because of sensitive periods in which a child may be biologically or psychologically ready for particular kinds of input that will influence future growth (see Chapter 2; Nelson, 1996; cf. Johnson et al., 1989). Clark emphasizes that the outcomes of various language-cognition-experiential interactions may be altered at later points in development but will develop more "laboriously" and may never develop to a comparable level of sophistication. From this position, it is important to consider how changes in one area synergistically impact development in all other areas, both directly and indirectly through bidirectional feedback loops.

Clark notes that early mismatches between many deaf children's communicative needs and their hearing parents' communicative abilities can result in relatively poor language skills prior to entering early intervention or more formal educational programs. Plasticity in development provides for later resilience, as language skills accelerate in more contextually appropriate environments, but there are lingering questions about whether or not late-learned language skills are the same as early-learned language skills (see Chapter 4; Newport, 1990) and, for that matter, about when "late" begins (e.g., Mayberry, 1993; Mayberry & Eichen, 1991). Not only are early-developing mechanisms such as discrimination and generalization forerunners of classification skills and category knowledge; they also play a central role in children's perceptions and conceptions of who they are and who (or what) significant others are in the world (see Chapter 2). The early environments of deaf children in hearing families may be just as rich as those of hearing children in hearing families or deaf children in deaf families, but the nature of their experiences are certainly different. The extent to which those differences are theoretically important as a precursor of later development can be determined only through the kinds of research described by Siple, Lillo-Martin, and Campbell. Before moving on to those chapters, we turn briefly to some background research that has helped to guide the current discussion and the current research that each of the authors brings to bear.

THE ROLE OF LANGUAGE IN THE COGNITIVE FUNCTIONING OF DEAF CHILDREN: EMPIRICAL FINDINGS

This section is not intended to be a comprehensive summary of research on cognition or language in deaf children but only a partial picture of research that has crossed the boundary between the two. In this context, we intentionally avoid issues relating to problem solving (Marschark & Everhart, 1995), intelligence (Marschark, 1993, chap. 7; see Braden, 1994), and creativity (Everhart & Marschark, 1988; Marschark & Clark, 1987), which we have dealt with elsewhere.

Looking over the existing literature, it appears that a lack of understanding about deaf children's language competencies and their role in cognitive development has led to a variety of methodological confounds and theoretical misunderstandings. Most notable is the fact, mentioned previously, that some investigators conducted studies with deaf children allegedly to examine cognitive development *in the absence of language.* Hans Furth, for example, who conducted pioneering research on the cognitive development of deaf children, saw his work as being generally enlightening for cognitive development precisely because it was conducted with children who "do not acquire functional language competence, even after undergoing many years of intensive training" (Furth, 1966, p. 13). The failure of many investigators to recognize (in both senses of the word) that deaf children might have language that was not spoken led down a garden path that still attracts educators and researchers around the world.

Perhaps the most popular paradigm for the study of deaf children's cognitive development and the possible impact of language has been the Piagetian *conservation task.* The success or failure of children in conservation was one hallmark of cognition for Piaget because it revealed children's understanding of the concepts underlying what they see, as opposed to their acceptance of the world in terms of its perceived attributes. In early studies of conservation, Furth (1964, 1966) found that school-aged deaf children lagged behind hearing peers in conservation performance by two to four years. He attributed such performance primarily to a lack of experiential diversity but claimed that language deficits were ultimately to blame because they prevented deaf children from having normal interpersonal interactions with others (cf. Vygotsky, 1934/1986). Rittenhouse and Spiro (1979), in contrast, attributed deaf children's difficulty with conservation tasks directly to the linguistic demands of the tasks. They found that hearing schoolchildren performed significantly better than deaf peers on a variety of conservation tasks and that deaf children enrolled in day school programs performed significantly better than deaf children in residential schools. Importantly, when the (signed) instructions were made explicit with regard to the dimension of interest, performance increased in all three groups and the observed differences were no longer reliable.[3] Nonetheless, a marginally significant advantage for hearing children over the residential schoolchildren led Rittenhouse and Spiro to argue that "the substantial amount of non-oral behavior to which deaf students in state residential schools are exposed because of the predominant use of sign language" leads to "cognitive confusion in the deaf student" (p. 509).

That conclusion is refuted (albeit not in a positive way) by the results of a British study by Lister, Leach, and Wesencraft (1988), who examined the conservation performance of hearing children as compared to deaf children who were exposed only to spoken language. They found that deaf children in day school programs and residential schools still lagged behind the younger hearing children by three to four years, with no differences related to school program. Those results suggest that "non-oral behavior" is unlikely to be the locus of conservation failure (see also Rittenhouse & Kenyon, 1991). Still unclear is the extent to which language fluency, rather than language modality, might be linked to conservation performance as well as other cognitive skills. That is, even if we cannot account for these findings with children in terms of the use of sign language or spoken language, we may still be able to explain some of the variance by examining fluencies within one's primary mode of communication. Until further research with younger children becomes available, we need to look to older students to address that question.

Parasnis and Long (1979) examined concrete and abstract reasoning and language abilities in a large group of deaf college students. They found that deaf males performed below what would be expected from 12th-grade norms for hearing males on a test of abstract reasoning, but there were no other reliable differences. Degree of hearing loss also was related to reading, writing, and abstract reasoning in males but not females. Sign language receptive skill was not related to performance on either reasoning task, but Simultaneous Communication (SC) receptive ability was strongly related to performance on both reasoning tasks for both males and females. This pattern of results suggests that better speech comprehension may be related to better cognitive functioning in deaf college students, although there are some gender effects. Arnold and Walter (1979) compared a group of deaf college students to a group of hearing students in a sign language interpreter training program. The two groups did not differ reliably in their receptive skills for either lipreading or Manually Coded English (MCE), but the deaf students performed significantly worse on tests of abstract reasoning and verbal reasoning drawn from the Differential Aptitude Test battery. Rather than attributing those differences to any cognitive differences between the two groups, Arnold and Walter concluded that the poor performance of the deaf students resulted in part from difficulties in understanding the printed English instructions.

Parasnis (1983) compared the concrete and abstract reasoning skills of deaf students who learned ASL at an early age from their deaf parents; deaf students who had learned to sign between the ages of 6 and 12 and had hearing parents; and a group of hearing students with hearing parents. Overall, she found no differences among the groups nor any interactions with gender on either of the cognitive tests. As in the Parasnis and Long (1979) study, abstract reasoning was related to SC receptive skills but not to sign language receptive skills. Abstract reasoning was significantly related to reading only in the early ASL learners, whereas it was strongly related to writing only in the later sign language learners. Concrete, spatial reasoning was not related to either reading or writing in any group. Overall, the finding that the native users of ASL and later ASL learners did not differ in their concrete or abstract reasoning skills suggested to Parasnis that having deaf parents and being exposed to manual communication at an early age do not have differential effects on the cognitive abilities of deaf learners. Zweibel (1987), however, reached the opposite conclusion. He examined measures of cognitive development and intelligence in three groups of deaf children coming from either families with deaf parents and deaf siblings, families with hearing parents and deaf siblings, or hearing parents and hearing siblings. Zweibel found that the deaf children with deaf parents and siblings (who used sign language in the home) performed better than the other deaf children and were comparable to hearing children on most measures. He concluded that early exposure to sign language is responsible for the "cognitive superiority" of deaf children of deaf parents (but see Marschark, 1993, chap. 7, for a review).

Finally, Dolman (1983) investigated the relationship between English syntactic comprehension and cognitive development, as assessed by tests of conservation, classification, seriation, and numeration. Using instructions that clearly indicated the dimension of interest in each task, he found that 7–15-year-old deaf children who succeeded in conservation tasks also had better syntactic skills. No differences were found among the deaf children as a function of whether they had early exposure to ASL or MCE. However, children who had learned ASL as their first language (from deaf parents) performed better on both English grammar and conservation tasks than children who had not received consistent exposure to any single communication method.

More recently, we have examined the problem-solving skills of deaf and hearing children using a form of the Twenty Questions game. In our first experiment, children in three age groups (7–8 years, 10–11 years, 13–14 years) played the game three times, using a board that had 42 colored drawings of possible "targets." Across all three age groups, deaf children were successful in the game (i.e., they found the target) significantly less frequently than hearing age-mates. The pattern of their questions revealed that, unlike hearing peers, the deaf children did not make use of constraining questions like "Is it an animal?" Instead, they tended to make specific guesses about which of the possible choices was correct. No consistent questioning strategies were found across children in the deaf samples (e.g., based on location, perceptual, or functional features), and results from an administration of the Porteus Mazes showed that the findings were not the consequence of any differences in impulsivity between the deaf and hearing groups, as there were no reliable differences found on that test. Interestingly, there was a significant interaction in performance related to whether or not the children had reported having played the Twenty Questions game before: deaf and hearing children who were familiar with the game performed equally well; when they were unfamiliar with the game, however, the hearing children nonetheless were able to play it successfully while the deaf children were not. Regardless of whether this interaction reflects general differences in problem-solving ability or differences specific to game situations (a possibility suggested to us by Elissa Newport), the result would seem to indicate a more flexible approach to novel problems in the hearing than the deaf subjects.

Further research on the use of category knowledge and hierarchical organization among deaf children remains to be done, but the fact that we found comparable overall differences in performance in an experiment involving deaf and hearing college students suggests that there are some basic differences in problem-solving strategies to be found between deaf and hearing individuals. In particular, preliminary results in another project suggest that category labels (and, we presume, category organization) may be less salient for deaf students than for hearing students. The fact that categories tend to be culturally determined and reflected in a society's language is not an irrelevant fact here, but the link between category representation within sign language and the representation of categories within the semantic memories of people who are deaf is still unclear.

Taken together, the above studies suggest that cognitive performance of deaf children and young adults does not depend specifically on fluency within spoken or written English, as some investigators have claimed, although it may be linked in some ways to language skill more generally (see Chapter 8). Clearly, however, there are a variety of contradictory findings across several popular paradigms. Some nonverbal paradigms sometimes have eliminated differences between deaf and hearing students on relevant tasks, but in other cases, significant differences remain. Delays in cognitive domains can be found for children who are exposed primarily to spoken language, as well as for those who are exposed to sign language (Marschark, 1993, chap. 7). Thus, although deaf children of deaf parents and hearing children of hearing parents would be expected to show equivalent performance on most cognitive tasks, that is not always the case. At the very least, such findings appear to rule out any causal link between language modality and cognitive abilities in deaf children (cf. Zweibel, 1987). Nevertheless, differences in the processing strategies employed by deaf and hearing children might provide for both advantages and disadvantages for deaf children in various domains. These strategies, in turn, might involve language coding (MacSweeney, Campbell, & Donlan, 1996; see Chapter 8).

In the coming chapters, Pat Siple, Diane Lillo-Martin, and Ruth Campbell provide broader and more in-depth examinations of the above issues as they relate to language development and cognitive development as well as language-cognition relations. More generally, Pat Siple first brings to bear her perspective as a cognitive psychologist who has conducted programmatic research in the psycholinguistics of ASL, as well as cognitive and developmental work relating to individuals who are deaf. Siple's first book, *Understanding Language through Sign Language Research* (1978), serves as a benchmark for many of the issues discussed in this volume. Here, she describes the similarities between signed and spoken languages and the ways in which the two affect language development at large. The relations between linguistic universals and cognitive universals are at the core of many issues raised in this book, and Siple's exposition of them provides a history of sign language research from the perspective of one who has long seen crosslinguistic studies as fertile ground for new discoveries. Focusing on the grounding of language development in cognitive development at several levels, she provides clear directions for future research pursuing the complex interplay of both domains and experiential-environmental factors.

As a linguist, Diane Lillo-Martin brings a different perspective to some of the issues raised in the present chapter and in Siple's. While most of her research has concerned the structure of ASL as it bears on linguistic theory (and vice versa), here Lillo-Martin takes a somewhat different turn, pursuing the question of whether signed and spoken languages might differentially affect cognitive development. She considers several levels of cognition, from perception to problem solving, in the corresponding contexts of differing levels of language analysis. In this venue, Lillo-Martin wrestles with the long-standing issue of whether cognitive differences observed between deaf children with deaf parents and those with hearing parents are related to having early exposure to sign language or are the result simply of having exposure to fluent language in any modality. The question is very much linked to her view of language and thought as independent, influencing each other only at relatively low levels. Presenting a model of bimodal language development within an amodal language module, Lillo-Martin provides several interesting counterpoints to the chapters by Siple and Campbell.

Ruth Campbell comes to the question of the relations of language and thought as someone who seeks to integrate neuropsychology and development with our understanding of language and cognitive processes. Drawing on her work with deaf and hearing children, as well as clinical neuropsychological cases, Campbell considers the ways in which being deaf might affect social functioning, perception, and memory. Separating auditory and linguistic components of spoken language from each other and from other aspects of communication, she also provides the perspective of a researcher in the United Kingdom, where educational and empirical approaches to deafness differ considerably from those familiar in North America (see Campbell,

1996). Campbell uses studies of lipreading and language perception to high-light points of convergence and divergence in the language and cognitive growth of deaf and hearing children. Her broad view of the influences of neuropsychological functioning on both domains provides additional insights into the issues raised by Siple and Lillo-Martin and brings an additional level of explanatory power (and complexity) to the discussion.

To the extent that spoken and signed languages follow the same lines of development, most observers would expect that they should broadly stand in similar relation to cognitive development. Depending on one's theoretical preference, however, hypotheses about the direction and degree of influence between language and thought may vary considerably. The following chapters clearly represent differences in such preferences and provide a wealth of information from alternative points of view. As the contributors will demonstrate, the theoretical questions are clear, even though the answers may be difficult. This situation motivates us to seek a common ground and a common understanding of the interplay of language and thought in children and adults. Throughout the remainder of this book, the points of convergence are put into sharp perspective by points of divergence. How completely the primary issues are resolved remains to be seen, and we therefore withhold further comments until the end.

NOTES

1. This change also resulted in the relatively sudden awareness of Deaf culture by the hearing community, even though deaf individuals have been making important contributions to society for a long time (e.g., Lang, 1993; Lang & Meath-Lang, 1995). But that is a different story.

2. Carl Sagan has noted that the information included on the *Voyager* and *Pioneer* spaceships was intended more for earth-bound American taxpayers than any alien cultures; it is extremely unlikely that those ships will ever be encountered by anyone or anything.

3. A variety of related findings have indicated that deaf children and younger hearing children sometimes fail Piagetian tasks either because they do not understand the language (e.g., marked and unmarked bipolar adjectives) or because they fail to recognize the particular dimension of interest. Neither of these indicates a lack of ability to conserve, even if it results in conservation failure.

REFERENCES

Arnold, P., & Walter, G. (1979). Communication and reasoning skills in deaf and hearing signers. *Perceptual and Motor Skills, 49,* 192–194.

Bates, E., Benigni, L., Bretherton, I., Camaioni, L., & Volterra, V. (1977). From gesture to the first word: On cognitive and social prerequisites. In M. Lewis and L. A. Rosenblum (Eds.), *Interaction, conversation, and the development of language* (pp. 247–308). New York: Academic Press.

Bates, E., Bretherton, I., & Snyder, L. (1988). *From first words to grammar.* New York: Cambridge University Press.

Braden, J. P. (1994). *Deafness, deprivation, and IQ.* New York: Plenum Press.

Brown, R. (1973). *A first language.* Cambridge, MA: Harvard University Press.

Campbell, R. (1996). Cognition and development. *Journal of Deaf Studies and Deaf Education, 1,* 215–216.

Carmichael, L., Hogan, H. P., & Walters, A. A. (1932). An experimental study of the effect of language on the reproduction of visually perceived form. *Journal of Experimental Psychology, 15,* 73–86.

Case, R. (1992). *The mind's staircase.* Hillsdale, NJ: Lawrence Erlbaum Associates.

Ceci, S. J. (1990). *On intelligence—more of less: A bio-ecological treatise on intellectual development.* Englewood Cliffs, NJ: Prentice-Hall.

Chomsky, N. (1965). *Aspects of the theory of syntax.* Cambridge, MA: MIT Press.

Clark, M. D. (1993). A contextualist/interactionist model and its relationship to deafness research. In M. Marschark & M. D. Clark (Eds.), *Psychological perspectives on deafness* (pp. 353–362). Hillsdale, NJ: Lawrence Erlbaum Associates.

Cromer, R. (1994). A case study of dissociations between language and cognition. In H. Tager-Flusberg (Ed.), *Constraints on language acquisition: Studies of atypical children* (pp. 141–153). Hillsdale, NJ: Lawrence Erlbaum Associates.

Curtiss, S. (1981). Dissociations between language and cognition: Cases and implications. *Journal of Autism and Developmental Disorders, 11,* 15–30.

Dolman, D. (1983). A study of the relationship between syntactic development and concrete operations in deaf children. *American Annals of the Deaf, 128,* 813–819.

Dunlea, A., & Andersen, E. S. (1992). The emergence process: Conceptual and linguistic influences on morphological development. *First Language, 12,* 95–115.

Everhart, V. S., & Marschark, M. (1988). Linguistic flexibility in the written and signed/oral language productions of deaf and hearing children. *Journal of Experimental Child Psychology, 46,* 174–193.

Furth, H. G. (1964). Research with the deaf: Implications for language and cognition. *Psychological Bulletin, 62,* 145–164.

Furth, H. G. (1966). *Thinking without language.* New York: Free Press.

Goldin-Meadow, S., & Mylander, C. (1984). Gestural communication in deaf children: The effects and noneffects of parental input on early language development. *Monographs of the Society for Research in Child Development, 49,* serial no. 207, nos. 3–4.

Gopnik, A., & Meltzoff, A. (1993). Words and thoughts in infancy: The specificity hypothesis and the development of categorization and naming. *Advances in Infancy Research, 8,* 217–249.

Harris, P. L. (1982). Cognitive prerequisites to language? *British Journal of Psychology, 73,* 187–195.

Intons-Peterson, M. J. (1996). Integrating the components of imagery. In M. de Vega,

M. J. Intons-Peterson, P. N. Johnson-Laird, M. Denis, & M. Marschark, *Models of visuospatial cognition* (pp. 20–89). New York: Oxford University Press.

Jenkins, J. J. (1969). Language and thought. In J. F. Voss (Ed.), *Approaches to thought* (pp. 211–237). Columbus, OH: Merrill.

Johnson, J., Fabian, V., & Pascual-Leone, J. (1989). Quantitative hardware stages that constrain language development. *Human Development, 32,* 245–271.

Karmiloff-Smith, A. (1989). Quantitative hardware stages that constrain language development. *Human Development, 32,* 272–275.

Lang, H. G. (1993). S*ilence of the spheres: The deaf experience in the history of science.* Westport, CT: Bergin & Garvey.

Lang, H. G., & Meath-Lang, B. (1995). *Deaf persons in the arts and sciences.* Westport, CT: Bergin & Garvey.

Lister, C., Leach, C., & Wesencraft, K. (1988). Sequence in hearing impaired children's development of concepts. *British Journal of Educational Psychology, 89,* 142–146.

Macnamara, J. (1972). On the cognitive basis of language learning in infants. *Psychological Review, 79,* 1–13.

MacSweeney, M., Campbell, R., & Donlan, C. (1996). Varieties of short-term memory coding in deaf teenagers. *Journal of Deaf Studies and Deaf Education, 1,* 249–262.

Marschark, M. (1993). *Psychological development of deaf children.* New York: Oxford University Press.

Marschark, M. (1997). *Raising and educating a deaf child.* New York: Oxford University Press.

Marschark, M., & Clark, D. (1987). Linguistic and nonlinguistic creativity of deaf children. *Developmental Review, 7,* 22–38.

Marschark, M., & Everhart, V. S. (1995). Understanding problem solving by deaf children. In T. Helstrup, G. Kaufmann, & K. H. Teigen (Eds.), *Problem solving and cognitive processes* (pp. 315–338). Bergen, Norway: Fagbokforlaget.

Mayberry, R. I. (1993). First-language acquisition after childhood differs from second-language acquisition. *Journal of Speech and Hearing Research, 36,* 1258–1270.

Mayberry, R. I., & Eichen, E. B. (1991). The long-lasting advantage of learning sign language in childhood: Another look at the critical period for language acquisition. *Journal of Memory and Language, 30,* 486–512.

Meier, R. P. & Newport, E. L. (1990). Out of the hands of babes: On a possible sign advantage in language acquisition. *Language, 66,* 1–23.

Nelson, K. (1973). Structure and strategy in learning to talk. *Monographs of the Society for Research in Child Development, 38,* serial no. 149, nos. 1–2.

Nelson, K. (1996). *Language in cognitive development.* New York: Cambridge University Press.

Newport, E. L. (1990). Maturational constraints on language learning. *Cognitive Science, 14,* 11–28.

Parasnis, I. (1983). Visual perceptual skills and deafness: A research review. *Journal of the Academy of Rehabilitative Audiology, 16,* 161–181.

Parasnis, I., & Long, G. (1979). Relationships among spatial skills, communication skills, and field independence in deaf students. *Perceptual and Motor Skills, 49,* 879–887.

Piatelli-Palmarini, M. (1994). Ever since language and learning: Afterthoughts on the Piaget-Chomsky debate. *Cognition, 50,* 315–346.

Rittenhouse, R. K., & Kenyon, P. L. (1991). Conservation and metaphor acquisition in hearing-impaired children. *American Annals of the Deaf, 136,* 313–320.

Rittenhouse, R. K., & Spiro, R. J. (1979). Conservation performance in day and residential school deaf children. *Volta Review, 81,* 501–509.

Siple, P. (1978). *Understanding language through sign language research.* New York: Academic Press.

Slobin, D. I. (1973). Cognitive prerequisites for the development of grammar. In C. A. Ferguson and D. I. Slobin (Eds.), *Studies of child language development* (pp. 175–208). New York: Holt, Rinehart, Winston.

Tager-Flusberg, H. (1994). *Constraints on language acquisition: Studies of atypical children.* Hillsdale, NJ: Lawrence Erlbaum Associates.

Thal, D. J. (1991). Language and cognition in normal and late-talking toddlers. *Topics in Language Disorders, 11,* 33–42.

Vygotsky, L. (1934/1986). *Thought and language.* Cambridge, MA: MIT Press.

Zweibel, A. (1987). More on the effects of early manual communication on the cognitive development of deaf children. *American Annals of the Deaf, 132,* 16–20.

CHAPTER 2

Universals, Generalizability, and the Acquisition of Signed Language

Patricia Siple

SOCRATES: And here I will ask you a question: Suppose that we had no voice or tongue, and wanted to communicate with one another, should we not, like the deaf and dumb, make signs with the hands and head and the rest of the body?

—PLATO, *Cratylus*

"Why do you study sign language?" That question is asked a surprising number of times of someone like me who did not grow up with deaf relatives and was trained as an experimental psychologist. There are two parts to my answer. In the applied arena, a solid base of fundamental research on the acquisition and use of sign language is crucial for making informed decisions about educational and social issues of concern to deaf people. The importance of this responsibility cannot be underestimated by the sign language researcher. It is the theoretical part, though, that brought me into sign language research, and it is the theoretical reasons for studying sign language that are the focus of this chapter.

The stage for the current theoretical interest in sign language was set in the 1960s by the pioneering work of William Stokoe. Stokoe (1960) argued that American Sign Language (ASL), while produced in a different modality, could be studied using the same principles employed to study spoken languages. He demonstrated that ASL signs were not irreducible holistic units but could be analyzed as composed of discrete elements corresponding to a phonetic and phonological description of language. Stokoe's work, resulting in *A Dictionary of American Sign Language on Linguistic Principles* (Stokoe, Casterline, & Croneberg, 1965), brought sign language to the attention of linguists and psycholinguists across the United States and, along with the work of Bernard Tervoort (e.g., Tervoort & Verberk, 1967), around the world.

Stokoe challenged American linguists to consider giving language status to ASL. Some accepted the challenge, and contemporary sign language research began as a search for cross-modality language universals. Language universals—properties shared by all languages—define what it means to be a language. If these universals could be demonstrated for ASL, then ASL, by definition, was a language. Fischer (1974a), working in this domain, assessed the language status of ASL against the universals set down by Chomsky and Halle (1968), Greenberg (1963), Hockett (1963), and Osgood (1963). In her paper, Fischer demonstrated that, with few exceptions, ASL followed the grammatical universals proposed by these authors. Exceptions included, of course, Hockett's (1963) universal that "the channel for all linguistic communication is vocal-auditory" (p. 8). Fischer concluded her paper with the suggestion that the proposed universals that also hold for sign language are true universals and that the others were "universal only within a given modality" (p. 204). With this kind of work, ASL quickly gained language status, and theoretical work on ASL began to focus on the modality question.

The major difference between spoken languages and ASL (and other sign languages) is the difference in modality of language perception and production. The question of interest became, "To what extent are proposed linguistic and cognitive structures and processes dependent on modality, or stated differently, which of these posited structures and processes are modality independent?" (Siple, 1978a, p. 3). This question characterizes the theoretical direction of most sign language research over the past two decades.

The logic of the theoretical work that focused on the modality question was straightforward. In the typical study, the goal was to determine whether some (set of) purported universal(s) that had been shown to hold for spoken languages also held for signed languages. If a characteristic of spoken language was also shown to hold for sign language, the characteristic was taken to be universal. If the characteristic was not shown to hold for sign language, it was described as modality dependent. The goal of this research was only partially met, however, in actual studies. The typical study usually contrasted one sign language (initially only ASL) with one or more spoken languages or sometimes with an actual proposed universal.

The gap between the typical study design and the goal of the work produced potentially flawed overgeneralization. The mechanisms of one sign language were taken to be characteristic of all sign languages; and in some cases, the sign language under study was contrasted with only one spoken language. There is nothing wrong with such a design, of course. The problem occurred in the generalization—the sweeping claim of universality, or even of modality dependence, when only one sign language was being considered. In many ways overgeneralized conclusions are understandable. Beliefs that reigned in the early days of sign language research certainly had an impact on the researcher. Manual gestures seemed more fundamental and therefore were believed to be more universal. The number and variety of sign languages has only recently become apparent with the rise of an international community of sign language researchers. A second factor that influenced sign language researchers was the belief that the structure of sign language was based on or dependent on the structure of the spoken language of the community within which it was embedded. Early sign language researchers would agree that many regularities were missed because of this common belief and because we were steeped in the knowledge of the linguistic structure of English and languages closely related to English. After intense study, we now know that ASL and other sign languages are often very different from the languages of their associated speech communities.

The languages of the world can be classified in many different ways, and universals that generalize to a particular language type have also been proposed: if a language is of type X, then property Y will hold. Languages are classified as to dominant order (subject-verb-object, for example), and languages with different dominant orders display different properties. Language modality is another type of classification. Generalization, then, may occur at different levels. Absolute universals hold, or have a strong tendency to hold, for all languages. Other characteristics of languages generalize to languages of a particular type. Still other characteristics generalize only to a specific language. As we will see, the level of generalization must be understood before it is possible to make claims about the fundamental question of the origins of language structures and processes.

In the present chapter, generalizations about language acquisition will be considered in an exploration of the relation of language acquisition to general cognitive development. An argument will be made that the issue of generalization must be considered for all characteristics of acquisition that are studied. In a final section of the chapter, a tentative conclusion will be reached that there is greater generalization, a greater probability of universality, at earlier and/or more abstract levels or stages of language analysis or processing and that generalization becomes more constrained at later and less abstract levels or stages.

WHY SEARCH FOR UNIVERSALS?

The search for universals has been undertaken with the primary purpose of providing information about the fundamental question of the origins of language behavior. Is language acquisition governed primarily by heredity and biological maturation, or is it governed by the environment of the child acquiring language? Universals of language acquisition, invariant patterns of acquisition across varying environments, provide support for genetic or biological origins. The search for modality independent universals—universals that hold for both signed and spoken languages—has generally been seen as a search for an innate, abstract language capacity, a capacity proposed to be uniquely human. Universals tied to modality of perception and production have generally been attributed to cognitive constraints on perception and production systems, whereas modality independent universals have been described as the result of innate, abstract principles of language acquisition. There is, of course, another possibility. Modality independent universals may result from innately determined, abstract cognitive constraints that are not sensitive to modality. Arguments in addition to modality independence are necessary to specify the origins of absolute universals.

The role of deafness and sign language has been considered in discussions of the origins of language and cognition and the relation between them at least since the time of Plato. Plato believed that knowledge is innate and that sensory experience merely serves to inform the individual about which of the things that are innately known are in the currently experienced environment. Because, according to Plato, knowledge is not obtained through the senses, lack of one sense should not affect one's capacity to possess language and knowledge. Aristotle, who argued that knowledge was derived from experience, forecast a different fate for deaf individuals. Lane (1976) says that Aristotle called the deaf "irremediably ignorant" (p. 79). If knowledge is derived through the senses, the absence of experience through one of the senses will deprive cognition. Whether language should be likewise impaired depends on the status of signed language vis-à-vis spoken language.

After a long history in philosophy, these two approaches to epistemology found their way into the newer fields of experimental psychology and psycholinguistics. At least four distinct positions on the origins of language and cognition and the relation between them have been described, and arguments about deafness and sign language have been produced in support of each position. Positions include (1) complete independence of language and thought, (2) dependence of thought on language, (3) dependence of language on thought, and (4) complete interdependence.

William James (1890) presented the position consistent with Plato that knowledge cannot arise from experience alone but must have an innate component. While the route to knowledge may differ from individual to individual, the knowledge is the same, and the route can be verbal or nonverbal. James cites a case of a deaf man who "had a very extensive command of abstract, even of metaphysical conceptions, when as yet his only language was pantomime confined to practical home affairs" (1892, p. 613). The account of this man, he argues, provides evidence of abstract thought without words and thus thought without, or before, language. Because the thought of this man is like that of others with different (language) experience, the structure of cognition, it can be argued, is innate.

Behaviorists have generally taken the position that thought and language are completely interdependent and acquired through experience. Watson, the "father" of behaviorism and champion of "blank slate" epistemology, described thought, or cognition, and language as one and the same thing (Watson, 1930). According to Watson, thought is talking to ourselves, and language (spoken or signed) is learned muscle habits. Evidence of covert, subvocal speech motor activity during thinking has been used to support this point of view. Interestingly, Watson also presented evidence of manual responses during the thinking of deaf people and described the presence of "finger language" during the dreams of a deaf-blind woman in support of his position.

The view on the relation between cognition and language that perhaps has had the most profound influence on educational and social decisions concerning deaf individuals has been a folk belief in the Sapir-Whorf hypothesis that we think in language and that cognitive ability depends on language. Thus, deaf people, who often do not fully acquire use of a so-called conventional language, were perceived as deficient thinkers. A corollary belief that sign language could only be used for communication about concrete objects and events added to the perception of deficiency. With this as the backdrop, the movement set in motion by Stokoe to bestow language status on ASL was especially significant. If ASL provided the capacity to communicate about abstract concepts and events and could be fully acquired by deaf people, there was no longer any reason to posit inevitable cognitive deficit.

While these positions are historically important, current thinking in psychology on the origins of language and cognition draws primarily from interactionist and contextualist positions that examine relative contributions of genetics and environment to the development of cognition and language. The interactionist position, following from Piaget, gives heavy emphasis to genetics. Development is described as the maturational unfolding of a genetic plan, with each new step, or stage, requiring input from (interaction with) the environment to "release" it. The primary data used to support the Piagetian position are the findings of an invariant order of acquisition of intellectual abilities across varying environments. The contextualist position, on the other hand, cedes a role to genetics but holds that the primary influence on language and cognitive development is the general environment or culture of the child. In this view, the course of development is determined by environment and culture; an invariant order of acquisition can occur only if the environmental determinants of development are similar from culture to culture. This view is exemplified in the Russian psychology of Luria (1961) and Vygotsky (1962, 1978), and in the work of Bruner (1975, 1983).

Furth (1966, 1973), working within the interactionist framework of Piaget, studied extensively the intellectual abilities of deaf students to provide evidence on the relation between cognition and language. Furth began with the premise that the majority of deaf children "do not acquire functional language competence" (1966, p. 14), where language is taken to be the spoken language of the larger community. He then developed nonverbal methods to test whether deaf students acquired each Piagetian stage, independent of language ability, and, if so, whether the same invariant order of stages applied to these deaf students "without language." Piaget (1955, 1962; Flavell, 1963) has argued that cognition is fundamental and can occur without language, at least up to the stage of formal operations. Intellectual ability is first acquired and expressed as sensorimotor representations and responses. Later, the stages of acquisition of sensorimotor intellectual ability are recapitulated in symbolic representations and language behavior. Furth demonstrated that deaf students do acquire the intellectual abilities set down by Piaget in the order he described. Acquisition was slower, however, and Furth ascribed this to the different sociocultural environment of the deaf child, which often does not generally permit the interaction necessary for intellectual advancement. Thus, Furth's results were consistent with Piaget's theory that cognitive, intellectual abilities are acquired in an invariant sequence, following a genetic plan, and that specific types of interaction with the environment are necessary to progress through the sequence. Language is not necessary for cognitive development but builds on it.

In disagreement with Piaget over the role of genetics in development, Vygotsky (1962, 1978) presented a theoretical approach to cognitive development within the contextualist framework. Vygotsky, too, turned to deafness in support of his position. According to Vygotsky, some types of thought are rooted in biology; they are consistently found across cultures and can be traced phylogenetically. Up to a point, thought is biologically determined. Language—that of others as well as one's own—can change the course of development, however, and language differs across environment and culture. Cognitive activity that is guided by language is, thus, determined by environment and culture. Language, according to Vygotsky, determines conceptual development and knowledge representation. Deaf children, because of their reduced verbal ability, will develop different conceptual representations of the world and may never achieve abstract conceptual thought. White (1987), taking a Vygotskian perspective, argues that deaf children are different from hearing children, not just delayed relative to them, because of their lack of conventional language during development.

In addition to interactionist and contextualist positions, the contemporary study of language acquisition has been greatly influenced by the nativist theory of Chomsky (1965, 1982, 1986). Chomsky has proposed that language knowledge is modular and independent of cognition. The innate language module, or Universal Grammar (UG), proposed by Chomsky includes general and abstract universal principles of all languages, supplemented by a set of parameters within UG that limit and specify options for classes of languages. Parameters have default values and are otherwise set through interaction with specific language input. Thus, Chomsky's position most closely resembles Piaget's, except that language is fundamental and on an equal footing with cognition for Chomsky, whereas, for Piaget, cognition is fundamental and language is dependent on earlier cognitive development. Since the universal principles and parameters described by Chomsky are abstract, they should hold for signed as well as spoken languages, and signed languages provide an important test of the theory (Lillo-Martin, 1991; Lillo-Martin & Klima, 1990).

Few today would argue that all knowledge is innate or that all knowledge is derived from experience. The complex interaction of "nature" and "nurture" on the development of cognition and language, however, has yet to be worked out. Does input merely act to unleash a predetermined sequence of development? Or does input shape the very nature of language and cognition, relying on a few innate processes to get things going? One's epistemology has implications for one's attitudes toward deafness and the use of sign language, and the study of cognitive and language development in deaf children serves to inform epistemology. The question is made more difficult, as well, by the fact that linguistic and cognitive activities have some relation to each other and can serve as input to each other. Few would take the position that cognition and language are either totally independent or totally dependent on each other. This relation also needs to be worked out.

Data from deaf individuals and the study of sign language have been provided in support of all of the major positions on the origins of cognition and language and the relation between them. Can all but one of these arguments be wrong? Or is it that the positions that have been put forward are too sweeping? That none of the positions hold all of the time, but each of them may hold sometimes? As we sort through arguments concerning the relations among deafness, language, and cognition in language acquisition, we will see that the latter is more likely. When and how input influences language acquisition is not constant but differs for different aspects of language development.

DETERMINING THE NATURE OF GENERALIZATION: UNIVERSALITY TO SPECIFICITY

Whatever the epistemological position taken, arguments about the relative influence of biology and input rest to a great extent on arguments about universals or the lack of them. Universals are taken to result from innate or maturational origins. Universals can arise in different ways depending on the relation between cognition and language (Slobin, 1986b). Universals of language acquisition can result from an innate, formal language device. Mechanisms proposed to arise from a formal innate language module are taken to be unrelated to cognition. Alternatively, language acquisition can be dependent on cognitive developmental principles that are themselves innate. These cognitive mechanisms are prerequisites for language acquisition.

The strongest types of data used to support proposed universals of language acquisition, whether they result from an innate language system or innate cognitive capacities, are crosslinguistic data. Crosslinguistic data are the only type that are presented in support of formal universals, those purported to result from an innate language acquisition device. Acquisition of grammatical universals posited to form a universal grammar (Chomsky, 1965, 1982, 1986) generally fall into this class. The claim of universality of formal language acquisition principles requires the study of the acquisition of a large number of languages that represent different language types in order to avoid the problem of overgeneralization from too few language contrasts. Slobin's (1986–1992) three-volume series represents a major effort to compile the kinds of data needed to make inferences about the universality of language acquisition processes.

When a language acquisition universal is proposed to result from an underlying universal cognitive capacity, additional supportive arguments are provided to relate the principle of language acquisition to some underlying cognitive capacity. Three types of potential universal cognitive prerequisites have been described (Johnston, 1986). One type is fully available before language emerges. The influence of cognitive universals of this type on language acquisition remains constant throughout language development. An example of this type of universal is Jakobson's (1941/1968) proposal that the chronology of phonological acquisition is governed by motoric complexity, or ease of production, of phonological contrasts. The ability to produce the sounds of language exists long before their use in language is acquired; they occur in early babbling. Cognitive, motoric complexity is, however, correlated with the ordering of later acquisition of productive language use. A second type of cognitive prerequisite is one that emerges over the course of language acquisition. This type of prerequisite can be seen in interactionist approaches to developmental theory that posit an invariant order of acquisition of cognitive structures (e.g., Flavell, 1963; Piaget, 1955, 1962). Piaget (1962) argued, for example, that language emergence is dependent on completion of the sensorimotor period of development. Studies attempting to assess this relationship have looked for correlations between the timing of aspects of sensorimotor cognitive development and language emergence (Bates, Benigni, Bretherton, Camaioni, & Volterra, 1979). These two types of cognitive prerequisites shape language acquisition directly.

The third type of cognitive prerequisite influences language acquisition indirectly, through interaction with output of the formal language acquisition system. These prerequisites—memory and attentional limitations, for example—exist at the beginning of language learning and have a continuing influence throughout development. Because these cognitive capacities often themselves develop, their influence on language acquisition can change over time. Working memory span increases with age, for example, and a working memory span of a particular size may be necessary for acquisition of a specific language structure determined by the innately given formal language acquisition system.

Theoretical studies of sign language acquisition have generally compared the performance of native sign language users with native spoken language users, with the goal either of establishing language or processing universals of acquisition or of determining the effects of language modality (signed vs. spoken) on language acquisition. Generalization across modality has been taken as a strong argument for universality. Similarity of language acquisition across modality is particularly important because at least some aspects of input and processing change with modality. Generalization across modality implies that the universal is either formal linguistic in nature or results from an abstract cognitive mechanism. Dependence of language acquisition on language modality can implicate peripheral cognitive capacities of perception and production, though it need not (O'Connor & Hermelin, 1978).

All too often, studies claiming to provide test cases for cross-modality, absolute universals have examined one sign language and sometimes have compared acquisition of that sign language with the acquisition of only one, or a small set of, spoken language(s). Modality specific universals are, of course, a form of universal that generalizes to a subset of languages or language types. Sometimes the question posed assumes a cognitively based universal and asks whether that cognitive universal is abstract (modality independent) or dependent on the specific nature of perceptual and production systems involved. A tight theoretical argument about the relation between underlying cognitive capacity and language acquisition provides some reason to accept the generalization, but it does not completely substitute for solid crosslinguistic data.

Ignoring the need for crosslinguistic data can lead to overgeneralization or undergeneralization in theoretical accounts of language acquisition principles. Overgeneralization can result from concluding that some aspect of language acquisition is universal when similarities between the acquisition of one signed language and one spoken language are found. Generalization may only extend to a language type that includes both the signed language and the spoken language under study. On the other hand, undergeneralization or inaccurate description of language acquisition mechanisms can occur when differences are found between a signed language and a spoken language and conclusions are based only on a contrast of the two languages studied. Crosslinguistic data are necessary to determine whether the two languages originally contrasted are different because they represent different subsets of languages (i.e., different language types) or whether the mechanism under study is actually language specific.

A particularly striking example of inaccurate description occurred, for example, when some investigators began to attempt descriptions of ASL grammar. Trained that arbitrariness was a defining characteristic of language, many were struck by the seemingly apparent iconicity of ASL. True, many signs are totally arbitrary, and it is impossible to understand the meanings of the vast majority of signs without some training. Still, there are a set of signs, often called *mimetic,* that seem to directly represent attributes of real-world objects. American linguists trained in transformational grammar tended to use English as their model when approaching ASL. Mimetic signs seemed to capture large units of grammar (NP, VP, and even S) holistically rather than through sequentially ordered, rule-governed strings of morphemes. This led some (e.g., DeMatteo, 1977, and others in Friedman, 1977) to propose that descriptions of ASL would require analog rules that would be unique to signed language. Others agreed that some instances of analog representation changed meaning but argued that these were nonlinguistic examples of aspects such as stress and demonstration (e.g., Coulter, 1977). Only when ASL was compared with classifier languages (Allan, 1977) did it become clear that the grammar of ASL could be captured by rule-governed systems operating on discrete units like those systems described for spoken languages (McDonald, 1983, 1985; Newport & Supalla, 1980).

Classifier languages are languages that include morphemes called *classifiers,* whose function is to classify nouns according to inherent characteristics of their referents (Allan, 1977). The characteristics denoted by classifiers are related to physical and perceptual attributes of the noun referent (e.g., shape, size, or location). ASL can be characterized as a polysynthetic language in that single signs are often composed of several distinct morphemes. It has been shown that the signs once thought to be indivisible units can be described by a discrete set of morphemes, some of which are classifiers (e.g., McDonald, 1983, 1985; Newport & Supalla, 1980). Thus, some of the differences between the grammars of ASL and English occur because ASL is a classifier language and English is not rather than because the two languages differ in modality.

In the following section, comparisons of the acquisition of signed and spoken language will be considered relative to issues of generalizability and the relation between language and cognition. While the survey is by no means complete, enough instances are described to conclude that no one position on these issues is correct but that the level of generalizability and nature and degree of dependence on underlying cognition depend on the type of language mechanism.

GENERALIZING FROM STUDIES OF SIGNED LANGUAGE ACQUISITION

Settings for language acquisition are more heterogeneous for deaf children than for hearing children. Spoken language is not acquired "naturally" by deaf children. Because of the greatly reduced auditory processing, alternative strategies of language perception must be taught, and these provide only a restricted range of input to the child. The vast majority of deaf adults use sign language, but only about 10 percent of deaf children are born into households where at least one parent is deaf. Also, because the spoken language of the culture is the dominant language, all children growing up in households where the primary language is signed become bilingual at some point, and this point varies from child to child. For these and related reasons, the studies on signed language acquisition selected for review are those that replicate as closely as possible the typical settings in which spoken language acquisition has been studied. In the ideal case, these are singleton, first-born children living in monolingual, middle-class households. In this type of setting, the hearing status of the child (deaf, hard of hearing, or hearing) can be relaxed because the environment fosters native acquisition of the sign language of the parents.

Studies have also been selected to show the range of aspects of language acquisition that have been investigated and to make illustrative points about generalization rather than to provide a comprehensive survey of signed language acquisition. First, issues related to the emergence of language are considered. Then, illustrative studies are described for phonological, semantic, morphological, syntactic, and pragmatic development. The fact that acquisition can be described at each discrete level of language analysis is itself a proposed universal that appears to generalize across all sign languages studied to date.

Emergence of Language

Timing of first words has been taken as an important index of the emergence of language. Hearing children acquiring a spoken language produce their first spoken words between 10 and 15 months of age (de Villiers & de Villiers, 1978), acquire a 10-word vocabulary at about 15.1 months of age (Nelson, 1973), and begin to form 2-word combinations between 18 and 21 months of age (Gesell & Thompson, 1934). Treated as universals, these milestones of the emergence of language are used diagnostically to assess language delay. The timing of the emergence of language has been described as determined by an innate language acquisition mechanism (Chomsky, 1965) or as tied to the achievement of specific cognitive prerequisites (Lenneberg, 1967; Piaget, 1962). The universal status of these milestones was challenged, however, by early and persistent reports that sign language emerged earlier than spoken language both for deaf children acquiring sign language monolingually and hearing children acquiring signed and spoken languages bilingually.

Age of appearance of first signs has been reported to occur at least 2 to 3 months earlier than the age of appearance of first words for both deaf and hearing children exposed to sign language. Schlesinger (1978; Schlesinger & Meadow, 1972) reports the first signs of two deaf children occurring at 10 and 12 months; and the first signs of two hearing children at 5.5 and 10.5 months. Other indices of language emergence were reported for one of these children; her vocabulary included over 100 signs by 18 months of age (over twice that of the typical child acquiring spoken language), and she began to form 2-sign combinations at 17 months. In an extensive study of language in a deaf child of deaf parents, McIntire (1974, 1977) reports that the child began to sign at 9 months, produced 2-sign combinations at 10 months, and had a vocabulary of more than 85 signs at 13 months. In the most extensive study to date, Bonvillian and his colleagues (Bonvillian, Orlansky, & Novack, 1983; Bonvillian, Orlansky, Novack, Folven, & Holley-Wilcox, 1985; Bonvillian & Folven, 1993) have reported language emergence data for 22 children (20 hearing and 2 deaf) with at least one deaf parent. The average age of first signs for these children was 8.5 months; a 10-sign vocabulary was achieved at 13.3 months; and sign combinations were first produced at 16.7 months.

Two general approaches have been taken in trying to interpret these data. One approach accepts modality dependence and attempts to provide explanations for the modality difference. In these approaches, interpretations of the data are based on assumptions about the mechanisms underlying the emergence of language. Depending on the view, the modality difference is seen as a sign advantage or a speech disadvantage. Another approach questions whether a difference exists at all. Questions raised by this later approach suggest the possibility that language emerges in an orderly fashion, following an invariant timetable, independent of language modality.

A sign advantage or speech disadvantage?   In one of the earliest proposals of a sign advantage, Brown (1977) suggested that signs may be acquired earlier because early signs tend to be iconic, preserving certain attributes or actions associated with the referent of the sign. Orlansky and Bonvillian (1984), investigating the proportion of iconic signs in early sign vocabularies, argue that other features of sign production may play a greater role in sign emergence since only about a third of the signs in a signing child's early vocabulary are iconic. Taking a similar position, Wilbur (1979; Hoffmeister & Wilbur, 1980) has suggested that signs may emerge earlier because neuromuscular development of the systems used in signing occurs earlier than development of the systems used for speaking. Meier and Newport (1990), in a review of the data on emergence of sign language, suggest two ways in which modality can play a role. In one view, language acquisition is guided by a set of underlying language mechanisms that differ for different aspects of language. Some underlying language mechanisms, like those governing emergence of lexical units, may be modality dependent, whereas others, like those governing acquisition of syntax, may be language independent. A second view, closer to that of Chomsky, interprets modality influences on the emergence of lexical units as the result of differences in the time course of perceptual and cognitive development in the two modalities. In this view, children are ready to produce words before the speech mechanisms have developed enough for intelligible word production. On this interpretation, speech is disadvantaged in production of first lexical units.

Whatever the underlying mechanism(s), these arguments suggest that the timing of language emergence is modality dependent, governed by the development of production and perception systems, rather than the result of abstract, cognitive, or formal universals. In an interactionist framework like that of Piaget, however, abstract cognitive universals do not necessarily appear according to a strict chronological timetable. Order of emergence of aspects of development is predetermined, but age of achievement varies, depending on the interaction of the specific stage of development with the child's experience. It is possible that the early experience of children exposed to sign language produces earlier achievement of the cognitive prerequisites proposed for language emergence.

Bonvillian and his colleagues (Bonvillian et al., 1983; Bonvillian et al., 1985) set out to determine whether cognitive prerequisites of language emergence, suggested within a Piagetian framework, were correlated with and preceded indices of first signs in children growing up in sign language environments. As a result of their work, they concluded that the relation predicted by the Piagetian framework did not hold. Piaget (1962) proposed that emergence of first words should occur at the end of Stage VI of the sensorimotor period and suggested that the development of object permanence was the primary prerequisite for acquisition of first words. Bates et al. (1979), arguing from a similar perspective, suggested that imitation and means-end relations, rather than object permanence, were the Stage VI cognitive prerequisites of language emergence. Bonvillian and his colleagues examined the relation between indices of language emergence and stage of cognitive development as measured by the subscales of the Uzgiris and Hunt (1975) battery. Results indicated that first signs occurred when children were in Stages III, IV, and V on object permanence and means-end relations. Only a few children were in Stage VI when they achieved a 10-sign vocabulary, and only about half were in Stage VI when they began to combine signs. Concluding that "children learning a visuomotor language typically acquire the first steps of language usage several months before children learning to speak," Bonvillian et al. (1985) suggest that "future investigators should be cautious about making claims about prerequisites for, or precursors to, language if their claims are based exclusively on studies of spoken language" (p. 22).

Bonvillian's conclusion of modality dependence of language emergence has not gone unchallenged. Other investigators, including Volterra and Caselli (1985), have pointed out Piaget's (1962) proposal that auditory "ges-

tures" can appear prior to completion of the sensorimotor period. These vocalizations may be overinterpreted by language researchers, but according to
Piaget, they lack representational content and are therefore not linguistic.
The possibility exists, then, that some early "signs" used by children acquiring a signed language are not truly linguistic but are part of larger sensorimotor routines. This seems even more likely since children acquiring spoken
language use manual gestures referentially prior to the emergence of first
words (Bruner, 1975; Bates et al., 1979). Volterra and Caselli (Caselli, 1983;
Volterra, 1983; Volterra & Caselli, 1985) have argued that both crosslinguistic and cross-modal data must be considered, using the same criteria for all
language comparisons, to establish language emergence.

The gestures used by children acquiring spoken language are initially
deictic in nature, and their use is dependent on context. With development,
these children begin to use referential gestures—gestures that refer to specific referents and come to be used independent of specific contexts. Caselli
(1983) compared the early gestures of three deaf children acquiring ASL and
one deaf child acquiring Italian Sign Language (LIS) with the gestures produced by two hearing children acquiring spoken Italian. The development of
the use of gestures was the same for all five children. The first gestures
produced by all of the children were deictic, context-bound gestures.
Context-bound referential gestures followed the use of deictic gestures. With
time, the use of referential gestures became decontextualized, and the children acquiring spoken language began to produce words. Since all of the
children show the same pattern of development of gestures, Caselli argues
that there is no good reason to call one set of gestures prelinguistic gestures
and the other set, linguistic signs. Instead, Caselli's results support the conclusion that decontextualized referential gestures are produced both by children acquiring spoken language and by children acquiring signed language.

Volterra (1983), comparing the gestures and words of three hearing children acquiring spoken Italian with a deaf child acquiring LIS and spoken
Italian, presented a strategy to test for the possibility of modality effects in
language emergence. Since children in both signed and spoken language
environments produce manual gestures, Volterra argued that it is necessary
to compare and contrast the functional use of the gestural productions of
these children. The point where the manual gestures of children growing up
in sign environments diverges from those of children in spoken language
environments can then be used to distinguish the point where input language
begins to have its effect on language development. This point should distinguish prelinguistic from linguistic use of gestures. When production modality (oral or manual) was ignored, the communicative acts of the four children followed the same course of development beyond two years of age.

The similarity of one-item productions for similar children was described above (Caselli, 1983). Two-item combinations were also used in similar ways, up to a point. All four children produced two deictic gestures in combination, deictic gestures and words in combination, deictic gestures and referential gestures in combination, and two-word sequences. The only difference among the productions of the children was that the deaf child in a bilingual, bimodal setting was the only child who produced combinations of two referential gestures. In similar situations, children acquiring only spoken language produced at least one spoken word. Volterra (1983) suggests that input language begins to have its effect on language acquisition only when children "have to use the symbolic and the combinatorial capacity simultaneously" (p. 114).

From the work of Caselli (1983) and Volterra (1983), hearing children appear to have equal potential for signed and spoken language acquisition. Their use of gestures parallels that of deaf children in a sign environment. Only at the point of combining two symbols do children acquiring spoken language differ from children acquiring signed language. Volterra and Caselli (1985) suggest that most vocal and gestural productions up to this point may be nonlinguistic and that additional criteria are necessary to distinguish gestures from words and signs. They provide four criteria: reference to objects or events that are not present, reference to the same entity in different contexts, reference to different instances of the same class, and occurrence in combination with other symbols. When the development of children acquiring signed and spoken languages are compared using these criteria, both prelinguistic, communicative development and language development occur following the same stages and on similar timetables. Volterra and Caselli (1985) conclude that symbolic, linguistic use of words and signs "depends on the child's cognitive maturity" (p. 8) and is therefore governed by underlying cognitive universals of development.

Bonvillian (Bonvillian & Folven, 1993) has analyzed his data with respect to function and content, as well as form, and these analyses confirm some of the conclusions of Volterra and Caselli (1985). Early signs were imitations and requests, and the first referential use of signs occurred at approximately the same age as that reported for spoken language acquisition. In addition, the semantic content of early vocabularies was similar to the semantic content of early spoken language vocabularies in terms of semantic categories represented, specific items within category, and number of instances within category. Bonvillian and Folven (1993) report that timing and rate of vocabulary development and timing of first sign combinations are accelerated compared to spoken language acquisition. It is likely, however, that this difference would disappear if manual gestures, as well as vocalization, were taken into account in the spoken language data. Volterra and Caselli (1985) found that similar functional combinations occurred at the same age when gestures, words, and signs were considered.

Thus, while early sign language acquisition research challenged the hypothesis that the timing of the emergence of language was governed by underlying universals, the research generated by this challenge has served to reinforce the proposal of universal cognitive prerequisites for language emergence. Crosslinguistic evidence from both signed and spoken language acquisition supports the conclusion that early productions are prelinguistic (mostly manual but sometimes vocal) gestures. Symbolic use of language (words and signs) requires the achievement of a specific level of cognitive development as a prerequisite.

Phonological Development

Language must be easily produced and perceived for efficient communication to occur. From the study of auditory and articulatory phonetics, we know that the phonological structure of spoken language is shaped both by the perceptual ability of the listener and by the capacities and limitations of the systems used in production. Studies of ASL and Belgian Sign Language indicate that the capacities and limitations of the perceptual and production apparatus for signed language shape phonological structure in the manual modality (Battison, 1974; Loncke, 1985; Siple, 1978b).

The specific structures and mechanisms of language perception and production must, of course, differ for signed and spoken language. Still, discrete sublexical units of production have been described for sign languages that function similarly to the phonological units of production in spoken languages. Originally called *cheremes* by Stokoe (1960; Stokoe et al., 1965), the phonemes, or parameters, of ASL and other signed languages fall into four broad classes: the handshapes used to make the sign, the location where the sign is made, the movement involved in making the sign, and the orientation of the hands. Studies of the phonology of several sign languages, including ASL (e.g., Battison, 1978; Klima, 1975; Stokoe, 1960; Stokoe et al., 1965), Chinese Sign Language (Yau, 1977), LIS (Corazza et al., 1985), and British Sign Language, or BSL, (reported in Kyle & Woll, 1985), indicate that a total of 50 to 100 of these parameters are necessary to describe the signs of a particular language. Also, while there is a great deal of overlap among the parameters of different sign languages, each language of those studied employs a distinct set. At a more abstract level, then, questions about universals can be asked.

One of the most influential and comprehensive theories of phonological development in spoken languages was presented by Jakobson (1941/1968).

Jakobson's theory addressed the order of acquisition of productive use of the phonemes of the language being acquired. Jakobson proposed that a small universal set of features forms the basis for the phonological systems of all the world's (spoken) languages. According to Jakobson, the universal feature system is implicational; that is, if a sound Y occurs in a language, then X does as well. This same system also governs the order of acquisition of speech sounds; so that for X and Y above, X will be acquired before Y. Jakobson argued that the chronological order of phonological development is related to the frequency of occurrence of the units of phonology across languages. The phonological units that are acquired first, he argued, are those that occur in all, or nearly all, of the (spoken) languages of the world. These first-acquired units are also easiest to produce. The most complex phonological units are acquired last, and they also occur in the smallest number of (spoken) world languages. Thus, ease of production is correlated with the chronological order of phonological development in Jakobson's theory. In its strongest form, this theory predicts that the order of acquisition of phonological units is invariant and universal across spoken languages.

While ease of production is predicted to be related to acquisition order, motor development is not the basis of it, according to Jakobson. All of the sounds of language are produced by children in an earlier babbling stage, but they are soon "lost." Full productive use of the sounds occurs much later. Thus, Jakobson's theory is an interactionist one with more abstract, cognitive laws or rules of motoric structure guiding phonological development. Many phonologists, following Jakobson, have taken the position that an innate system governs the order of acquisition of phonological units. Some have attributed the constraints on phonological acquisition to innate cognitive or physiological processes of perception and production (e.g., Stampe, 1969), whereas others have implicated a specialized language acquisition system (e.g., Chomsky & Halle, 1968).

Comparative data from widely varying languages strongly support the general ordering of acquisition of phonological units proposed by Jakobson (Macken, 1995). Macken (1995) provides additional evidence that this ordering is guided by constraints on perception and production. The universal ordering is more statistical than absolute, however. There are individual differences among children and some unexpected differences between languages that are related to input context and problem-solving strategies of the child. There is, however, a correlation between the chronological order of phonological acquisition, the frequency of occurrence in the spoken languages of the world, and motoric complexity, as predicted by Jakobson.

One of the first aspects of phonological development studied for signed language was the acquisition of productive control of the handshape parameters, or phonemes, of ASL. In an early working paper, Boyes-Braem (1973) presented a model of handshape acquisition derived from a featural analysis of ASL handshapes that was based on anatomical and motor development properties. Boyes-Braem argued that the infant form of the closed fist, the A handshape, is the most unmarked form because it is the most relaxed and occurs earliest in development. Applying a set of seven abstract, motoric features (including thumb opposition, finger extension, and contact of fingertip with thumb), Boyes-Braem grouped together the handshapes of ASL into four sets, ordered in difficulty and complexity. Using arguments similar to Jakobson (1941/1968), Boyes-Braem predicted that handshape acquisition would be influenced by this ordering of anatomical complexity, or ease of production, along with a cognitive factor of preferred finger order and a set of secondary influences that include context and feedback.

To test the theory, Boyes-Braem (1973) examined the sign production of a deaf child, aged 2 years, 7 months, acquiring ASL from her deaf parents. While handshapes from all four groups, or stages, proposed by Boyes-Braem were produced, more handshapes were from the earlier stages than from the later stages. More important, many errors in handshape were made, and these errors were predominately substitutions of simpler handshapes from earlier stages, as would be predicted by Jakobson's theory applied to sign languages. Other errors could be attributed to secondary influences such as context and feedback.

McIntire (1974, 1977) provided further confirmation of the general Boyes-Braem model with longitudinal data from a deaf child from 13 to 18 months of age. The vast majority of this child's signs were produced with Stage I handshapes. In McIntire's data, 88 percent of signs requiring a Stage I handshape were produced with the correct handshape, whereas only 4 percent of signs requiring handshapes beyond Stage I were produced with the correct handshape. Incorrect handshapes were used for 186 signs, and 182 of these substitutions (98%) were from Stage I.

McIntire examined Stage I handshapes substituted for other Stage I handshapes to further test the Boyes-Braem model. Like Jakobson, Boyes-Braem proposes that substitutions will be based on an invariant order of acquisition, predicted from the operation of the proposed feature set on the set of phonemes in the child's current repertoire. On the basis of this analysis, McIntire (1977) offered a revised feature set based on the work of Lane, Boyes-Braem, and Bellugi (1976). With this revised set of rules and the secondary factors described by Boyes-Braem, McIntire was able to account for the majority of Stage I substitutions.

While the work of Boyes-Braem (1973) and McIntire (1974, 1977) supports a Jakobson-like model of phonological acquisition, crosslinguistic data are clearly needed. Until these data are available, however, two other types of data provide further support for such a model. First, Jakobson proposed that the first sounds (and by extension, first handshapes) acquired are those common to most or all of the world's languages. If McIntire's modifications of Boyes-Braem's model are taken into account, both Chinese and Italian Sign Language appear to include all of the handshapes of Stage I (Yau, 1977, and Corazza et al., 1985, respectively) and British Sign Language has all but one (Kyle & Woll, 1985).

Another important feature of Jakobson's theory is that motor development is not the underlying factor guiding phonological acquisition. Children have the ability to produce all of the sounds of their language long before they gain productive use of them in the language. This is not as clear for some of the handshapes of sign languages. ASL, however, is a classifier language, and several handshapes do double duty, serving as handshapes for single morpheme signs and as classifiers in multimorphemic signs. Classifier acquisition begins at about 3 years of age and is not complete until 8 or 9 years of age. Handshape classifiers are acquired after children have gained the use of the same handshapes in single morpheme signs, yet the order of acquisition of the earliest classifiers corresponds to that predicted by Boyes-Braem (1973), Kantor (1980), and McIntire (1974, 1977).

Thus, while other factors influence the chronological order of phonological acquisition, Jakobson's (1941/1968) proposal that cognitive structural complexity is a primary influence appears to hold for both signed and spoken language. There is general support for a universal order of acquisition for spoken language phonemes and for sign language parameters. Both of these universal orderings are related to motoric complexity and ease of production. It appears, then, that an abstract, innate cognitive universal guides phonological acquisition, though secondary factors like phonological context and feedback also influence the chronological order of acquisition.

Semantic Development

Because it can be argued that a primary index of the emergence of language is the combination of symbols, discussion of semantic development will focus on the semantic relations expressed by early word and sign combinations. Brown (1973, 1980) has suggested that when children begin to put two words together, the combinations are used to express a small set of semantic relations. A small set of two-term semantic relations accounts for two-word combinations produced in Brown's Stage I of acquisition for a variety of languages, representing different language types. Furthermore, Brown has demonstrated that longer utterances are built out of the two-term relations through processes of stringing two relations together or expanding one term into a combination of two others. For example, the English utterance "Daddy throw ball" can be analyzed as a stringing together of (AGENT + ACTION) and (ACTION + OBJECT), deleting one repetition of the action, to produce a three-term relation (AGENT + ACTION + OBJECT). An example of expansion in English acquisition is the utterance "Bring my shoe," which expands the object of (AGENT + OBJECT) into (POSSESSOR + POSSESSED) to form the three-term relation (ACTION + POSSESSOR + POSSESSED). Because the semantic relations and the rules for combining them generalize across several language types, Brown (1973) suggests that they are universal.

Early work on the acquisition of ASL demonstrated that similar two-term and three-term semantic relations are produced by children acquiring ASL in a native language environment (Bellugi & Klima, 1972; Fischer, 1974b; Klima & Bellugi, 1972; Nash, 1973; Prinz & Prinz, 1981; Schlesinger, 1978; Schlesinger & Meadow, 1972). In addition, Newport and Ashbrook (1977) found that the order of acquisition of semantic relations in ASL is the same as that reported for English by Bloom, Lightbown, and Hood (1975). Thus, the nature of semantic relations expressed in early language acquisition and the more complex relations expressed as utterance length increases appears to be universal across language modality.

The early semantic relations produced by children express relations related to the sensorimotor schemata of the child described by Piaget (Brown, 1980). Piaget (1955, 1962; Flavell, 1963) argued that stages of language acquisition essentially recapitulate sensorimotor development, and Bates and her colleagues (1979) have demonstrated that early semantic relations are initially produced in gesture and play. Thus, early acquisition of semantic relations is correlated with and appear to be guided to some extent by the course of cognitive development.

Morphological and Syntactic Development

Grammar is used to express semantic relations like reference to time, negation, and the distinction between agent and object. While the grammars of all languages convey semantic relations, they differ in the mechanisms used to indicate specific semantic relations. Some languages (e.g., English) depend heavily on word order to express semantic relations, whereas other languages (e.g., Serbo-Croatian) rely on complex morphological systems like case marking. The specific systems used to convey semantic relations define classes of languages or language types. ASL is a polysynthetic language with a rich and complex morphology.

As described earlier, one of the most perplexing problems for linguists attempting to describe the grammar of ASL was the existence of iconic or mimetic signs—signs that appeared to directly represent attributes of referent objects and events. It is now clear from the work of Newport and Supalla (1980; Newport, 1982), McDonald (1983, 1985), and others that ASL is a language of a particular type, a predicate classifier language (Allan, 1977). The grammar of ASL, including mimetic signs, can be described structurally, with mechanisms operating on discrete units similar to those mechanisms described for spoken languages.

The classifier system of ASL is embedded within a complex morphological system as it is for spoken language (Newport, 1982). The organization of the morphological system for spoken languages and for ASL has a shell-like structure. The core, or central morpheme, is called the root. If the language is of the predicate classifier type, like ASL, classifiers operate on certain verb stem roots. Derivational morphology operates at the next level to change grammatical category. Finally, inflectional morphological processes signal things like tense, number, or aspect. The morphology of ASL verbs of motion and location has a similar structure (Newport, 1982). For verbs of motion and location, a small set of handshape classifiers that represent attributes like the size and shape of referent objects combine with a small set of root morphemes that represent motion or location of the referent objects. Other classifier operations may also occur. For example, the nonactive hand may be used as a classifier to represent the location of a secondary object; other morphemes indicate manner of movement. These morphemes make up a verb stem to which derivational morphological processes can be applied. Supalla and Newport (1978) have described morphological processes similar to those for spoken languages by which nouns are derived from verbs. Following derivational processes, inflectional processes inflect the nouns or verbs for things like aspect or number.

While mimetic signs of ASL can be analyzed as part of a predicate classifier system, their iconic properties can also be easily observed. Because of this, iconic descriptions or derivations (often apocryphal) of ASL signs are typically given to adult learners to help them remember vocabulary. An important question, then, is how children acquiring ASL as a native language acquire the ASL classifier system. Children acquiring spoken classifier languages as first languages acquire the complex classifier system through a morphological analysis process. Children acquiring ASL have alternative inductive processes available to them (Newport, 1988), based on holistic rather than analytic strategies. Mimetic signs could be learned as holistic units representing real-world events iconically. In this case, children should vary these signs continuously, in analog fashion, to express real-world relations. Alternatively, these multimorphemic, mimetic signs could be learned holistically by rote through reference to real-world events as monomorphemic signs are learned. In this case, children should only acquire and use "citation" forms of the signs and lack the ability to use the morphological system productively.

While iconicity and holistic strategies are available to the child learning ASL, Newport and Supalla (1980) report that children with deaf parents acquiring ASL natively use a strategy based on morphological analysis to acquire the complex movement morphology of the ASL classifier system. Children first produce simple, monomorphemic signs. Signs requiring complex movements are replaced either by frozen, citation form signs that do not vary in different contexts or by incorrect nonfrozen forms. The incorrect nonfrozen forms include one or more correct movement morphemes but omit one or more movement morphemes. At a later period of development, children may produce all of the movement morphemes of a multimorphemic sign, but sequentially rather than simultaneously, as is required for some signs. Sequential productions like these would not have occurred in the child's input. Finally, the child produces correct adult forms.

The pattern of acquisition of movement morphology in the classifier system mirrors morphological acquisition of spoken language. Children begin by producing unanalyzed forms, then they analyze those forms into discrete morphological units, and finally they combine the units into adult, complex forms. The time frame for this development is lengthy and is similar to that for spoken language morphological development. Children begin the acquisition process at age 2 years, 6 months, and all forms are used correctly by age 5. Errors continue to be made, however, up to 7 or 8 years of age (Newport & Meier, 1986).

Acquisition of the handshapes of the classifier system also shows prolonged development, and acquisition processes mirror those of other classifier languages (Schick, 1990). Schick describes three types of classifier predicates based on the relation of the handshapes to the referent objects. In one type of ASL classifier predicate, handshapes specify classes or categories of objects (e.g., vehicle); in another, handshapes represent size and shape features of referent objects; and in a third type, handshapes represent the general shape of the hand necessary to handle or hold referent objects. These three types of classifier predicates (handshapes plus movement morphemes) also differ in the syntax and semantics represented by the predicate. Within predicate classifier type, specific predicates differ in morphological complexity. In the early stages of acquisition, the order of access of classifier handshapes is correlated with motoric complexity (Kantor, 1980). Acquisition is also sensitive, however, to both syntactic and semantic structure as represented by the three types of classifier predicates, as well as morphological complexity within classifier predicate type (Schick, 1990). Schick's results parallel those for acquisition of spoken classifier languages. She reports, for example, that classifiers that represent classes of referents are acquired before classifiers that represent attributes of referents for Thai and Japanese as well as for ASL.

Thus, aspects of morphosyntactic acquisition of ASL, a predicate classifier language, are similar to those reported for spoken classifier languages. The processes of acquisition of classifier systems, then, generalize across language modality. Specific aspects of acquisition (acquisition order of some types of classifiers, for example) generalize to language type (Schick, 1990), whereas the more general processes of morphological development (analysis of previously unanalyzed units into morphemes, with later integration of these units into a productive morphological system) appear to generalize across all languages.

Two types of explanations have been offered for the origins of these universals of morphosyntactic acquisition (Newport, 1988, 1990). In one type of explanation, universals of morphological acquisition are attributed to attentional and memorial limitations of the child. Somewhat paradoxically, it is suggested that the child attends to pieces of the complex form and relates those pieces to units of meaning (i.e., carries out a morphological analysis) because the child's cognitive processing system is not yet developed enough to record and integrate complex relationships of form and meaning for complex morphophonemic signs and words. By this account, native learners should demonstrate acquisition based on morphological analysis because they lack the cognitive capabilities to use holistic strategies. Morphological analysis strategies of language learning, according to this account, are not programmed into the child. Instead, they are the only or easiest way the child has to carry out the task of acquiring complex morphological forms, given the child's level of cognitive development. Older language learners with more developed cognitive processing systems have the capacity to use holistic strategies and should, therefore, use them when learning ASL.

Data on early versus late acquisition of ASL tend to support a cognitive limitations explanation of morphological development. Newport (1988, 1990) has reported that the morphological forms used to express complex movement and location relations differ among groups of adult signers depending on whether they began to learn ASL natively, between 4 and 6, or at age 12 or after. Only native learners use the complex verbal classifier system of ASL productively. Later learners show some productive use but more typically use frozen citation forms in situations where signs with complex classifier morphology are more appropriate. Sign use based on holistic, rote strategies is more typical the later ASL acquisition is begun. Iconicity-based holistic strategies are used neither by children nor by adults acquiring ASL.

Additional data in support of a critical period for the acquisition of productive use of ASL morphology was presented by Galvan (1989). In Galvan's study, verbs requiring complex morphology in ASL were elicited from 3- to 9-year-old children acquiring ASL natively and from 5- and 9-year-old children who had begun signing between 2 and 4 years of age. Qualitatively different patterns of acquisition were demonstrated by the two groups of children, depending on their age of acquisition. Classifier use and aspectual marking increased with age for native signers, for example, but decreased for later learners. Later learners tended to use frozen forms and signs with little morphological complexity.

Mayberry (1993a, 1993b; Mayberry & Eichen, 1991), using memory and repetition techniques to assess ASL fluency, has provided a more complex view of age of learning effects on ASL acquisition, including acquisition of complex morphological forms. Mayberry has examined the ability to repeat and remember ASL sentences in adult signers who learned ASL as a first language natively, in early childhood, and in late childhood and in adult signers who learned ASL as a second language in late childhood after learning English as a first language. Mayberry's results for learners of ASL as a first language parallel those reported by Newport (1988, 1990). Productive use of ASL mechanisms decreased with age of acquisition, with only native learners showing full productive use. Data from late-childhood second-language learners, however, was similar to that of adults who learned ASL as a first language in early childhood. Evidently, learning a first language natively provides a basis for later second-language learning, even if the second language differs in modality and grammatical structure from the first. Still, none of the non-native learners of ASL, either as a first or second language, achieve full productive use of ASL grammar, and this seems particularly true for the complex morphological system.

A second explanation for universals of morphosyntactic acquisition (Newport, 1988, 1990; Lillo-Martin, 1991) begins with the assumption that the child comes with an innate language module that governs the child's acquisition of grammar (Chomsky, 1965, 1982, 1986). This module consists of general universal principles of language structure, including abstract principles that produce morphological analysis during language acquisition. In addition, the innate language module proposed by Chomsky includes sets of parameters for different language mechanisms. Each parameter for a particular grammatical relation specifies a different structural option for expressing the underlying semantic relation with a specific grammatical mechanism.

Children acquiring language begin language use with a default parameter value; if necessary, they acquire the parameter value for the particular language being acquired through interaction with specific language input. Principles licensing specific parameters are acquired when positive evidence of the parameter's use exists in the child's input and the parameter is set. It can be argued that parameters should be set relatively early in acquisition since evidence of their use should be readily available in the typical child's input. Thus, by this account, the child's acquisition of grammar is accomplished through the application of innate structural principles that generalize to language type and are independent of cognitive ability.

Lillo-Martin (1991) has provided an account of the acquisition of a different part of the complex ASL system of verbal morphology within this Principles and Parameters framework of Universal Grammar (UG) (see also Chapter 3). She has demonstrated that ASL has two types of verbs that can have null arguments: those that can be marked for agreement with spatial referencing morphology and those that cannot. In order to account for certain aspects of children's acquisition of null arguments in ASL, as well as cross-linguistic data on the use of null arguments in spoken languages that do and do not have them, Lillo-Martin has added further specifications to the Principles and Parameters Theory. More important to our discussion, she also had to separate out the acquisition of the morphological system from the setting of parameters in the syntactic system. According to Lillo-Martin, the acquisition of syntax is guided by the innate language module of UG. Morphology, as well as pragmatics and discourse rules, takes longer to acquire, and acquisition of these systems may be related to the development of the cognitive processing system. Thus, Lillo-Martin argues that null argument parameter setting occurs very late in ASL acquisition because acquisition of the complex verbal morphology system is required prior to parameter setting, and acquisition of ASL verbal morphology requires development of the cognitive processing system.

If parameter setting is sensitive to and possibly interacts with morphological development processes, it is unclear why the vast machinery of UG is necessary to account for acquisition of syntax. It is possible to account for some aspects of syntactic development with more general rules of cognitive processing, and Newport (1988) has proposed that the general operating principles set out by Slobin (1986a) can be viewed as cognitive strategies that guide the child's acquisition of language under conditions of limited attention and memory. The case for UG seems considerably weaker when the data from age of acquisition of ASL studies are considered.

Studies of both adult use and child acquisition indicate that there is a sensitive period during which ASL acquisition must begin if the user is to have full productive use of the ASL system of morphology (Galvan, 1989;

Mayberry, 1993a, 1993b; Mayberry & Eichen, 1991; Newport, 1988, 1990). It appears that the acquisition of the complex morphology of ASL must begin before 2–4 years of age for correct parameter setting to be achieved for ASL according to UG theory. An innate language module that works only in early childhood seems somewhat arbitrary. A more parsimonious account would relate all of morphosyntactic development to underlying cognitive developmental processes. In this kind of account, acquisition of productive morphology could occur only during the time when the child is analyzing and organizing his or her perceptual world and relating perceptual attributes to semantic representations. Once the application of these semantic systems has become automatic, or proceduralized, it may be impossible to access the semantic distinctions necessary to build a complex system of morphology like that found in ASL. Once the morphological system of ASL is acquired, it may be possible to account for further syntactic development using these forms with operating principles like those proposed by Slobin (1986a).

The discussion of acquisition of morphology and syntax has focused on studies of ASL acquisition because there is little information about acquisition of these systems in other sign languages. Crosslinguistic data from other sign languages is needed, especially since the use of classifiers appears to be more typical of signed than spoken languages. The use of classifier-like morphemes has been described for BSL (Kyle & Woll, 1985), Danish Sign Language (Engberg-Pedersen & Pedersen, 1985), and Swedish Sign Language (Wallin, 1990). More complete descriptions of movement and location verbs are available for LIS (Corazza, 1990) and Thai Sign Language (Collins-Ahlgren, 1990), and both of these sign languages appear to be of the predicate classifier type. Interestingly, spoken Thai is also a classifier language, but it is a numeral classifier language, not a predicate classifier language (Allan, 1977). Collins-Ahlgren (1990) suggests that, while spoken Thai and Thai Sign Language share features in their classifier systems, these are general features of classifier languages, and the functions of classifiers differ in the two languages. Thus, she argues, the classifier systems of spoken Thai and Thai Sign Language have developed independently. Acquisition data would be particularly interesting for bilingual children acquiring these two languages.

Pragmatic Development

The structure of words and sentences appears to be governed to a great extent by cognitive and formal universals, producing a great deal of similarity among languages or classes of languages. Language is primarily used for communication, however, and the rules governing social interaction vary greatly from culture to culture and thus language to language. Some very general rules of conversation, like the conversational postulates described by Grice (1975), the given-new contract investigated by Clark and Haviland (1977), and the principle of relevance proposed by Sperber and Wilson (1986), may generalize to most or all languages. Even these may need to be learned, however, and the specific forms used to instantiate the rules differ greatly among languages. Development of these conversational skills would be expected to generalize to language types defined by aspects of culture or to be language specific (e.g., Ferguson, 1976). Because the skills are acquired through learning in context, development should be guided by a complex interaction of the specific mechanisms used in the language, the development of underlying cognitive skills necessary to abstract these rules from language input, and the specific language input environment of the child.

Learning the rules of conversation includes acquiring the skills used to regulate conversation. The child must learn to initiate and maintain interactions, negotiate turn taking, and change topics in conversation. These skills require attention to extralinguistic information, as well as structural aspects of language. In spoken language, many of the devices used to regulate conversation occur in the gestural-visual channel (Argyle & Cook, 1976). Linkage of the vocal-auditory and gestural-visual channels permits simultaneous processing of linguistic and nonlinguistic information. Gaze, for example, plays a key role in regulating conversation. Speakers of English use gaze to initiate and terminate interaction, to negotiate turn taking, and to add information to the linguistic message. Gaze and other devices used to regulate conversation differ from culture to culture, however, and vary depending on the other functions they serve (Argyle & Cook, 1976).

In signed language communication, the gestural-visual channel carries the linguistic content. It is also used in ASL to provide extralinguistic information that functions to regulate conversation (Baker, 1977; Baker & Padden, 1978; Wilbur & Petitto, 1983). The devices used in ASL differ somewhat from those used in English, however, and must be learned by hearing individuals learning ASL as a second language (Baker, 1977; Swisher, 1991). Because the same channel is used to convey linguistic and conversation-regulating information in ASL, it might be expected that interference would occur, changing the nature of conversation or making it more difficult. This does not appear to be the case, however. The general structure of adult ASL conversation appears to be similar to the structure of conversation in spoken languages (Baker, 1977; Wilbur & Petitto, 1983), and children acquiring ASL learn to structure conversation similar to adult ASL users by the time they are about 12 years of age (Prinz & Prinz, 1985).

Few direct comparisons of the development of conversation skills in spoken and signed languages have been made, however, and it is in this area that modality effects might be expected. Even though smooth conversation skills are eventually achieved in sign languages, differences between the auditory and visual channels and coordination of so much information in the visual channel might be expected to affect the course of development. Taking a position like that of Bruner (1975, 1983)—that input and interaction provide necessary contexts that guide language development—Harris (1992) has argued that constraints arising from dependence on the visual channel for both linguistic and context information will produce a slower rate of language acquisition in deaf children.

One way that the visual and auditory communication channels differ is in how attention getting can be achieved. Unlike much of the paralinguistic information used to regulate spoken conversation, attention getting generally occurs in the auditory channel rather than the visual channel. Common ways to initiate conversation in spoken languages are to say the addressee's name, produce an auditory cue that signals the beginning of an utterance, or simply begin talking. Auditory attention-getting cues can be heard within a wide, multidirectional radius of the speaker and grab the receiver's attention so that the speaker can begin to talk immediately. Because signed language requires the visual attention of the addressee and visual attention is directional in nature, it is necessary for the signer to gain the visual attention of the addressee before beginning the signed message. If the addressee is not already looking toward the signer, attention getting is achieved by waving a hand in front of the addressee, touching or patting the person, or tapping a table or other nearby object (Baker, 1977; Stokoe et al., 1965).

Children acquiring a sign language must understand the need for joint visual attention with the addressee and be able to establish it before they can successfully initiate conversation. Attention getting is more complex in the visual channel than in the auditory channel. A general set of visual, tactile, and vibratory cues are used to get an addressee's attention. The child must understand the need to establish the visual attention of the addressee, as well as learn that this set of cues signals interaction. Siple and her colleagues (Siple, Akamatsu, & Loew, 1990; Siple, Richmond-Welty, Howe, Berwanger, & Jasper, 1994) have argued that the increased need for metacognitive awareness and the greater complexity of visual attention getting may delay child-initiated interaction in ASL. The Siple et al. (1994) study examined language interactions in two sets of twins: one hearing-impaired set acquired ASL monolingually; the other hearing set acquired both ASL and spoken English from infancy. The communication patterns of the two sets of twins were very similar, with the exception that the monolingual ASL set did not initiate as many language interactions with adults or with each other as the bilingual set. Examination of the attention-getting devices used by the two sets of twins indicated that the bilingual twins acquired and used auditory attention-getting devices before either set of twins began to use ASL-appropriate attention-getting devices.

Swisher (1991, 1993) has provided additional support for the important role of learning in establishing joint mutual attention in signed conversation. Swisher (1991) has demonstrated that hearing parents who learn sign language to communicate with their deaf children tend not to use attention-getting strategies appropriate to the visual-gestural modality. In these situations, joint mutual attention is not established before signing begins, with the result that the children often miss part or all of the message. Fluent adult signers may be able to "catch" the onset of signing in their periphery and understand the message. Children, who are less familiar with the signs being used, cannot as readily take advantage of the less detailed peripheral visual information (Swisher, 1993).

Very little is known about the development of conversational interaction in signed language. The few studies that exist, however, suggest that the nature of visual communication may change the course of development, leading to modality-dependent acquisition processes. Thus, generalization to modality, or to language groups within modality, is expected in the acquisition of communication skills related to the regulation of conversation. Further, the acquisition of these modality-dependent skills is most likely rooted in the development of the underlying cognitive ability to understand that such regulation is necessary, interacting with the complexity of the system of regulation itself.

CONCLUSIONS

This survey, comparing signed and spoken language acquisition for selected aspects of language structure and processing, leads us to an interrelated set of conclusions concerning universality and the origins of language acquisition. First and perhaps most important, a large body of crosslinguistic data from both signed and spoken languages representing different language types is necessary to establish that a particular aspect of language acquisition is universal. Comparisons of too few languages of restricted types can lead to both overgeneralization and undergeneralization. Some acquisition processes generalize to all languages, constituting universals. Other acquisition processes generalize to language types, where type can refer to classification based on formal structure, modality, or the culture within which a language is embedded. In addition, there are language-specific acquisition processes.

Aspects of language acquisition that are universal tend to be more abstract and to occur at earlier levels or stages of acquisition, though they can occur at any level. These universals include principles governing the chronological order of phonological acquisition and the order of acquisition of semantic relations. Because environments differ so greatly, universals provide strong support for innate capacity for some components of language acquisition. The universals described here appear to result primarily from innate cognitive universals rather than from formal language universals, though this survey includes too few examples to rule out formal universals.

Languages can be classified in many ways, and universals specific to language types abound. Interestingly, these universals tend to generalize across language modality. Acquisition of the complex morphology of predicate classifier languages, for example, is similar for signed and spoken languages and appears to be governed by the development of general cognitive conceptual structures and problem-solving strategies. Generalization across modality implicates abstract principles of development rather than more peripheral aspects of perception and production, though the abstract principles may be cognitive or formal linguistic in nature.

Language modality, signed versus spoken, defines a language typology, but generalization of language acquisition processes appears to occur rarely to modality. While the building blocks of signed language are gestural-visual rather than vocal-auditory, acquisition processes generalize across modality. Exceptions appear to occur at the level of pragmatics where acquisition of the devices used to regulate the flow of conversation may be modality dependent. Modality-dependent language acquisition processes are governed by more peripheral cognitive processes related to perception and production.

Logically, there is the possibility of generalization to language type within modality. At this point there are too few crosslinguistic studies of sign language acquisition to determine whether these occur, however. Many generalizations to language type have been described for spoken languages, but in most cases, it is unclear whether sign languages of these types exist and, if they do, whether acquisition processes generalize within or across modality. It is possible that future sign language research will demonstrate generalization to language types within the gestural-visual modality.

Universality, generalization to language type, and language specificity can occur at all levels and stages of language acquisition, though there is a tendency toward greater generalization of acquisition processes at more abstract or at lower levels or stages of processing. To the extent that these tendencies hold, the influence of genetic factors appears to be greater at lower levels or stages of language acquisition. At higher levels or stages, the child's environment plays a larger role in shaping language acquisition.

In sum, the relation between language and cognition is complex. No one general theory accounts for language acquisition. The great variety of results in crosslinguistic studies of specific language acquisition phenomena for both signed and spoken language implicates different types of mechanisms for different aspects of acquisition. When more is known, it may be possible to further characterize the types of processes that rely more on innately determined cognitive and linguistic structures and processes and those that are influenced to a greater extent by the child's environment.

REFERENCES

Allan, K. (1977). Classifiers. *Language, 53,* 285–311.

Argyle, M., & Cook, M. (1976). *Gaze and mutual gaze.* Cambridge: Cambridge University Press.

Baker, C. (1977). Regulators and turn-taking in American Sign Language. In L. A. Friedman (Ed.), *On the other hand: New perspectives on American Sign Language* (pp. 215–236). New York: Academic Press.

Baker, C., & Padden, C. A. (1978). Focusing on the nonmanual components of American Sign Language. In P. Siple (Ed.), *Understanding language through sign language research* (pp. 27–58). New York: Academic Press.

Bates, E., Benigni, L., Bretherton, I., Camaioni, L., & Volterra, V. (1979). *The emergence of symbols: Cognition and communication in infancy.* New York: Academic Press.

Battison, R. (1974). Phonological deletion in ASL. *Sign Language Studies, 5,* 1–19.

Battison, R. (1978). *Lexical borrowing in American Sign Language.* Silver Spring, MD: Linstok Press.

Bellugi, U., & Klima, E. S. (1972). The roots of language in the sign talk of the deaf. *Psychology Today, 6,* 61–64, 75–76.

Bloom, L., Lightbown, P., & Hood, L. (1975). Structure and variation in child language. *Monographs of the Society for Research in Child Development, 40,* serial no. 160, no. 2.

Bonvillian, J. D., & Folven, R. J. (1993). Sign language acquisition: Developmental aspects. In M. Marschark & M. D. Clark (Eds.), *Psychological perspectives on deafness* (pp. 229–265). Hillsdale, NJ: Lawrence Erlbaum Associates.

Bonvillian, J. D., Orlansky, M. D., & Novack, L. L. (1983). Early sign language acquisition and its relation to cognitive and motor development. In J. G. Kyle & B. Woll (Eds.), *Language in sign: An international perspective on sign language* (pp. 116–125). London: Croom Helm.

Bonvillian, J. D., Orlansky, M. D., Novack, L. L., Folven, R. J., & Holley-Wilcox, P. (1985). Language, cognitive, and cherological development: The first steps in sign language acquisition. In W. Stokoe & V. Volterra (Eds.), *SLR '83: Proceedings of the III International Symposium on Sign Language Research* (pp. 10–22). Silver Spring, MD: Linstok Press.

Boyes-Braem, P. (1973). A study of the acquisition of the dez in American Sign Language. Unpublished manuscript.

Brown, R. (1973). *A first language: The early stages.* Cambridge, MA: Harvard University Press.

Brown, R. (1977). Why are signed languages easier to learn than spoken languages? In *Proceedings of the First National Symposium on Sign Language Research and Teaching* (pp. 9–24). Washington, DC: National Association of the Deaf.

Brown, R. (1980). Development of a first language in the human species. *American Psychologist, 28,* 97–106.

Bruner, J. S. (1975). From communication to language. *Cognition, 3,* 255–287.

Bruner, J. S. (1983). *Child's talk: Learning to use language.* New York: W. W. Norton.

Caselli, M. C. (1983). Communication to language: Deaf children's and hearing children's development compared. *Sign Language Studies, 39,* 113–144.

Chomsky, N. (1965). *Aspects of the theory of syntax.* Cambridge, MA: MIT Press.

Chomsky, N. (1982). *Some concepts and consequences of the theory of government and binding.* Cambridge, MA: MIT Press.

Chomsky, N. (1986). *Knowledge of language: Its nature, origin, and use.* New York: Praeger Press.

Chomsky, N., & Halle, M. (1968). *The sound patterns of English.* New York: Harper & Row.

Clark, H. H., & Haviland, S. E. (1977). Comprehension and the given-new contract. In R. O. Freedle (Ed.), *Discourse production and comprehension* (pp. 1–40). Norwood, NJ: Ablex.

Collins-Ahlgren, M. (1990). Spatial-locative predicates in Thai Sign Language. In C. Lucas (Ed.), *Sign language research: Theoretical issues* (pp. 103–117). Washington, DC: Gallaudet University Press.

Corazza, S. (1990). The morphology of classifier handshapes in Italian Sign Language (LIS). In C. Lucas (Ed.), *Sign language research: Theoretical issues* (pp. 71–82). Washington, DC: Gallaudet University Press.

Corazza, S., Radutzky, E., Santarelli, B., Verdirosi, M. L., Volterra, V., & Zingarini, A. (1985). Italian Sign Language: General summary of research. In W. Stokoe & V. Volterra (Eds.), *SLR '83: Proceedings of the III International Symposium on Sign Language Research* (pp. 289–298). Silver Spring, MD: Linstok Press.

Coulter, G. R. (1977). Continuous representation in American Sign Language. In *Proceedings of the First National Symposium on Sign Language Research and Teaching* (pp. 247–257). Washington, DC: National Association of the Deaf.

DeMatteo, A. (1977). Visual imagery and visual analogues in American Sign Language. In L. A. Friedman (Ed.), *On the other hand: New perspectives on American Sign Language* (pp. 109–136). New York: Academic Press.

De Villiers, J. G., & de Villiers, P. A. (1978). *Language acquisition.* Cambridge, MA: Harvard University Press.

Engberg-Pedersen, E., & Pedersen, A. (1985). Proforms in Danish Sign Language: Their use in figurative signing. In W. Stokoe & V. Volterra (Eds.), *SLR '83: Proceedings of the III International Symposium on Sign Language Research* (pp. 202–209). Silver Spring, MD: Linstok Press.

Ferguson, C. A. (1976). The structure and use of politeness formulas. *Language in Society, 5,* 137–151.

Fischer, S. D. (1974a). Sign language and linguistic universals. In C. Rohrer & N. Ruwet (Eds.), *Actes du colloque franco-allemand de grammaire transformationelle* vol. 2, *Etude de semantique et autres* (pp. 187–204). Tubingen: Niemeyer.

Fischer, S. D. (1974b). The ontogenetic development of language. In E. W. Straus (Ed.), *Language and language disturbances: The Fifth Lexington Conference of Pure and Applied Phenomenology* (pp. 22–43). Pittsburgh: Duquesne University Press.

Flavell, J. (1963). *The developmental psychology of Jean Piaget.* Princeton, NJ: Van Nostrand.

Friedman, L. A. (1977). *On the other hand: New perspectives of American Sign Language.* New York: Academic Press.

Furth, H. G. (1966). *Thinking without language: Psychological implications of deafness.* New York: Free Press.

Furth, H. G. (1973). *Deafness and learning: A psychosocial approach.* Belmont, CA: Wadworth Publishing Company.

Galvan, D. (1989). A sensitive period for the acquisition of complex morphology: Evidence from American Sign Language. *Papers and Reports on Child Language Development, 28,* 107–114.

Gessell, A., & Thompson, H. (1934). *Infant behavior: Its genesis and growth.* New York: McGraw Hill.

Greenberg, J. H. (1963). Some universals of grammar with particular reference to the order of meaningful elements. In J. H. Greenberg (Ed.), *Universals of language* (pp. 73–113). Cambridge, MA: MIT Press.

Grice, H. P. (1975). Logic and conversation. In P. Cole & J. L. Morgan (Eds.), *Speech acts* (pp. 41–58). New York: Academic Press.

Harris, M. (1992). *Language experience and early language development.* Hove, East Sussex, UK: Lawrence Erlbaum Associates.

Hockett, C. F. (1963). The problem of universals in language. In J. H. Greenberg (Ed.), *Universals of language* (pp. 1–29). Cambridge, MA: MIT Press.

Hoffmeister, R., & Wilbur, R. B. (1980). The acquisition of sign language. In H. Lane & F. Grosjean (Eds.), *Recent perspectives on American Sign Language.* Hillsdale, NJ: Lawrence Erlbaum Associates.

Jakobson, R. (1941/1968). *Child language aphasia and phonological universals* (A. R. Keiler, Trans.). The Hague: Mouton.

James, W. (1890). *The principles of psychology* (vols. 1–2). New York: Henry Holt & Co.

James, W. (1892). Thought before language: A deaf-mute's recollections. *Philosophical Review, 1,* 613–624.

Johnston, J. R. (1986). Cognitive prerequisites: The evidence from children learning English. In D. I. Slobin (Ed.), *The crosslinguistic study of language acquisition,* vol. 2, *Theoretical issues* (pp. 961–1004). Hillsdale, NJ: Lawrence Erlbaum Associates.

Kantor, R. (1980). The acquisition of classifiers in American Sign Language. *Sign Language Studies, 28,* 193–208.

Klima, E. S. (1975). Sound and its absence in the linguistic symbol. In J. F. Cavanagh & J. E. Cutting (Eds.), *The role of speech in language.* Cambridge, MA: MIT Press.

Klima, E. S., & Bellugi, U. (1972). The signs of language in child and chimpanzee. In T. Alloway, L. Krames, & P. Pliner (Eds.), *Communication and affect.* New York: Academic Press.

Kyle, J. G., & Woll, B. (1985). *Sign language: The study of deaf people and their language.* Cambridge: Cambridge University Press.

Lane, H. (1976). *The wild boy of Aveyron.* Cambridge, MA: Harvard University Press.

Lane, H., Boyes-Braem, P., & Bellugi, U. (1976). Preliminaries to a distinctive feature analysis of handshapes in American Sign Language. *Cognitive Psychology, 8,* 263–289.

Lenneberg, E. H. (1967). *Biological foundations of language.* New York: John Wiley & Sons.

Lillo-Martin, D. (1991). *Universal grammar and American Sign Language: Setting the null argument parameters.* Dordrecht, The Netherlands: Klewer Academic Publishers.

Lillo-Martin, D., & Klima, E. S. (1990). Pointing out differences: ASL pronouns in syntactic theory. In S. D. Fischer & P. Siple (Eds.), *Theoretical issues in sign language research: Linguistics* (pp. 191–210). Chicago: University of Chicago Press.

Loncke, F. (1985). Sign phonemics and kinesiology. In W. Stokoe & V. Volterra (Eds.), *SLR '83: Proceedings of the III International Symposium on Sign Language Research* (pp. 152–158). Silver Spring, MD: Linstok Press.

Luria, A. R. (1961). *The role of speech in the regulation of normal and abnormal behavior.* London: Pergamon Press.

Macken, M. A. (1995). Phonological acquisition. In J. A. Goldsmith (Ed.), *The handbook of phonological theory* (pp. 671–696). Oxford: Blackwell.

Mayberry, R. I. (1993a). First-language acquisition after childhood differs from second-language acquisition: The case of American Sign Language. *Journal of Speech and Hearing Research, 36,* 1258–1270.

Mayberrry, R. I. (1993b). The first language timing hypothesis as demonstrated by American Sign Language. *Child Language Research Forum, 25,* 76–85.

Mayberry, R. I., & Eichen, E. B. (1991). The long-lasting advantage of learning sign language in childhood: Another look at the critical period for language acquisition. *Journal of Memory and Language, 30,* 486–512.

McDonald, B. (1983). Levels of analysis in signed languages. In J. G. Kyle & B. Woll (Eds.), *Language in sign: An international perspective on sign language* (pp. 32–40). London: Croom Helm.

McDonald, B. H. (1985). Productive and frozen lexicon in ASL: An old problem revisited. In W. Stokoe & V. Volterra (Eds.), *SLR '83: Proceedings of the III International Symposium on Sign Language Research* (pp. 254–259). Silver Spring, MD: Linstok Press.

McIntire, M. L. (1974). A modified model for the description of language acquisition in a deaf child. Master's thesis, California State University at Northridge, Northridge, CA.

McIntire, M. L. (1977). The acquisition of American Sign Language hand configurations. *Sign Language Studies, 16,* 247–266.

Meier, R. P., & Newport, E. L. (1990). Out of the hands of babes: On a possible sign advantage in language acquisition. *Language, 66,* 1–23.

Nash, J. E. (1973). Cues or signs: A case study in language acquisition. *Sign Language Studies, 3,* 79–92.

Nelson, K. (1973). Structure and strategy in learning to talk. *Monographs of the Society for Research in Child Development, 38,* serial no. 149, nos. 1–2.

Newport, E. L. (1982). Task specificity in language learning? Evidence from speech perception and American Sign Language. In E. Wanner & L. R. Gleitman (Eds.), *Language acquisition: The state of the art* (pp. 450–486). Cambridge: Cambridge University Press.

Newport, E. L. (1988). Constraints on learning and their role in language acquisition: Studies of the acquisition of American Sign Language. *Language Science, 10,* 147–172.

Newport, E. L. (1990). Maturational constraints on language learning. *Cognitive Science, 14,* 11–28.

Newport, E. L., & Ashbrook, E. (1977). The emergence of semantic relations in American Sign Language. *Papers and Reports on Child Language Development, 13,* 16–21.

Newport, E. L., & Meier, R. (1986). The acquisition of American Sign Language. In D. I. Slobin (Ed.), *The crosslinguistic study of language acquisition,* vol. 1, *The data* (pp. 881–938). Hillsdale, NJ: Lawrence Erlbaum Associates.

Newport, E. L., & Supalla, T. (1980). Clues from the acquisition of signed and spoken language. In U. Bellugi & M. Studdert-Kennedy (Eds.), *Signed and spoken language: Biological constraints on linguistic form* (pp. 187–212). Weinheim, West Germany: Verlag Chemie.

O'Connor, N., & Hermelin, B. (1978). *Seeing and hearing and space and time.* London: Academic Press.

Orlansky, M. D., & Bonvillian, J. D. (1984). The role of iconicity in early sign language acquisition. *Journal of Speech and Hearing Disorders, 49,* 287–292.

Osgood, C. E. (1963). Language universals and psycholinguistics. In J. H. Greenberg (Ed.), *Universals of language* (pp. 299–322). Cambridge, MA: MIT Press.

Piaget, J. (1955). *The language and thought of the child.* Cleveland, OH: Meridian.

Piaget, J. (1962). *Play, dreams, and imitation in childhood.* New York: W. W. Norton.

Plato (1892). *The dialogues of Plato* (vol. 1, B. Jowett, Trans.). New York: Macmillan. (Publication date of original work unknown.)

Prinz, P. M., & Prinz, E. A. (1981). Acquisition of ASL and spoken English by a hearing child of a deaf mother and a hearing father: Phase II. Early combinatorial patterns. *Sign Language Studies, 30,* 78–88.

Prinz, P. M., & Prinz, E. A. (1985). If only you could hear what I see: Discourse development in sign language. *Discourse Processes, 8,* 1–19.

Schick, B. (1990). The effects of morphosyntactic structure on the acquisition of classifier predicates in ASL. In C. Lucas (Ed.), *Sign language research: Theoretical issues* (pp. 358–374). Washington, DC: Gallaudet University Press.

Schlesinger, H. S. (1978). The acquisition of bimodal language. In I. M. Schlesinger & L. Namir (Eds.), *Sign language of the deaf* (pp. 57–93). New York: Academic Press.

Schlesinger, H. S., & Meadow, K. P. (1972). *Sound and sign: Childhood deafness and mental illness.* Berkeley: University of California Press.

Siple, P. (1978a). Linguistic and psychological properties of American Sign Language: An overview. In P. Siple (Ed.), *Understanding language through sign language research* (pp. 3–23). New York: Academic Press.

Siple, P. (1978b). Visual constraints for sign language communication. *Sign Language Studies, 19,* 97–112.

Siple, P., Akamatsu, C. T., & Loew, R. C. (1990). Acquisition of American Sign Language by fraternal twins: A case study. *International Journal of Sign Linguistics, 1,* 3–13.

Siple, P., Richmond-Welty, D., Howe, J. N., Berwanger, P., & Jasper, J. E. (1994). Gaze, joint attention, and interaction in twins with deaf parents. Paper presented at the annual meeting of the Boston Child Language Conference, January, Boston, MA.

Slobin, D. I. (1986a). Crosslinguistic evidence for the language-making capacity. In D. I. Slobin (Ed.), *The crosslinguistic study of language acquisition,* vol. 2, *Theoretical issues* (pp. 1157–1256). Hillsdale, NJ: Lawrence Erlbaum Associates.

Slobin, D. I. (1986b). Introduction: Why study acquisition crosslinguistically? In D. I. Slobin (Ed.), *The crosslinguistic study of language acquisition,* vol. 1, *The data* (pp. 3–24). Hillsdale, NJ: Lawrence Erlbaum Associates.

Slobin, D. I. (Ed.) (1986–1992). *The crosslinguistic study of language acquisition* (vols. 1–3). Hillsdale, NJ: Lawrence Erlbaum Associates.

Sperber, D., & Wilson, D. (1986). *Relevance.* Oxford: Blackwell.

Stampe, D. (1969). The acquisition of phonemic representation. In *Proceedings of the Fifth Regional Meeting of the Chicago Linguistics Society* (pp. 443–454). Chicago, IL: University of Chicago Press.

Stokoe, W. C., Jr. (1960). *Sign language structure: An outline of the visual communication systems of the American deaf* (Studies in Linguistics: Occasional Papers 8). Buffalo, NY: University of Buffalo, Department of Anthropology and Linguistics.

Stokoe, W. C., Jr., Casterline, D. C., & Croneberg, C. G. (1965). *A dictionary of American Sign Language on linguistic principles.* Washington, DC: Gallaudet College Press.

Supalla, T., & Newport, E. (1978). How many seats in a chair?: The derivation of nouns and verbs in American Sign Language. In P. Siple (Ed.), *Understanding language through sign language research* (pp. 91–132). New York: Academic Press.

Swisher, M. V. (1991). Conversational interaction between deaf children and their hearing mothers: The role of visual attention. In P. Siple & S. D. Fischer (Eds.), *Theoretical issues in sign language research: Psychology* (pp. 111–134). Oxford: Oxford University Press.

Swisher, M. V. (1993). Perceptual and cognitive aspects of recognition of signs in peripheral vision. In M. Marschark & M. D. Clark (Eds.), *Psychological perspectives on deafness* (pp. 209–227). Hillsdale, NJ: Lawrence Erlbaum Associates.

Tervoort, B. T., & Verberk, A. J. (1967). *Analysis of communicative structure patterns in deaf children.* Groningen, The Netherlands: Z. W. O. Onderzock, NR.

Uzgiris, I., & Hunt, J. M. (1975). *Assessment in infancy: Ordinal scales of psychological development.* Urbana: University of Illinois Press.

Volterra, V. (1983). Gestures, signs, and words at two years. In J. G. Kyle & B. Woll (Eds.), *Language in sign: An international perspective on sign language* (pp. 109–115). London: Croom Helm.

Volterra, V., & Caselli, M. C. C. (1985). From gestures and vocalizations to signs and words. In W. Stokoe & V. Volterra (Eds.), *SLR '83: Proceedings of the III International Symposium on Sign Language Research* (pp. 1–9). Silver Spring, MD: Linstok Press.

Vygotsky, L. S. (1962). *Thought and language.* Cambridge, MA: MIT Press.

Vygotsky, L. S. (1978). *Mind in society* (M. Cole, V. John-Steiner, S. Scribner, & E. Souberman, Eds.). Cambridge, MA: Harvard University Press.

Wallin, L. (1990). Polymorphemic predicates in Swedish Sign Language. In C. Lucas (Ed.), *Sign language research: Theoretical issues* (pp. 133–143). Washington, DC: Gallaudet University Press.

Watson, J. B. (1930). *Behaviorism* (rev. ed.). Chicago: University of Chicago Press.

White, S. J. (1987). Lost for words: A Vygotskyian perspective on the developing use of words for hearing-impaired children. *Quarterly Newsletter of the Laboratory of Comparative Human Cognition, 9,* 111–115.

Wilbur, R. B. (1979). *American sign language and sign systems.* Baltimore, MD: University Park Press.

Wilbur, R. B., & Petitto, L. A. (1983). Discourse structure in American Sign Language conversations (or, How to know a conversation when you see one). *Discourse Processes, 6,* 225–241.

Yau, S. C. (1977). *The Chinese signs: Lexicon of the standard sign language for the deaf in China.* Wanchai, Hong Kong: Chiu Ming Publishing Co.

CHAPTER 3

The Modular Effects of Sign Language Acquisition

Diane Lillo-Martin

LANGUAGE AND THOUGHT 1: THE SAPIR-WHORF HYPOTHESIS

One of the topics that introductory linguistics courses almost always cover is the Sapir-Whorf hypothesis. According to the textbooks, around 1930 Edward Sapir (see Sapir, 1949) and (somewhat later) Benjamin Lee Whorf (Whorf, 1956) made two proposals: "First, that all higher levels of thinking are dependent on language. Second, that the structure of the language one habitually uses influences the manner in which one understands his environment. The picture of the universe shifts from tongue to tongue" (Chase, 1956, p. vi).

Careful reviews of this position usually point out that Sapir and Whorf were not the originators of such ideas, nor did they even put them so strongly (see Hill, 1988, for a nice review). But the idea that language shapes thought—or cognition—has been debated in various forms over the years and now usually goes by the name of the Sapir-Whorf hypothesis.

Despite their popular appeal, the two hypotheses, linguistic determinism and linguistic relativity, have been largely discredited by thorough crosslinguistic study and experimentation. The linguistic determinism hypothesis is the easiest to put to rest. The facts that (1) one can discover the patterns in a language other than one's own and that (2) cross-cultural miscommunications are frequent even among speakers of the same language attest to the ability of human cognition to think outside of language (cf. Hill, 1988).

The linguistic relativity hypothesis has been subject to greater scrutiny. Whorf's famous example of the Hopi view of time ("becoming later") as embodied in the linguistic system (e.g., the absence of tense marking on verbs) has frequently been discredited, in terms of both the actual linguistic system and the relationship between such a system and such a worldview.

A more particular example of potential linguistic relativity comes from the study of color terms. In a widely cited work, Berlin and Kay (1969) argued that perception and memory of colors are more closely related to a universal human capacity to perceive color than to the various ways in which different languages break apart and label the color spectrum. While their work has been subject to some criticism (Hill, 1988), it stands as one example of the failure of a strong form of linguistic relativity.

In large part, then, the strongest forms of the Sapir-Whorf hypothesis cannot be true. Although languages differ, and cultures differ, it is usually concluded that where differences exist between languages, they may be entirely accidental or they may reflect—not determine—speakers' worldviews. However, in at least one way, the relativity hypothesis does receive support. As Hill (1988) points out: "The original demonstrations by Boas . . . and Sapir . . . , that the sound patterning of our languages constrains our perception of speech sounds, have never been refuted" (p. 31).

Sapir showed that a speaker's perception of speech sounds was influenced by the role these sounds played in the native language. To an untrained native speaker, it is difficult to distinguish the various phones that make up one phoneme. For example, the /p/ in "pot" and the /p/ in "spot" are pronounced very differently, but native speakers of English to whom this fact has never been pointed out are rarely even aware of it. Sapir (1933) remarked: "I have come to the practical realization that what the naive speaker hears is not phonetic elements but phonemes. . . . It is exceedingly difficult, if not impossible, to teach a native to take account of purely mechanical phonetic variations which have no phonemic reality for him" (pp. 47–48). That is, by virtue of having learned to speak, the way we perceive speech is affected. There are two aspects of this phenomenon we should examine more closely.

First, there is abundant evidence that adults perceive linguistic contrasts from their own native language much differently from their perception of contrasts not in their own language (in addition to Sapir's work, see Lisker & Abramson, 1964, 1970; and Miyawaki et al., 1975). This effect of linguistic experience can be observed not only in adults but even in very young children. A series of studies has found that children as young as 1 year old differentially perceive sounds from their own language as compared with sounds from other languages (see Eimas, 1991, and Werker, 1991, for reviews of many of these studies). It seems, however, that the very youngest infants tested have not yet narrowed down their phonetic inventories. That is, they perceive all contrasts in the way that adult native speakers of the languages using these contrasts do. Hence, the perception of specific phonetic contrasts is clearly an area in which language acquisition affects perception. In this sense, linguistic relativity is correct: the way we perceive the world (in particular, the way we perceive speech sounds) is strongly affected by the characteristics of our native language.

The second issue to consider has not been tested, but it is even more germane to the point of this book. Does having learned spoken language affect the perception of speech in general? That is, are there aspects of speech perception that depend on early exposure to spoken language but not on early exposure to a particular language? Even more broadly, does having learned spoken language in general affect any other aspect of perception or cognition? Is there some aspect of our perception that has been influenced by the fact that we have been exposed to spoken language—something that would be different if we had not been exposed to speech?

It is reasonable to bring up the possibility that exposure to spoken language affects perception or cognition. In comparison, we know that exposure to the vertical and horizontal lines normally present in the environment affects the development of a kitten's visual perception (Blakemore, 1974). Why shouldn't exposure to the special acoustic properties of speech affect perception, especially auditory perception?

It is easy to see why this issue has not been tested. In order to see whether the acquisition of spoken language affects perception or cognition, it is necessary to compare individuals who have acquired spoken language with individuals who have not. Unfortunately for the experiment, individuals who have not acquired spoken language are rare, and there is always a reason for their lack of spoken language that would invalidate the comparison. Only people who have suffered from severe mental, social, or auditory deprivation fail to acquire a spoken language. It would be possible to experimentally test the hypothesis by keeping neurologically normal children in a rich, loving environment with sound but not speech (cf. the kittens). However, this is, of course, impossible.[1]

Thus, we cannot directly test the question of whether the acquisition of spoken language affects the perception of language or other cognitive functions (aside from the particular phonetic contrasts found nonuniversally). But we can raise the issue with slightly different particulars, resurrecting the Sapir-Whorf hypothesis by virtue of the recognition that human language is not confined to the oral and aural modality. We can now ask: Does growing up with exposure to a signed language affect cognition? If so, how?

I will take it as well proven that the natural signed languages of the deaf are fully developed human languages on a par with naturally developed spoken languages (see Chapter 2). The conclusion that American Sign Language (ASL) is an independent, noncontrived, fully grammatical human language comparable to any spoken language has been supported by over 30 years of research. Recent research has shown that ASL displays principles of organization remarkably like those for spoken languages, at discourse, semantic, syntactic, morphological, and even phonological levels (see, e.g., Klima & Bellugi, 1979; Wilbur, 1987; and Sandler & Lillo-Martin, forthcoming, for reviews). Furthermore, it is acquired (Lillo-Martin, forthcoming), processed (Emmorey, 1992), and even breaks down (Poizner, Klima, & Bellugi, 1987) in ways analogous to those found for spoken languages. The similarities between signed and spoken languages are strong enough to make the differences worth investigating. In the third section of this chapter, I will argue that although there are differences in detail, the similarities are strong enough to conclude that essentially the same language mechanism underlies languages in either modality.

Then, if we accept the proposition that language reflects rather than determines thought, we might expect that signed languages will have no more of an effect on thought (or cognition) than Hopi or English. There are even further theoretical reasons not to expect such effects, to be discussed in the next section. There, I will outline the modularity hypothesis, which maintains that language is served by a processor independent in specific ways from other cognitive devices. I will briefly discuss the basic evidence for this hypothesis from consideration of spoken languages and suggest that it is a viable hypothesis for signed languages as well. If one and the same module underlies the acquisition and processing of spoken and signed languages, then we are led to expect signed languages to have certain characteristics but not others. In the third section, I will discuss the basic characteristics of signed languages and argue that they are consistent with the modularity hypothesis. Thus, our prediction will be that acquisition of a signed language does not affect cognition.

However, as I will summarize in the fourth section, there have been claims made that significant differences are found between the cognitive processes of deaf/signing children or adults and those of hearing/speaking ones. Does this mean Whorf was right after all? Are there, as he maintained, innumerable variations among languages that lead to innumerable cognitive variations among groups of speakers? In the final section, I will show that the credible differences that have been claimed are tightly limited in domain, and I will argue that this is exactly what is expected to follow from the model presented. In so doing, I will often speculate and raise questions for future research.

THE VIEW FROM THE MODULARITY HYPOTHESIS

To begin with, let us consider a hypothesis about the human faculty for language (based solely on studies of spoken languages): the modularity hypothesis, as described by Jerry Fodor (1983). According to Fodor, language has the characteristics of an "input system"—more similar to visual processing than to higher order thinking.[2] That is, the cognitive mechanisms that subserve language are specialized, automatic, and domain specific; according to this hypothesis, language is not served by the same cognitive devices that are used for problem solving or reasoning. Of course, the output of the language processor must feed general cognition, just as the output of the visual processor provides input to thought processes; and our responses to language can be mediated by such factors as whether or not we believe what we hear, just as our responses to what we see can be influenced by our knowledge of the world. But we hear language as language whether we believe it or not, just as we see a tiger as a tiger even if it is in the living room.

Let us use the diagram in Figure 3.1 to illustrate. The diagram shows the language processor operating as an input system: like the visual processor

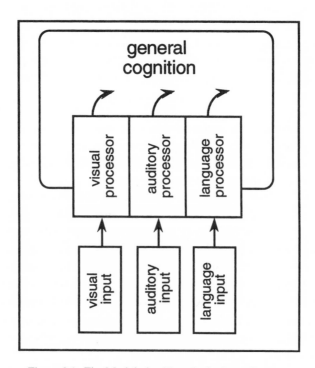

Figure 3.1. The Modularity Hypothesis: Input Systems

and the auditory processor, it takes input, processes it, and sends the output of its processing to general cognition. (Many additional processors, of course, have been omitted from the figure.) General cognition does not guide the processing of the input systems; it does not even have access to deep representations. Only the output of the input processors is available for the operations of general cognition.

To be more specific, Fodor (1983) provided a list of characteristics that he claimed modular systems display. Modules are domain specific, so the module for visual processing is distinct from the module for linguistic processing (cf. note 2). Their operation is mandatory, so we can't help but hear linguistic input as language. There is limited central access to the representations of a module; although the final output of a module's processing is available to central cognition, its internal layers of representations are not. The operation of a module is fast, but the operations of problem solving are frequently not fast. Modules are informationally encapsulated; that is, information from outside the module is not available during the module's processing.[3] Modular systems have shallow outputs; that is, they conduct only a minimal amount of processing before sending output to the central processors. They are associated with fixed neural architecture; specialized brain regions subserve language and other input systems. Modules exhibit characteristic and specific breakdown patterns, as in the aphasias and agnosias. Finally, the ontogeny of modules exhibits a characteristic pace and sequencing, such as the well-known milestones children go through in acquiring (spoken or signed) language.

My hypothesis is that natural signed languages are served by the same language module that serves spoken languages. That is, the domain specificity of the linguistic processor refers to language processing, not speech processing.[4] If so, sign language processing should display the same characteristics as other modules, such as having mandatory, fast operation with limited central access to shallow outputs, displaying informational encapsulation, and being served by a fixed neural architecture with characteristic breakdown and ontogeny. There is some evidence that this is so. For example, the processing of American Sign Language is as mandatory and fast as spoken language processing; signers experience sign language aphasias after damage to similar neural areas as those implicated in spoken language aphasias, and children acquiring ASL go through the same stages and pass the same milestones as those acquiring spoken languages (see, e.g., Klima & Bellugi, 1979; Emmorey, 1992; Poizner et al., 1987; Newport & Meier, 1985; and Lillo-Martin, forthcoming).

What more can be said about the language processor specifically? Let us make a combination of Fodor's modularity and Noam Chomsky's modularity (1981). Unlike Fodor, Chomsky proposes that the operations of the phonological, morphological, syntactic, and semantic components may themselves be modular. See Figure 3.2 for illustration. The figure shows that the language module receives input and passes its output to the processing of the central systems (general cognition) without receiving feedback from the latter. The language module itself consists of Universal Grammar (UG) and is divided into submodules, here represented as phonology, morphology, syntax, and semantics. This representation is not meant to be exhaustive but is illustrative of the internal workings of the language module.

Now, if the same Universal Grammar explains signed and spoken languages, then its principles should be abstract enough to hold across modalities. As linguistic information is input (from whatever modality), it is processed by the amodal submodules and output to general cognition, displaying the characteristics of an input system/module.

What evidence can be adduced in regards to the modularity hypothesis? An important class of evidence for domain specificity comes from studies of the perception of speech, many of which have been undertaken at Haskins

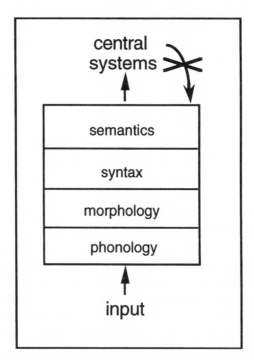

Figure 3.2. The Modularity Hypothesis: The Language Module

Laboratories (see, e.g., Liberman, Cooper, Shankweiler, & Studdert-Kennedy, 1967; Mann & Liberman, 1983; Mattingly & Liberman, 1985; and Mattingly & Studdert-Kennedy, 1991). As Fodor (1983, p. 49) points out, these experiments show that "the very same signal that is heard as the onset of a consonant when the context specifies that the stimulus is speech is heard as a 'whistle' or 'glide' when it is isolated from the speech stream. The rather strong implication is that the computational systems that come into play in the perceptual analysis of speech are distinctive in that they operate only upon acoustic signals that are taken to be utterances." These results support the hypothesis that a specialized processor analyzes acoustic information in very particular ways only if the input is linguistic (the modularity hypothesis).

Fodor cites a study by Marslen-Wilson and Tyler (1981) as evidence for the mandatoriness of the language module: "Even when subjects are asked to focus their attention on the acoustic-phonetic properties of the input, they do not seem to be able to avoid identifying the words involved. . . . This implies that the kind of processing operations observable in spoken-word recognition are mediated by automatic processes which are obligatorily applied" (Marslen-Wilson & Tyler, 1981, p. 327, cited in Fodor, 1983, p. 53).

Fodor acknowledges that some individuals, such as trained phoneticians or painters, can "undo the perceptual constancies" and "hear their language as something like a sound-stream," or see the world "as a two-dimensional spread of color discontinuities varying over time" (1983, p. 54). But he argues that such highly skilled processing is qualitatively different from normal processing and should not be taken as a counterargument to the claim of mandatoriness. Furthermore, in his 1985 précis, Fodor argues that experiments that demonstrate particular points using non-normal processing (such as the perception of speech in noise) cannot necessarily be taken to provide evidence about normal processing and therefore cannot be used as counterevidence to the modularity hypothesis.

As for limited central access, Fodor cites two of the numerous experiments that demonstrate that only meaning is maintained for long after sentence processing; the exact syntax becomes lost momentarily (see Sachs, 1967). We can, by employing extra processing, force ourselves to recall certain aspects of processing. Other, lower levels might never be accessible, but their impact can still be seen in processing. For example, Pisoni and Tash (1974) found that reaction times to same/different judgments for pairs of sounds that are perceptually indistinguishable were different depending on whether the stimuli were actually acoustically identical or differed only in noncontrastive (subphonetic) acoustic properties. It is, at best, very difficult to access lower levels of language processing; in normal processing, these levels are used but are not available for conscious report.

Fodor provides similar kinds of evidence for his other claimed character-istics of modules, which I will not summarize here. Let me put forward that the evidence for the hypothesis is strong and consider what implications it would have, if it is correct, for signed languages. First, however, I would like to discuss another hypothesis that also has bearing on the questions raised here.

Modularity and Language Acquisition

Although it is theoretically independent, another hypothesis is often con-nected with the modularity hypothesis: the nativism hypothesis. According to the nativism hypothesis, some aspects of the language module are innate. The nativism and modularity hypotheses can be presented together with the principles and parameters theory of grammar (e.g., Chomsky, 1981), which maintains that the principles and parameters of Universal Grammar are in-nately given. Because the parameters allow for linguistic variation, the child must be exposed to a particular language to "set" them at the appropriate values. However, since the range of possible linguistic variation is limited, the child's job is greatly reduced in comparison to hypothesis testing or other theories of learning.

Just what does the child need to learn? One important proposal is the lexical hypothesis (Borer, 1983). According to this hypothesis, the range of linguistic variation is restricted to the lexicon. Surely children need to learn the words of their language, since there is a wide variety between languages in lexical items (although even within the lexicon, there must be universals, such as the types of lexical or functional categories that are available, lexical redundancy rules, argument structure and lexical semantics, etc.). According to the lexical hypothesis, all variation is in the lexicon. Parameter settings, according to this view, are associated with particular lexical items.

What evidence can be adduced in regards to the nativism hypothesis? One of the strongest theoretical motivations for the nativism hypothesis is known as Plato's problem. The problem is this: How is it that we know so much, given our limited experience? This question can be raised in numer-ous domains (Plato raised it in connection with geometry), but there is clear evidence for it within language. By the time a child has an adultlike gram-mar (say, by age 3), the child obviously "knows" things in his or her mental grammar for which he or she never received evidence. Many studies of the child's language acquisition circumstances have made it clear that negative evidence—that is, input that certain strings are not grammatical sentences—

cannot be part of the input the child brings to the language acquisition task (see, e.g., Morgan & Travis, 1989, and Lasnik, 1989). But without innate knowledge, negative evidence would be crucial for the child to respect constraints, such as the constraint that rules out example (1d) below. In the lack of negative evidence, a constraint must prevent the child from ever trying to produce (1d), even on analogy with (1b), for example.

(1)   a. I like ice cream with chocolate.
       b. What do you like ice cream with?
       c. I like ice cream and chocolate.
       d. *What do you like ice cream and?

The existence of constraints in the adult grammar has led many researchers to hypothesize that they must be part of the innate endowment that children bring to the language acquisition task (see, e.g., Chomsky, 1986, and Hornstein & Lightfoot, 1981). Other researchers have tested this hypothesis by looking at young children's language, and they have found overwhelming support for the innateness hypothesis. Children as young as 3 years can be shown to respect these constraints—in fact, they show this as soon as they can be tested on the appropriate structures. Although children make mistakes like saying "goed" for "went," they never produce sentences like (1d). (See Crain, 1991, for a review of evidence that children do respect constraints at an early age.)

So constraints, apparently, must be a part of Universal Grammar. Principles governing limited crosslinguistic variation are also proposed to be part of UG. Individual lexical items, on the other hand, are clearly not part of UG. Where is the line drawn between good and poor candidates for inclusion?

Three hallmarks of innateness have been proposed by Stephen Crain (1991). First, knowledge in the absence of experience is a candidate for innateness. Any constraint that is not learnable on the basis of positive evidence must be part of UG. Second, the proposed principles of UG should be universal. We therefore do not expect languages to differ in unlearnable ways. Third, early emergence in the course of acquisition is expected of universal principles (that is, there should be evidence that the child respects universals as soon as they can be tested). These hallmarks show us that language-particular, learnable facts are not candidates for UG, and thus, this is where languages can be expected to vary.

Suppose that this innate language module serves both spoken and signed languages. What predictions are made? There are two general predictions we should consider. First, what predictions are made regarding the structure of signed languages? Second, what predictions are made regarding the influence of language on cognition?[5]

If one and the same module serves languages in either the visual or the auditory modality, then modality must be unspecified in the module (see Chapter 4). This means that the linguistic principles found to operate in signed languages cannot be significantly different from those found to operate in spoken languages. More precisely, taking the modularity hypothesis together with the nativism hypothesis, if any differences are found between signed and spoken languages, they must be learnable on the basis of the positive evidence that young children receive. This will be the topic of the next section.

Aside from this prediction concerning the structure of signed languages, the model presented has implications for the question of whether or not language (modality) affects cognition. Under the model, by the time the output reaches general cognition, information about the modality is no longer present. Hence, the modality of language use can have no influence on cognition. This hypothesis will be discussed in the final section of this chapter.

SIGN AND SPACE

If the same module that underlies the acquisition and processing of spoken languages underlies signed languages, what predictions can be made about the structure of signed languages? Signed languages should display the same characteristics as spoken languages, at least insofar as these characteristics are dependent on the hardwired specifications of the language module. In other words, signed languages should be different from spoken languages only as much as spoken languages are different from each other. If this is the case, then we are justified in claiming that the language module is amodal—principles of organization must be abstract enough to apply to either signed or spoken languages.

It is important to clarify which characteristics of language are dependent on the module. In studies of spoken languages, it has been found that certain (abstract) characteristics hold universally. Such properties are candidates for Universal Grammar, the hardwired specifications of the language module with which we are most concerned. Constraints that specify which elements of a sentence cannot be related by rules are prime candidates for UG, especially because they are not learnable. On the other hand, the presence of an optional rule (for example, the scrambling rule, which reorders constituents in Japanese) is learnable since positive input will be present in the linguistic environment in the form of sentences in which the rule has been applied.

Thus, signed languages may well have some properties distinct from those of spoken languages and still be consistent with the modularity hypothesis, provided that the evidence for those properties is clearly available in the input. We would not expect, however, to find modality differences below the surface—that is, aspects of signed languages that are crucially different from spoken languages yet unlearnable in the sense described above.

Let us now briefly examine some characteristics of the structure of signed languages (in particular, ASL) to see how well the predictions of the modularity hypothesis fit with the facts. I will focus the discussion on those areas most likely to exhibit modality effects to see whether or not purported effects are learnable.

Syntax

The research that has been done to investigate the syntax of ASL has in general found that it does adhere to the principles of UG. For example, Susan Fischer (1974) found that ASL obeys Ross's Complex NP Constraint (1967); Carol Padden (1983) found that ASL obeys Ross's Coordinate Structure Constraint; and I (Lillo-Martin, 1991) found evidence for both of these constraints as well as the Wh-Island Constraint and other subcases of Subjacency and the Empty Category Principle. Recent studies have proposed that ASL is not distinct from spoken languages in general in its phrase structure (e.g., Aarons, Bahan, Kegl, & Neidle, 1992; Boster, 1996; Liddell, 1980; Padden, 1983; Petronio, 1993), in wh-movement (Lillo-Martin & Fischer, 1992; Petronio & Lillo-Martin, 1997), and in other areas, although in many of these areas, ASL may be more akin to Chinese or Hungarian than English.

One area of ASL syntax that has attracted a considerable amount of discussion concerns the use of pronouns and other referential devices. In this domain there is the potential for strong modality effects, as evidenced by the term *spatial syntax,* which is frequently applied (e.g., Bellugi, vanHoek, Lillo-Martin, & O'Grady, 1988; Bellugi, Lillo-Martin, O'Grady, & vanHoek, 1990). Let me first describe this area in some detail to illustrate its spatial effects and then provide a nonspatial analysis.

When reference is made to people (or things) physically present in a signed discourse, pronoun signs referring to those people take the form of an index finger directed toward the referent. In simpler terms, for signers to refer to themselves, they point to their own chest; to refer to an addressee, they point to the addressee's chest; and to refer to some third person, they point to that person's chest. To refer to people (or things) not present, a signer chooses a location for that referent and either "imagines" that the referent is located there or fixes the referent in that location, using the same pointing gestures (Liddell, 1990). These pronoun signs are illustrated in Figure 3.3.

This system is spatial in that spatial locations are used as locations toward which the pointing sign is made; unlike the locations of other signs (which are meaningless sublexical units), these locations are used to enable the signer to pick out different referents (i.e., meaningfully). (Liddell [1990] uses the terms *articulatory locations* and *location fixing* to distinguish between these two uses of space.) The result is that ASL pronoun signs seem to be quite different from the pronouns of spoken languages in four ways (see Lillo-Martin & Klima, 1990, for a discussion of the first three).

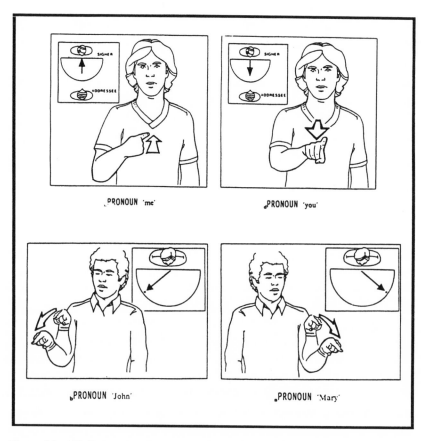

Figure 3.3. ASL Pronominal Signs (from Lillo-Martin & Klima, 1990; copyright, Dr. Ursula Bellugi, The Salk Institute)

First, there is apparently an infinite number of ASL pronouns. This results because any spatial location can be used as a location for a referent. Although signers do not, in practice, use more than around three distinct locations for different pronouns in any discourse segment (presumably because they or their conversational partner would forget who goes where if a large number of distinctions were used), in principle, between any two locations used, another location for a pronoun can be chosen. This situation would seem to entail an infinite lexicon—surely an undesirable state of affairs. It would not seem possible simply to omit specification of location in pronoun signs since the location serves to distinguish referents—a semantic function. It is also clearly impossible to list pronoun signs in every possible location as different signs.

The second way in which ASL pronouns seem to differ from spoken language pronouns is that they are unambiguous in reference. Once a location is fixed for a referent, a pronoun directed toward that location picks out that referent only. An example is given in (2). The pronoun "she" in the English example is ambiguous since it can refer back to either Karen or Susan. (In context, it might be clear which referent is intended, but structurally either one is possible.) In contrast, in the ASL example there is no way to be ambiguous. The ASL pronoun must be articulated toward location a or location b, clearly identifying the intended referent (t indicates a marker for topicalization).

(2) a. Karen saw Susan yesterday. She had already finished the paper.

$$\overline{\quad\quad t \quad\quad} \quad \overline{\quad\quad t \quad\quad}$$
   b. YESTERDAY, $_a$KAREN $_a$INDEX $_a$SEE$_b$ $_b$SUSAN.
   two possible continuations:

$$\overline{\quad t \quad}$$
PAPER $_a$PRONOUN WRITE FINISH.

$$\overline{\quad t \quad}$$
PAPER $_b$PRONOUN WRITE FINISH.

In spoken languages, pronoun signs frequently pick out a class of referents, identified by features such as person, number, and gender. Even in languages with more refined classes, such as the gender classes of Bantu languages, a pronoun will pick out one member of that limited class, and frequently the reference will be completely disambiguated by context, but the pronoun itself does not identify its referent unambiguously. Use of a pronoun in one class does not distinguish among multiple possible referents within that class. In ASL, on the other hand, the referent is unambiguously picked out by use of the pronoun signs.

Although ambiguity is still averted, the third way in which ASL pronouns differ from spoken language pronouns concerns what is called *referential shift*. Under certain conditions, the reference of a pronoun changes. This referential shift is signaled by a shift in the signer's body position. For example, if "John" has been established in a location to the signer's right, the signer can then shift his body toward that location, with the result that the reference of pronouns changes. In particular, what changes is the reference of pronouns directed at the signer. Although normally taken as first person in reference, such pronouns will be interpreted as referring to some other person, made syntactically explicit in the relevant contexts. An example of referential shift is given in (3), where POV indicates a marker for point of view.

$$\overline{}^{\,_{a}POV}$$

(3) $_a$JOHN $_a$POV $_1$PRONOUN LIKE $_b$JANE;

$$\overline{}^{\,_{b}POV}$$
$_b$POV LIKE $_a$PRONOUN.

John$_i$ (from his$_i$ point of view) I like Jane$_j$;
and (she$_j$) (from her$_j$ point of view) likes him$_i$.

A phenomenon similar to the ASL referential shift is direct discourse in speech; this type of context does give rise to pronoun shift in both types of languages. For example, both the English and the ASL versions of the sentence "John said, 'I'm leaving now' " contain an apparent first-person pronoun that has reference to someone other than the speaker/signer. However, in ASL the contexts for referential shift go far beyond direct discourse. Referential shift is used when the thoughts or actions of another are reported or when the report is made from another's point of view (Engberg-Pedersen, 1995; Lillo-Martin, 1995; Poulin & Miller, 1995). At first glance, this might seem quite different from the use of pronouns in spoken language and a use which is specifically available in the spatial modality.

The fourth difference between ASL pronouns and spoken language pronouns is that ASL pronouns apparently contain additional information about real spatial/topographical locations. When locations are fixed for nonpresent referents, there are two ways of going about choosing the locations to be used. In the first, the locations used are apparently arbitrary, and the choice of locations reflects a tendency for maximal perceptual salience. So, for example, "John" might be located to the signer's right side, and when "Mary," the next referent, is introduced, she might be located to the signer's left side (see Bahan & Petitto, 1980). The relative spatial relationships between John, Mary, and the signer are used purely syntactically and say nothing about their real physical locations.

However, apparently the same pronoun signs can be used with the intention of specifying exact physical locations. In this case, by establishing John on the right and Mary on the left, the signer is conveying the information that John was on his right and Mary on his left. This topographical use of space is utilized extensively to convey locative relationships. Furthermore, additional morpho-syntactic devices can make use of this same topographical space. For example, classifier signs, which have morphemes to represent the size and shape or semantic category of their referents, are frequently employed in this system to indicate precise physical locations. Although I am focusing on pronoun signs here, the same questions about the use of space can be raised for classifiers and other morphemes that use this system. This spatial representation of space would seem to be unique to the visual modality and a prime candidate for a true modality effect.

These differences between the ASL pronominal system and spoken language pronouns seem to stem directly from the spatial nature of ASL and therefore to undermine the strong modularity hypothesis outlined above. However, I will now present alternative explanations for the various effects of the ASL system. My alternative does involve modality effects of a sort, but they are learnable, and as I have argued, learnable modality effects do not pose significant problems for the modularity hypothesis.

First, following some of the arguments made in Lillo-Martin and Klima (1990) and Meier (1990), the ASL pronominal system can be analyzed as containing two pronouns: a first-person pronoun ($_1$PRONOUN) and a non-first-person pronoun (PRONOUN).[6] All NPs in ASL, like NPs in spoken languages, are marked with a referential index. The referential index determines coreference and noncoreference between NPs at a level of interpretation, and NPs so marked with indices are subject to universal linguistic constraints. In ASL, unlike spoken languages, the indices are realized on the surface. This is the modality effect: although referential indices are needed in the grammar of all languages, regardless of modality, most likely only in sign languages will the referential index be phonologically realized. To my knowledge, no spoken language shows an overt manifestation of referential indices, and all of the sign languages that have been reported on do show this.

The phonological realization of the index requires that all co-indexed pronouns be articulated at the same location; contra-indexing requires different locations. The location used for a referent will remain constant throughout a discourse until it is changed by a new location being assigned by the signer (when, for example, he or she forgets where a referent has been located) or by one of a set of verbs that trigger such a change. When locations do not represent physical positioning, the choice of location will be determined by the perceptual salience strategies referred to above. I will return to the instances in which locations for referents do represent physical locations.

The analysis presented so far accounts for the first and second differences between signed and spoken language pronouns: there are two pronouns in ASL, not an infinite list, and the reference of each pronoun is determined by the referential index. Given this, the third difference might pose a larger problem: if the location of a pronoun (R-locus) corresponds to its referential index, then how will the pronoun be able to refer to a different person?

The solution to the third problem lies in the analysis of referential shift. I have analyzed the body movement that signals the referential shift as a predicate, which indicates that the following material is presented from the point of view of the subject of that predicate (Lillo-Martin, 1995). To illustrate, reconsider sentence (3) above, repeated below.

$$\overline{}\ _a\text{POV}$$

(3) $_a$JOHN $_a$POV $_1$PRONOUN LIKE $_b$JANE;

$$\overline{}\ _b\text{POV}$$
$_b$POV LIKE $_a$PRONOUN.

John$_i$ (from his$_a$ point of view) I like Jane$_j$;
and (she$_j$) (from her$_j$ point of view) likes him$_i$.

In this sentence, there are two referential shifts. The first part of the sentence gives John as the subject, then the POV predicate appears, agreeing with John. From this point until the next POV predicate, the sentence is told from John's point of view. This means that any first-person pronouns will refer to John, not the signer. In the second conjunct, the matrix subject is null (cf. Lillo-Martin, 1986), but the reference of the null subject is unambiguous; since the POV predicate agrees with the location for JANE given in the previous conjunct, the subject of the second conjunct, and person whose point of view is taken in the remainder of the sentence, is Jane.

By what mechanism does the POV predicate allow the reference of pronouns in the following clauses to change? The ASL first-person pronoun following a POV predicate behaves much like the logophoric pronouns of West African languages such as Ewe and Gokana (cf. Clements, 1975; Hyman & Comrie, 1981; Koopman & Sportiche, 1989). Following the analysis of such logophoric pronouns proposed by Koopman and Sportiche, I (Lillo-Martin, 1995) have proposed that the ASL first-person pronoun can also act as a logophoric pronoun. The POV predicate takes a clausal complement that is headed by an operator. This operator binds all logophoric pronouns in its scope and therefore causes the shift in interpretation. Hence, the referential shift becomes fully accountable under the mechanisms already provided in UG.

A further point about the changes in reference under the POV predicate is required. Note that non-first-person pronouns do not change their reference.

This is important, as it shows that only the logophoric, first-person pronoun is affected by the operator. However, this might lead the reader to wonder what happens when first-person reference is desired (i.e., reference to the signer). One option would be to change the POV back to the signer; under the signer's point of view, the first-person pronoun would, of course, refer to the signer. However, if it is desired to make reference to the signer, still within someone else's point of view, the first-person pronoun will not do. Rather, the signer needs to be established at a new (non-first) location, and a non-first-person pronoun can be used to refer to him or her. In the unmarked case, the location used for the signer is not arbitrary, however, nor is it determined by the perceptual salience procedure. Rather, the signer's location will be established as the location that the signer occupied before the shift to another's point of view. So if under the shift the signer moved his or her shoulders to the right (facing toward the left), the new location for the signer under POV will be on the left. This new location falls within the use of linguistic locations for representing physical locations, to which I now turn.

There has been some debate in the ASL literature regarding whether or not there is a clear distinction between syntactic and topographical uses of space. (The main opponent of such a distinction is Liddell, 1990, 1995, but see Emmorey, 1996; Emmorey, Corina, & Bellugi, 1995; and Poizner et al., 1987, for evidence that the distinction is psychologically real.) Notwithstanding, both sides agree that spatial locations are in some cases strictly sublexical, but in others they convey information about locations. When location is used as a sublexical element, it need only be listed in the lexical entry for a particular sign—surely a learnable aspect of the language (later I will discuss sublexical aspects of ASL phonology in more detail).

When location is used to convey information about location, it is usually considered to have morphological status. Location is not different from hand configuration or movement in having this dual role—all three parameters can be sublexical or have morphological status. The only problem is that no detailed analysis of the location morphemes has been completed. Ted Supalla (1986) argued that the large variety of movements observed in classifier signs can be broken down into a small number of movement morphemes that combine sequentially or simultaneously to create more complex forms. However, he did not break down locations in the same way.

It is possible that location could be broken down into a small number of basic morphemes that can be combined in various ways. As with the movement morphemes proposed by Supalla, by utilizing simultaneous as well as sequential combinations of morphemes, a relatively small number of morphemes might be able to adequately represent the linguistically significant uses of spatial locations. Alternatively, Liddell and Johnson (1989) proposed an analysis of space using numerous vectors, distances, and heights that resulted in over 100 different points in space toward which a sign could be directed. Although large, this number is finite, and this system thus represents a possible way of breaking down the visual-spatial input into modality-independent morphemes.

I should note, however, that Liddell (1995) claims that even the Liddell and Johnson model is not sufficient for representing the spaces that can be used. He argues that the locations are unlimited—hence unlistable, non-morphemic. Instead, he claims that "linguistic features can be used to describe the handshape, movement, and certain aspects of the orientation of the hand, but the locations the signs are directed toward cannot be described through linguistic features" (p. 36). If this is correct, the specification of how the nonlinguistic information is represented or processed will require extensive analysis.

With a morphological analysis of location, on the other hand, it is clear that no learnability flags need be raised. The surface realizations of these morphemes give overt evidence for their existence and analysis. Presumably, children learning this system will use a morphological analysis and not even attempt to learn the system as an iconic, analog mapping of space to space. This presumption is based on the results of numerous studies of the acquisition of other aspects of ASL, in which it is clearly seen that the iconic bases of certain signs (including pronominals [Petitto, 1983] and verb agreement [Meier, 1982]) do not play a role in their acquisition (see also Lillo-Martin, forthcoming, for review). There are no modality-specific constraints required here.

With a morphological analysis of the input, the modularity hypothesis is not violated. It is important that by the time the input reaches the syntactic processor, no modality-specific information is necessary. If, literally, a picture of the visual input is necessary for syntactic analysis, this would contradict my claims. But notice that a mental picture that arises as a result of the linguistic structure is not contrary to the claims made here. It is expected that such a mental picture might be constructed from the meaning of the morphemes and their syntactic analysis, just as with spoken languages.

Morphology

ASL morphology is rich and productive. Temporal aspect, agreement with person and number, distribution, instrument, location, and other information can be marked by morphological processes. In its form, ASL morphology does reflect its visual-spatial modality. Most morphological processes in ASL do not use affixation; rather, the form of the root itself changes. For example, much of the verbal morphology uses characteristic changes in movement by altering the direction of the movement, changing the size of the movement, and/or adding repetition to the movement.

More specifically, ASL marks verb agreement with subject and object using the spatial syntax described above. An agreeing verb moves from the location associated with the subject to the location associated with the object, as illustrated in Figure 3.4.

I have already discussed aspects of the analysis of the spatial representation of (real or imagined) space, but there is still the issue of how the morphological combination is represented. This, too, was originally taken to be a modality-peculiar component of ASL grammar, and stress was given to the simultaneous nature of the morphological pieces (Klima & Bellugi, 1979).

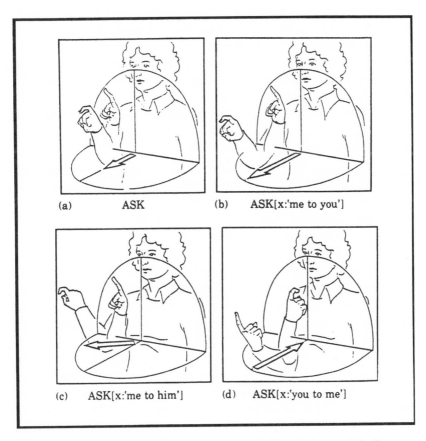

Figure 3.4. ASL Verb Agreement (from Klima & Bellugi, 1979; copyright, Dr. Ursula Bellugi, The Salk Institute)

However, although spoken languages do frequently use affixation for morphological processes, an analog to, analysis of, and representation of the ASL process is available by considering Semitic root-plus-vowel combinations in an autosegmental approach. For example, Liddell (1984b) proposed to represent ASL verbal roots as schemas with underspecified movements, with aspect as morphemes that can fill in the movement specifications. This kind of analysis indicates that ASL morphology isn't so strange after all. The analyses utilize the kinds of theoretical machinery that are necessary for spoken languages anyway, despite their superficially different appearance. The rules and principles of morphological combination—those aspects that would be part of UG—are constant across modalities.

Phonology

ASL signs have sublexical structure. (Stokoe [1960], wanting to be accurate in his use of roots, called the individual units *cheremes,* but currently researchers studying this level of ASL structure call it *phonology.*) For some time, the focus in describing sign sublexical structure was on the simultaneity of occurrence of the sign pieces. Signs can be described using one of a limited number of hand configurations, locations, and movements—all of which combine simultaneously (see, e.g., Stokoe, Casterline, & Croneberg, 1965). If simultaneous combination is a crucial part of sign structure, it might well seem to be a modality effect.

However, more recent research on ASL phonology has pointed out the importance of sequentiality (beginning with Liddell, 1984a), and almost all current accounts of ASL phonology include representations of both sequential and simultaneous information. In fact, current models of ASL phonology employ the same terminology, representational systems, and theoretical devices as current models of spoken language phonology (see, e.g., Brentari, 1990; Coulter, 1993; Liddell & Johnson, 1986; Padden & Perlmutter, 1987; Perlmutter, 1992; and Sandler, 1989, 1993). As one example, in Figure 3.5, I have reproduced a model of the structure of spoken language phonological representations from Clements (1985) alongside a model of the structure of ASL hand configuration representations from Sandler (1989).

The names of the features, the node labels, or the proposed tiers are often the only hints that the language whose phonology is being represented is potentially radically different. Here, of necessity, there is a modality effect, since the node labels are different and the skeleton itself has a different shape. But, importantly, the constraints on how to combine elements, what a hierarchy can and cannot look like, and what processes can apply are constant, regardless of modality. I take this as evidence that the same lan-

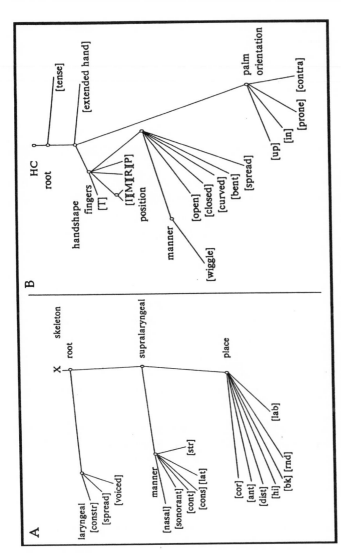

Figure 3.5. Spoken (A) and Signed (B) Language Feature Hierarchies (from Sandler, 1989). This model has been revised in Sandler (1995, 1996), where the terminal features shown here have been replaced by a smaller, more abstract set of unary components. The basic hierarchy of feature classes has remained unchanged.

guage module is employed in the processing of signed and spoken languages, once the most superficial input patterns can be translated into amodal, abstract units.

A Bimodal/Amodal Language Module

Let me put together the evidence reviewed so far and make my proposal more precise. I accept the arguments that language structure and processing display the characteristics of a module, roughly as defined by Fodor but amended following Chomsky to include submodules for different aspects of processing (including, in particular, auditory phonetic processing as one module that provides input to the next higher linguistic module). I take the similarities between signed and spoken language to be a good indication that the same computational system underlies both at some levels. In particular, those aspects of Universal Grammar that are amodal (including logical form, syntax, morphology, and parts of phonology and the lexicon) constitute modules that are common for signed and spoken languages. The input to the common modules must come through separate modules, processing auditory versus visual information. My proposed model is illustrated in Figure 3.6.

The diagram in Figure 3.6 shows separate phonetic processors for auditory and visual input. There is good evidence that auditory phonetic processing is modular. Some evidence for this was discussed in the previous section, and much of Fodor's book employs this kind of evidence. Whether or not there is a separate visual phonetic processor (and if so, how it develops) is less clear. Some research has pointed to specialized processing of sign linguistic information (e.g., Poizner, 1983; Poizner, Fok, & Bellugi, 1989), but more work is needed. I hypothesize the existence of a separate visual phonetic processor for sign languages, but this may turn out to need revision.

Does the proposal illustrated in Figure 3.6 violate domain specificity as Fodor intended it? Wendy Sandler (1992), in a very interesting paper on signed languages and modularity, has argued that signed languages do counterexemplify a Fodorian modularity, and the apparent violation of domain specificity provides part of her rationale. She does not consider a model like the one proposed here to be consistent with Fodor's claims since he argues for domain specificity and informational encapsulation of the language module using specifically auditory phonetic terms and evidence. However, I think the proposal made here is largely consistent with Fodor's proposal, and there is evidence that Fodor himself would agree. In the transcript of a panel discussion on the modularity of speech and language, published in

Mattingly and Studdert-Kennedy (1991), Fodor was asked about the kind of input that a module could accept. He replied:

> I think it is not only possible but entirely likely that the notion of domain that you want for specification for domain specific systems would be quite abstract. In fact, it's more interesting, if it turns out that way. You can imagine a possible world in which there aren't any psychophysical constraints on linguistic exchanges at all. People can do them with little rubber balls, by waving their hands, or making noises in the back of their throats, or by doing songs and dances. It doesn't matter. Would it follow from that that there is no modularity thesis for language in that world? No, not at all. . . . That wouldn't be the death of the modularity thesis; that would be extremely interesting. (pp. 369–370)

Sandler points out another issue that deserves discussion here. She notes that certain linguistic phenomena seem to cluster in signed languages. As one example, I pointed out earlier that it is likely that all signed languages, and only signed languages, have phonologically realized referential indices. Sandler discusses the infrequency of linear morphological processes in signed languages in comparison to spoken languages and the abundance of nonlinear devices (such as displayed in ASL verb agreement) in signed languages. She says "Though not outside the confines of forms and processes predicted by phonological theory, sign languages appear to be universally distinguished from spoken languages in the ways described" (p. 339). That is, these putative modality effects are not cases of processes that fall outside the boundaries of UG but tendencies for certain UG processes, but not others, to appear in signed languages. According to the modularity hypothesis defended here, such characteristics are completely accidental: there is nothing in the model that predicts that sign languages will have certain characteristics more than others. This is an issue that deserves further thought; these phenomena do remain unexplained under my proposed model.

In summary, in this section I have shown that those differences that do exist between ASL and spoken languages do not undermine the modularity hypothesis. Rather, although the differences are surely due to modality, they are learnable because they rely only on the surface characteristics of the input. They do not violate the observed principles of UG. Hence, the data show that the structure of ASL is consistent with the modularity hypothesis.

Given this, we can ask what predictions the modularity hypothesis makes regarding the influence of the acquisition of a signed language on cognition. It should be clear that under the modularity hypothesis no differences are expected. I have argued that information about modality is not present in the language processor past the initial phonetic/phonological processor. Thus, if

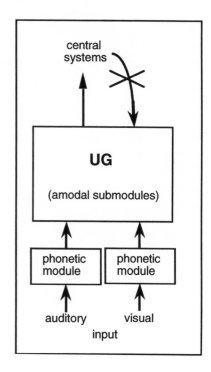

Figure 3.6. Amodal UG with Auditory
and Visual Input Modules

the information flow is strictly one way, no information about modality will
be present by the time linguistic information reaches general cognition,
hence no effect on cognition is expected for signed versus spoken input. Is
it the case that modality of language acquisition has no effect on cognition?
Some researchers have argued that it is not. In the next section, I will review
some of the arguments that have been made involving this matter. However,
in the final section, I will argue that the observed differences are consistent
with the modularity hypothesis, and I will show how to account for them.

SPATIAL LANGUAGE AND COGNITION

In order to look for possible effects of early sign language acquisition on
cognition, it is relevant to look at studies of cognition in deaf children and
adults. In this section, some such studies will be reviewed. However, it is
important to point out that many studies have not clearly distinguished between deafness and early sign language as background variables. For this
reason, many studies of deaf children and adults will turn out not to bear on

the issue under consideration. The discussion in this section will lead to and focus on studies that do make the distinction between deafness and early exposure to sign language.

Differences in Children

There was a time, not so long ago, when many researchers claimed that deaf children were "backwards" cognitively—that they displayed as much as several years' retardation in cognitive development compared to their hearing counterparts (for reviews, see, e.g., Hoemann, 1991; Marschark, 1993; and Wood, 1991). Such a difference might be attributed to the deaf children's early exposure to sign language, and the claim might then be made that language does indeed profoundly affect cognition. However, most of this earlier research failed to take fully into account the deaf subjects' language backgrounds. In fact, in many cases the putative intellectual (or achievement) delay was attributed to the deaf child's lack of language (i.e., spoken/written language), with very little, if any, attention paid to whether or not the student had been exposed to a signed language.

To my knowledge, it has not yet been firmly established to what extent language—any language—is a prerequisite for certain cognitive functions (see Chapter 1). Many scientists (including Piaget and Fodor) have recognized preverbal and nonverbal intelligence, leading to the conclusion that at least some thought is possible without language. However, the possibility that some other thought is dependent on the acquisition of language (but it doesn't matter which one) will not go away. Gale, deVilliers, deVilliers, and Pyers (1995) have resurrected this claim, with data indicating that language-delayed oral deaf children do not perform with age-matched controls on theory of mind tests, even when carefully tested nonverbally. Only when the students have passed certain complex grammatical tests of complementation do they pass the nonverbal tests.

But this finding is not about the effects of early exposure to a particular language; it concerns whether certain grammatical constructs, be they presented in English or ASL or Japanese, are prerequisites of certain cognitive functions. Here, I want to focus on the effects of early exposure to signed languages in particular, so I will try to avoid discussing claims that language very broadly affects cognition. This means that many early studies of cognition in deaf children will be excluded since they have ignored the presence or absence of signed languages versus spoken languages in the deaf students tested.

Other earlier studies were marred by the experimenters' failure to communicate with the child subjects; again, by ignoring signed languages, the experimenters did not take advantage of what would frequently be the most effective communication method. Still other studies tested linguistic competence instead of general intelligence, confusing the two. Such observations have led most researchers to the conclusion that the early studies were too flawed to conclude anything about the relationship between deafness or language use and cognition.

Recognizing this, Hans Furth (1961) and others demonstrated that the apparent differences between deaf and hearing subjects disappear when children are tested on nonverbal measures, taking into consideration the differences between language and cognition. For example, Furth (1961) showed in a series of experiments that when language experience is taken into account, deaf children do not display a significant lag in cognitive abilities compared to hearing children. As he summarized 30 years later: "Overall then, the studies reported . . . indicate no clear general deficiency in the logical development of profoundly deaf persons, if anything rather a great similarity. Yet they are massively different in experience and competence in societal language. What implications can be drawn from these results for a theory of thinking and language and their mutual relation?" (Furth, 1991, p. 219).

The implication, clearly, is that knowledge of a specific language—or, to Furth, knowledge of any language—is not a prerequisite to specific types of logic. In numerous studies (see, e.g., Braden, 1985; Rodda & Grove, 1987; and Hoemann, 1991), an overall finding of no difference in cognition between deaf (signers) and hearing children has been supported.

However, Furth points out that most of his subjects are deaf children who not only are delayed in their development of "societal language" (i.e., English) but also may fail to receive sufficient exposure to ASL to have developed it along the normal time course for language acquisition. This is a problem that has plagued many studies of deaf children's cognitive abilities, even after it became clear that the procedures for testing deaf children must take language abilities into consideration. That is, most studies of deaf children's cognitive abilities—even those employing tests that examined nonverbal or performance intelligence using nonverbal, gestured, or even signed instructions—report the results without a clear distinction between groups of children who have had early, late, or no exposure to ASL. Thus, it is very difficult to interpret these studies, especially as they bear on the question at hand: whether early exposure to a signed language affects cognitive development.

More recently, some consideration has been given to this issue, although it is still not adequately controlled in many studies. In several cases, researchers have compared groups of deaf children of deaf parents (DCDP) with deaf children of hearing parents (DCHP). When both groups are drawn from similar educational and social backgrounds, it is often assumed that only the DCDP have had early sign language exposure. While this is frequently the case, it should not be assumed that all DCDP have early exposure (usually only one deaf parent is required to classify a child as DCDP, but some deaf parents, especially those married to hearing people, do not sign or do not sign all the time), nor should it be assumed that no DCHP have early exposure, especially since this is becoming a more popular option in early intervention programs. Nevertheless, we can keep this in mind as we consider several studies comparing these groups.

What most studies comparing DCDP and DCHP have found is an advantage for early sign language exposure. Advantages have been claimed for educational and social achievement (e.g., Mayberry, Wodlinger-Cohen, & Goldin-Meadow, 1987; Meadow, 1967), as well as for cognitive functions. I will focus on the latter.

Carol Kusché and her colleagues (Kusché, Greenberg, & Garfield, 1983) noted previous studies that found an advantage for DCDP over DCHP and raised the important question, "Why?" Some studies explained the advantage as a function of the early use of manual communication (e.g., Meadow, 1967), while others appealed to differences in child-rearing practices between deaf and hearing parents of deaf children (e.g., Sisco & Anderson, 1980). Kusché et al. (1983) discussed a number of other factors that could be relevant and reasoned that a plausible, testable hypothesis was that genetic factors underlay the difference. In order to study this hypothesis, they collected data from 78 deaf high school students, including 19 DCDP and 19 DCHP controls, 20 deaf children with hearing parents but deaf siblings (DCDS) who were considered likely to have genetic deafness but not necessarily early sign language exposure, and 20 DCHP controls for the DCDS.

Kusché et al. (1983) found that the DCDP did outperform their DCHP controls on nonverbal IQ (WISC-R or WAIS) and reading (SAT) measures, and they furthermore found that the DCDS outperformed their DCHP controls on IQ and one SAT measure (language achievement). The DCDP were not significantly different from the DCDS on IQ. Since the DCDP self-reported earlier acquisition of sign language than the DCDS did, and the DCDS did not report earlier acquisition than their controls, Kusché et al. argued that "it is unlikely that better communication in infancy and childhood could explain" the higher intelligence of the DCDS compared to their controls and the lack of a difference between the DCDS and the DCDP. Instead, they offered a tentative genetic explanation: "We believe it is possible that natural, cultural, and/or historical selection have resulted in superior nonverbal intelligence for deaf individuals when genetic etiologies are involved" (p. 464).

There are, however, at least two reasons why the possibility that early sign language rather than a genetic advantage underlies the IQ difference between DCDP and controls should not yet be abandoned. One concerns the source of data on the subjects' early language acquisition. The high school subjects in this study were asked to complete a questionnaire that asked (among other things), "How old were you when you learned to sign?" The average age at which DCDP reported learning to sign was 3.11 years, and the age of acquisition was correlated with achievement scores. This indicates either that not all DCDP did have early exposure to sign (contrary to the previous assumption) or that the self-report was not always accurate. The second question concerns whether or not some of the DCDS did receive early input. Although their self-reported age of acquisition of sign language was 6.84 years, it is possible that some of these students had essentially early exposure to sign from older deaf siblings. Since the study does not report how many of the DCDS had older versus younger deaf siblings, the possibility that some of them had early exposure cannot be discounted.

To follow up on the question of whether early sign language or genetic factors plays a more important role in the observed advantage for DCDP over DCHP, Abraham Zwiebel (1987) studied 6–14-year-olds in Israel. His study included 23 deaf children with deaf parents and deaf siblings (DPDS), 76 deaf children with hearing parents and deaf siblings (HPDS), and 144 deaf children with hearing parents and hearing siblings (HPHS). All children were instructed orally; only the DPDS group could be expected to have had early exposure to sign language (Israeli Sign Language), while the HPDS group was considered to have had partial manual communication at home.

Zwiebel obtained scores for his subjects on three intelligence measures: the Snijders-Oomen Nonverbal Test for the Deaf, the Goodenough-Harris Human Figure Drawing Test, and teacher ratings of intellectual potential. He found that the DPDS group was superior to both of the other two deaf groups on all three intelligence measures used and equivalent to hearing controls (HC). He concluded: "It is the *environmental* variable that explains the superiority of the DpDs children" (1987, p. 19; emphasis in original).

If early exposure to sign language does confer an advantage on DCDP compared to DCHP, what kind of advantage is it? Is it simply the advantage of some language over no language, or is it more directly related to sign language per se? There are a few indications that it might be a particular advantage of exposure to a signed language rather than more simply any linguistic environment.[7]

Some studies of the putative performance IQ difference between deaf children with and without early ASL exposure have found that not only are DCDP superior to DCHP on some tests but also they are superior to HC. For example, Conrad and Weiskrantz (1981) cite Karchmer, Trybus, and Paquin (1978), who report nonverbal mean IQs for DCDP of 107.8 on the WISC; Sisco and Anderson (1980) found a mean of 106.7 on the WISC-R. If early exposure to sign language provides an advantage for DCDP simply because it allows them to have early, normal language acquisition, why should it result in scores higher than those for HC who also experience early, normal language acquisition?

Conrad and Weiskrantz (1981) argue that perhaps there is no advantage for DCDP over HC. They studied groups of 8–11-year-old DCDP (N = 38), DCHP (N = 19) with younger deaf siblings (who presumably have an inherited deafness with decreased chance of multiple handicaps but still no early exposure to sign language), and HC (N = 45) in Britain using the British Ability Scales. Unlike the earlier (U.S.) studies, they did not find significant differences among the three groups. They suggested that the earlier findings might have suffered from a sampling bias, although there is no direct evidence. Recall that Zwiebel also found that Israeli DCDP were equivalent to, not superior to, HC (although he also found them superior to DCHP, unlike Conrad and Weiskrantz).

On the other hand, Jeffrey Braden (1987) finds convincing the consistency of the finding that DCDP are superior to HC on performance IQ measures. However, he points out that it is imperative to separate the factors underlying intelligence scores in order to appropriately address the question of why DCDP should be superior to HC. He supposes that DCDP are faster in information processing than DCHP or HC. Although this was supported by his experiment with deaf high schoolers (31 DCDP, 31 DCHP, and 37 HC), his study also failed to replicate the advantage of DCDP over HC in IQ, tested using Raven's Progressive Matrices. Braden reports that the literature shows the highest scores for DCDP on timed IQ tests, while untimed tests such as the Progressive Matrices result in similar scores between DCDP and HC groups. Given the surprising nature of some of Braden's results, his hypothesis is not fully supported, but his observation that different components of nonverbal intelligence might be differently affected should be pursued.

Patricia Spencer and Linda Delk (1989), in a study comparing visual-spatial abilities and reading comprehension, discovered differential advantages and disadvantages for 77 DC (both DP and HP) compared to HC norms. Spencer and Delk found that deaf 7–8-year-olds performed significantly higher than HC norms on the Motor-Free Visual Perception Test

(MVPT), a test of receptive visual perception. On the other hand, the deaf subjects were significantly lower than HC norms on the Visual-Aural Digit Span Test (VADS), which tests recall memory for visually presented digit sequences. This comparison was not the point of Spencer and Delk's paper, and they do not attempt to explain it. However, it is the kind of difference that may turn out to be crucial to understanding what ways, if any, early sign language exposure may affect cognition.

One study that specifically addressed the ways in which early exposure to a signed language might differentially affect aspects of visual cognition in young deaf children was conducted by Ursula Bellugi and colleagues (Bellugi, O'Grady, et al., 1990). Since this study made specific hypotheses about how the particular superiorities displayed by DCDP over HC could be accounted for by early sign language exposure, I will discuss it in some detail.

Bellugi, O'Grady, et al. examined deaf children of deaf parents on a number of tests of spatial cognition and also found the deaf children to be superior to hearing children on some of them. It is important to point out that the subjects tested by Bellugi, O'Grady, et al. were exposed to ASL from birth by their deaf parents and/or older siblings. Thus, it is possible to connect any differences between the performance of the deaf children and the hearing children to the deaf children's early exposure to ASL. (Of course, with these populations it is impossible to rule out other possible explanations having to do with hearing loss itself; no deaf children without early exposure to ASL were tested as a control group in this study.)

One of the clearly striking differences was found on the Benton Test of Facial Recognition. In this test, the child sees black-and-white photographs of unfamiliar faces: in some conditions, a target must be matched from six alternatives; in other conditions, the alternatives are given with changes in angle or lighting. Norms are available for hearing children from the age of six years; but Bellugi, O'Grady, et al. tested deaf children as young as 3. They found that even the youngest of their 42 subjects performed better than the 6-year-old hearing norms, and the deaf 6–10-year-olds consistently outperformed the hearing norms.

Bellugi, O'Grady, et al. attribute the difference in performance between deaf and hearing children on this test to the importance of faces in ASL. In addition to conveying affect, as it does with hearing/speaking people, the face conveys grammatical information in ASL, and in many cases it is the sole source of such information (i.e., manual markers need not be present). Thus, deaf children exposed to ASL pay attention to faces more than hearing children do. They conclude, "This suggests that linguistic experience may impact on nonlinguistic cognitive development" (p. 293).

Another task that resulted in large differences between deaf and hearing children was developed by Bellugi, O'Grady, and colleagues. In this study, a film was made by attaching an LED to the fingertip of a consultant who traced pseudo-Chinese characters in a dark room. The resulting picture was a moving light in which some of the movements reflected the strokes of the character while others were transitions between strokes. Deaf and hearing Chinese first-graders were asked to write the symbol that each point-light display represented. As the responses to one item shown in Figure 3.7 make clear, the deaf children were much more adept at this innovative task than were the hearing children.

Alongside the results of these two tests supporting meaningful differences between deaf and hearing children, Bellugi, O,Grady, et al. also found no

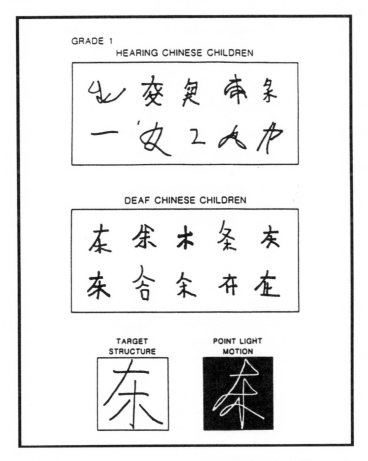

Figure 3.7. Chinese Pseudocharacters Test (from Bellugi et al., 1990; copyright, Dr. Ursula Bellugi, The Salk Institute)

differences between the groups on some tasks. For example, in tests of drawing, such as a subtest of the Boston Diagnostic Aphasia Exam and the Visual-Motor Integration Test, no obvious differences were found between deaf and hearing children. (Spencer and Delk [1989] also used the VMI in their study and similarly found no differences between deaf and hearing children.)

Putting together all of the evidence presented here, there is apparently some evidence for an advantage in some aspects of visual cognition among deaf children with early exposure to sign language. Certainly much more work is necessary to confirm this, especially with the aims of keeping the control groups consistent and investigating the nature of the supposed advantage more thoroughly. The advantage seems to be selective—only certain aspects seem to be enhanced. It is necessary to consider in more detail just which aspects are advanced and how precisely these effects could be related to early sign language exposure. More studies with children can help in addressing this question. In addition, some studies with adults have shed some light on it. We now turn to these studies.

Behavioral Studies with Adults

Karen Emmorey and colleagues (Emmorey, Kosslyn, & Bellugi, 1993) pursued the possibility that early exposure to a signed language would result in enhanced performance on some spatial cognitive tasks by testing three groups of subjects on a series of mental imagery and rotation tasks. Importantly, they were able to dissociate effects of early language exposure from effects of deafness by including a group of hearing children of deaf parents—native signers who are not deaf—in addition to a group of deaf signers and a group of hearing nonsigners.

In Emmorey et al.'s image generation task, subjects initially memorize the shape of printed uppercase alphabetic letters placed within a 4-by-5 square grid. During the task, they are presented with a lowercase written stimulus for which they are to generate the image of the previously learned letter. The test comes 500 milliseconds later, with an "X" placed somewhere on the grid (or within a set of brackets with no grid); subjects decide whether or not the "X" falls on a square occupied by the printed letter they recall. This test and its results are illustrated in Figure 3.8.

As is clear from the graph, both the hearing and the deaf signers are significantly quicker at this task than the hearing nonsigners but not significantly different from each other. On the other hand, the signers were not different from the nonsigners on an image maintenance task that used the

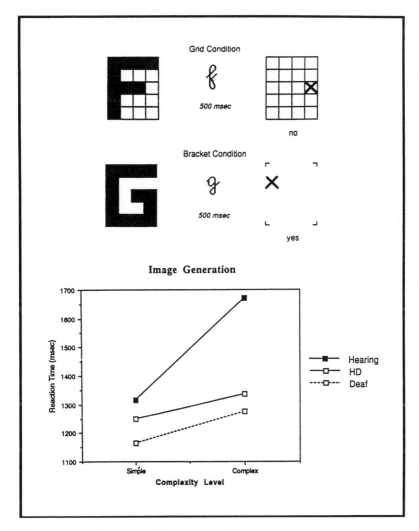

Figure 3.8. Image Generation Task: Sample and Results (from Emmorey et al., 1993; copyright, Dr. Ursula Bellugi, The Salk Institute)

same materials. In the maintenance task, the stimulus printed letter is presented to the subjects just before the probe "X" is presented.

The finding of a difference between the generation and maintenance tasks was followed up by a task examining mental rotation and mirror reversals. Subjects were presented with pairs of figures in which the left figure was upright and the right figure was rotated 0, 90, 135, or 180 degrees. Furthermore, the right figure was either the same pattern as the left or mirror-reversed. Subjects decided as quickly as possible whether the shapes were the same or a mirror-reversal. This test and its results are illustrated in Figure 3.9.

The results of this study showed that the deaf signing subjects were significantly faster than the hearing nonsigners at all degrees of rotation. As in the image generation task, the hearing native signers patterned like the deaf

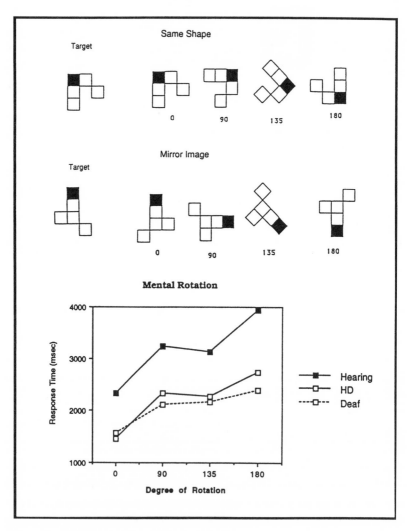

Figure 3.9. Mental Rotation Task: Sample and Results (from Emmorey et al., 1993; copyright, Dr. Ursula Bellugi, The Salk Institute)

signers—that is, they were significantly faster than the hearing nonsigners. Since the signers were faster than the nonsigners even in the 0 rotation condition, the results were interpreted as showing that the signers were superior to the nonsigners in detecting mirror reversals per se, not rotation.

How can the results of these behavioral studies be connected to the early exposure to sign language experienced by both the deaf and hearing native signers? As Emmorey et al. (1993) point out, both image generation and reversal interpretation are skills that would be frequently called on in the processing of a signed language. Referents in an ASL discourse are associated with locations in space and later referred to by use of these locations (see Liddell, 1990; Lillo-Martin, 1986; Lillo-Martin & Klima, 1990; Padden, 1983; and many others). In interpreting a pronoun, for example, that makes use of a location, a comprehender must recall the referent associated with that location or generate the image of the sign previously made there. Similarly, when locative relations are expressed in ASL through the use of the signing space, the signer typically uses the space from his or her own point of view, so the comprehender must mentally reverse the spatial relationships in order to compute the correct spatial array.

Hence, according to Emmorey et al. (1993), early exposure to sign language leads to an enhancement in spatial cognition, especially in certain domains that are crucially relied upon in sign language processing. This observation leads them to conclude: "Our findings suggest that the processing that underlies one sort of human language is not entirely modular. . . . Central aspects of ASL processing are not domain specific and are not insulated from other types of visual processing" (p. 30).

Is this conclusion necessary, given the model of modularity reviewed in the second and third sections of this chapter? Is there a way to make these observations compatible with the modularity hypothesis—and is there any reason to do so? Before addressing these questions in the final section, I would like to bring up one more type of data that suggests that early exposure to language does affect cognition, in spite of the predictions arrived at in the second section.

Evoked Potential Studies with Adults

Helen Neville (1991) used behavioral and electrophysiological methods to examine language and nonlanguage cognitive processing in the brains of deaf and hearing individuals, signers and nonsigners. In studies of language behavior, Neville and colleagues found that hearing nonsigners, hearing native signers, and deaf native signers all displayed characteristic left-hemisphere superiority for processing their native language, whether it was speech or sign. However, late learners of a language do not show the same patterns for processing that language as do native learners. Thus, early exposure to a language affects the brain's organization for processing that language.

In the domain of nonlinguistic spatial processing, Neville and colleagues report a distinctive dissociation, separating the effects of auditory deprivation from the effects of early exposure to a signed language. Only the deaf subjects they tested showed use of the areas usually used in the service of auditory processing for visual-spatial processing. Thus, auditory deprivation leads to brain reorganization independent of early language exposure. However, both the deaf subjects and the hearing native signers showed strong left-hemisphere involvement during a task that required the detection of the direction of movement of a square presented in the visual periphery. The hearing nonsigners tested did not show left-hemisphere specialization for this task. Thus, early exposure to sign language apparently affects the organization of the brain for certain nonlinguistic behaviors. As Neville (1991) summarizes: "The modality through which language is first acquired significantly impacts the fundamental specializations of the two hemispheres for nonlanguage processing" (p. 269). This strong conclusion demands a serious examination of the proposed modularity hypothesis and its relation to sign language.

LANGUAGE AND THOUGHT 2: MODULARITY AND MODALITY

How can the modularity hypothesis summarized in the second section be compatible with the results summarized in the previous two sections? If language processing is informationally encapsulated from general cognition, how can the particular language a child is exposed to influence cognition? By the time information input to the language module reaches general cognition, all information about the modality is no longer accessible. Conversely, there is limited central access by general cognition into the internal representations of the module. Must we conclude that the modularity hypothesis is incompatible with the facts about sign language?

It is not necessary to draw that conclusion. Let us examine the workings of the language module once again, paying attention to the input side of the module. Fodor (1983) draws a distinction between vertical and horizontal processing. The vertical processors are the input modules, such as visual processing, auditory processing, and language. The horizontal processors cut across domains. Fodor generally discusses them in relation to the central systems. Problem solving is a typical example of a horizontal faculty since it requires access to several domains. In addition to processes like problem solving, there are horizontal processes that are used in support of various systems, such as memory; Fodor calls these *computational resources.* There may well be competition across domains for limited computational resources, and Fodor admits to an uncertainty regarding just how autonomous they may be. In other words, the processors (including, for example, memory) that are used in the service of language may well be the same processors that are used for other, nonlinguistic tasks. Such a model would help to account for the results of multitask experiments, which show a decrease in, say, some aspect of language performance while engaging in a simultaneous nonlinguistic task, such as finger tapping.[8]

Since virtually all relevant studies have been concerned with the computational resources that underlie spoken language, the possibility that some aspects of spatial cognition count as computational resources for language has not been entertained within the modularity program. However, with the recognition of signed languages as natural human languages, and the resulting expectation that the same language module might underlie both signed and spoken languages, it should now be obvious that the computational resources that underlie sign language acquisition and processing might well include (specific) spatial cognitive processes. Let us consider this possibility using the diagram in Figure 3.10.

As the figure shows, input to the language module (UG) might come in either auditory or visual modalities, given the present hypothesis. Either way, computational resources are necessary in the service of the operations of the language module.[9] So for spoken languages, certain computational resources are called on that might be independent of those used in the service of signed languages. For example, spoken languages may use rapid temporal phonological processing. On the other hand, signed languages may employ computational resources not used by spoken languages, such as certain spatial cognitive processes.

Now it should become clear how early exposure to a sign language might affect cognition without violating the modularity hypothesis or proving the Sapir-Whorf hypothesis. If early exposure to a language leads to the development or enhancement of certain cognitive skills, they may be precisely those that are used as its computational resources. Extra practice or, more likely, use during a certain period of development might lead to selective enhancement. Neville (1991) was able to place her results within a framework of neurological development that makes sense of the present data and is also compatible with the modularity proposal made here. She reports that in the development of the sensory systems (and their neural substrates),

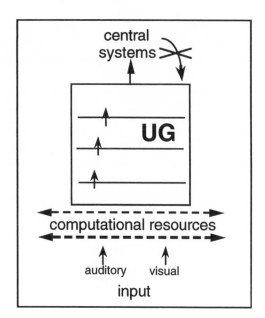

Figure 3.10. The Modularity
Hypothesis plus Computational
Resources

"there is an initial period of growth that is genetically influenced. . . .
Those initial biases are strongly determined . . . but they are not immutable.
. . . Following the early period of initial growth, there is a transient period
of redundancy. . . . The subsequent pruning of these diverse connections
occurs . . . as a direct consequence of activity that selectively stabilizes
certain connections, whereas others that do not receive input are eliminated
or suppressed" (p. 291).

It is in young childhood that the brain is most plastic, genetically driven
but allowing for experience to leave its mark. The suggestion being made
here is that early exposure to language may leave its mark not only in the
brain's specialization for language but also in other domains of the brain.

According to the picture being painted here, early exposure to sign language can lead to enhancement of the spatial cognitive functions that underlie sign language processing. The question might then be raised: Why
shouldn't early exposure to spoken language lead to similar enhance-
ments?[10] I think that it actually has been raised, but because of the ubiqui-
tousness of spoken language acquisition, it has not been asked in these
terms, nor can it be satisfactorily answered. To test the hypothesis that early
exposure to spoken language enhances the computational resources that underlie spoken language, it would be necessary to compare the workings of

these resources in children or adults who have acquired a spoken language during childhood with a control group who have not. The control group, who have not acquired spoken language in childhood, must have normal intelligence and normal socialization. To control for the effects of auditory deprivation, it is optimal that the control group not be deaf or perhaps that a deaf group and nondeaf group be compared. Fortunately for society, but unfortunately for this experiment, such a (nondeaf) group does not exist. Even the hearing children of deaf parents, who were an appropriate control for the effects of auditory deprivation in the experiments reported here, are not an appropriate control group for this thought experiment because they do acquire spoken language in childhood. The closest group would be deaf children or adults. Thus, we have come full circle. To turn our original question on its head: What effects on cognition does not acquiring a spoken language in early childhood have?

As we have seen earlier in this chapter, although earlier claims were made about deaf children's cognitive deficiencies in comparison with hearing children, there are strong reasons to doubt such reports. However, there is one domain in which there may be differences between deaf and hearing individuals, even when the language differences are taken into consideration during test design and implementation. (Note that in this case, we are considering possible effects of lack of early acquisition of a spoken language, so deaf children with or without early exposure to a sign language are included.)

It has frequently been found that some deaf subjects have shorter sequential memory spans in comparison to hearing subjects or that the mode of rehearsal in short-term memory might be different (see Marschark, 1993, and Rodda & Grove, 1987, for some discussion). For example, Klima and Bellugi (1979) found that deaf native signers showed a shorter memory span for signs than hearing controls did for spoken words. Similarly, Conrad (1970, 1972) found evidence for differences between deaf and hearing children in their coding of English letters; whereas the hearing children showed evidence for sound-based phonological coding, the deaf children in general showed evidence for visual-based coding. On the other hand, Hanson (1982) found evidence for both (sound) phonological and visual coding by native signers, depending on the task. Although the nature and extent of differences in short-term memory between deaf and hearing subjects are in need of more detailed study, the possibility of real, language-related differences cannot be excluded.

The strongest differences between deaf and hearing groups apparently appear in sequential, temporal memory tests. This is a domain that has frequently been cited as crucial to the processing of spoken language. So perhaps (hearing) individuals who are exposed to a spoken language in early childhood are at an advantage for certain types of short-term sequential memory processes, while individuals who are exposed to a sign language in early childhood are at an advantage for certain types of spatial cognitive processes. But, as Furth (1991) points out, "what effective difference does this behavioral difference make? It has been known for a long time that persons differ in their preferred imagery. . . . No evidence has yet been produced that these differences substantially affect important intellectual processes" (p. 223). In the model presented here, these differences in computational resources do not directly affect the central systems, which is the sense in which the language one grows up with does not affect cognition.

I conclude that the modularity hypothesis need not be abandoned, despite the results that indicate that exposure to a sign language in childhood may have as a consequence differences in certain areas of cognitive processing. Does this provide evidence in favor of the modularity hypothesis? Not directly. We started out with the modularity hypothesis by assumption or, more precisely, on the basis of the arguments put forth for it by others. We discussed evidence that some have taken to be in contradiction to the hypothesis and showed that these data are in fact compatible with it. This provides indirect support for the hypothesis, in that it is found to be consistent with data from a new domain, not considered in its original development. However, there are some areas that need to be more fully worked out, and I have not shown that a nonmodular account would be unable to explain the results presented here. There remains work for adherents of the modularity hypothesis to undertake to convince the reader that the hypothesis is not only viable but preferred. This is work I will endeavor to undertake. To cite one last quote: "Modularity is a potboiler" (Fodor, 1985, p. 33).

ACKNOWLEDGMENTS

This work was supported in part by research grant number 5 R01 DC 00183–12 from the National Institute on Deafness and Other Communication Disorders, National Institutes of Health. I would like to thank Karen Emmorey for discussing some of the issues presented here with me; Ignatius Mattingly and Wendy Sandler for helpful comments on an earlier version of this chapter; Laurel LaPorte-Grimes for indexing; Elizabeth Laurençot for her sharp editorial eye; and Michiko Nohara for literature search assistance. Portions of this work have been presented at colloquia at Brandeis University, the University of Chicago, the University of Connecticut, and the University of Maryland. I thank those audiences for the chance to try some things out and for helpful comments.

NOTES

1. In very few cases, hearing children of deaf parents might go through a period with limited exposure to spoken language, despite having normal physiology and loving parents. (In most cases, these children receive input in spoken language from relatives, neighbors, friends, television, etc.) A few studies have examined the acquisition of spoken language in this population; however, I know of no studies that have examined phonetic processing or other relevant types of perception in subjects totally without spoken language input.

2. Actually, although I may use comparisons of language processing and visual processing on several occasions, Fodor's notions of a module are much more specific than this. He proposes as candidates for modules "mechanisms for color perception, for the analysis of shape, and for the analysis of three-dimensional spatial relations" (1983, p. 47). Similarly, he suggests that "computational systems that assign grammatical descriptions to token utterances; or ones that detect the melodic or rhythmic structure of acoustic arrays" may be distinct modules. This fine-tuning of modules to quite specific tasks is important to keep in mind throughout this discussion, despite the broad language used in the text.

3. This is one of the most debated of Fodor's claims about language, pitting those who believe that semantic, pragmatic, or real-world information might influence sentence processing against those who believe that such information is only able to correct a misanalysis or to choose between several possible analyses.

4. Considering the caveat of note 2, I find it completely plausible that speech perception may be served by a modular processor as well, and indeed, much of the evidence that Fodor adduces for the modularity hypothesis concerns speech processing. What I am now evaluating is the possibility that the computational systems that assign grammatical descriptions to token utterances may operate independently of modality.

5. There are also predictions about the processing of signed languages that should be considered in the light of the modularity hypothesis. In the interests of the current focus, I will leave this task for another time.

6. Lillo-Martin and Klima (1990) argued, in fact, that the system has only one pronoun, but following Meier (1990), I will adopt the first/nonfirst distinction.

7. This is not to downplay the importance of early (sign) language exposure for deaf children. I put the question this way simply because the focus of this chapter is on whether early exposure to a signed language has an effect different from that of early exposure to a spoken language (for a hearing child).

8. Not all modularists agree with Fodor in this way. For example, Crain and Shankweiler (1987) specifically argue that the working memory underlying language is part of the language module. It is not inconceivable that the two views might be compatible, if, for example, there are language-particular and cross-systems components of working memory.

9. The computational resources may be a third-dimensional base underlying all components of the grammar, not just an input processor. I will leave this possibility aside for the present.

10. I thank Carol Fowler for raising this question.

REFERENCES

Aarons, D., Bahan, B., Kegl, J., & Neidle, C. (1992). Clausal structure and a tier for grammatical marking in American Sign Language. *Nordic Journal of Linguistics, 15*(2), 103–142.

Bahan, B., & Petitto, L. (1980). Aspects of rules for character establishment and reference in ASL storytelling. Unpublished manuscript. Salk Institute for Biological Studies, La Jolla, CA.

Bellugi, U., Lillo-Martin, D., O'Grady, L., & vanHoek, K. (1990). The development of spatialized syntactic mechanisms in American Sign Language. In W. H. Edmondson & F. Karlsson (Eds.), *SLR '87: Papers from the Fourth International Symposium on Sign Language Research* (pp. 183–189). Hamburg: Signum-Verlag.

Bellugi, U., O'Grady, L., Lillo-Martin, D., O'Grady, M., vanHoek, K., & Corina, D. (1990). Enhancement of spatial cognition in deaf children. In V. Volterra & C. Erting (Eds.), *From gesture to language in hearing and deaf children* (pp. 278–298). New York: Springer-Verlag.

Bellugi, U., vanHoek, K., Lillo-Martin, D., & O'Grady, L. (1988). The acquisition of syntax and space in young deaf signers. In D. Bishop & K. Mogford (Eds.), *Language development in exceptional circumstances* (pp. 132–149). Edinburgh: Churchill Livingstone.

Berlin, B., & Kay, P. (1969). *Basic color terms.* Berkeley: University of California Press.

Blakemore, C. (1974). Developmental factors in the formation of feature extracting neurons. In F. O. Schmitt & F. G. Worden (Eds.), *The neurosciences: Third study program* (pp. 105–113). Cambridge, MA: MIT Press.

Borer, H. (1983). *Parametric syntax: Case studies in Semitic and Romance languages.* Dordrecht: Foris.

Boster, C. T. (1996). On the quantifier-noun phrase split in American Sign Language and the structure of quantified noun phrases. In W. Edmondson & R. Wilbur (Eds.), *International Review of Sign Linguistics* (Vol. 1, pp. 159–208). Mahwah, NJ: Lawrence Erlbaum Associates.

Braden, J. P. (1985). The structure of nonverbal intelligence in deaf and hearing subjects. *American Annals of the Deaf, 130*(6), 496–501.

Braden, J. P. (1987). An explanation of the superior performance IQs of deaf children of deaf parents. *American Annals of the Deaf, 132,* 263–266.

Brentari, D. (1990). Theoretical foundations of American Sign Language phonology. Ph.D. dissertation, University of Chicago.

Chase, S. (1956). Foreword. In J. B. Carroll (Ed.), *Language, thought, and reality: Selected writings of Benjamin Lee Whorf* (pp. v–x). Cambridge, MA: MIT Press.

Chomsky, N. (1981). *Lectures on government and binding.* Dordrecht: Foris.

Chomsky, N. (1986). *Knowledge of language.* New York: Praeger.

Clements, G. N. (1975). The logophoric pronoun in Ewe: Its role in discourse. *Journal of West African Languages, 2,* 141–177.

Clements, G. N. (1985). The geometry of phonological features. *Phonology Yearbook, 2,* 225–252.

Conrad, R. (1970). Short-term memory processes in the deaf. *British Journal of Psychology, 61,* 179–195.

Conrad, R. (1972). Short-term memory in the deaf: A test for speech coding. *British Journal of Psychology, 63,* 173–180.

Conrad, R., & Weiskrantz, B. C. (1981). On the cognitive ability of deaf children with deaf parents. *American Annals of the Deaf, 126,* 995–1003.

Coulter, G. (Ed.) (1993). *Phonetics and Phonology,* vol. 3, *Current Issues in ASL Phonology.* San Diego: Academic Press.

Crain, S. (1991). Language acquisition in the absence of experience. *Behavioral and Brain Sciences, 14,* 597–650.

Crain, S., & Shankweiler, D. (1987). Reading acquisition and language acquisition. In A. Davidson, G. Green, & G. Herman (Eds.), *Critical approaches to readability: Theoretical bases of linguistic complexity.* Hillsdale, NJ: Lawrence Erlbaum Associates.

Eimas, P. D. (1991). Comment: Some effects of language acquisition on speech perception. In I. G. Mattingly & M. Studdert-Kennedy (Eds.), *Modularity and the motor theory of speech perception* (pp. 111–116). Hillsdale, NJ: Lawrence Erlbaum Associates.

Emmorey, K. (1992). Processing a dynamic visual-spatial language: Psycholinguistic studies of American Sign Language. *Journal of Psycholinguistic Research, 22,* 153–187.

Emmorey, K. (1996). The confluence of space and language in signed languages. In P. Bloom, M. Peterson, L. Nadel, & M. Garrett (Eds.), *Language and space* (pp. 171–209). Cambridge, MA: MIT Press.

Emmorey, K., Corina, D., & Bellugi, U. (1995). Differential processing of topographic and referential functions of space. In K. Emmorey & J. Reilly (Eds.), *Language, gesture, and space* (pp. 43–62). Hillsdale, NJ: Lawrence Erlbaum Associates.

Emmorey, K., Kosslyn, S. M., & Bellugi, U. (1993). Visual imagery and visual-spatial language: Enhanced imagery abilities in deaf and hearing ASL signers. *Cognition, 46,* 139–181.

Engberg-Pedersen, E. (1995). Point of view expressed through shifters. In K. Emmorey & J. Reilly (Eds.), *Language, gesture, and space* (pp. 133–154). Hillsdale, NJ: Lawrence Erlbaum Associates.

Fischer, S. D. (1974). Sign language and linguistic universals. In C. Rohrer & N. Ruwet (Eds.), *Actes du colloque franco-allemand de grammaire transformationnelle,* vol. 2, *Etude de semantique et autres* (pp. 187–204). Tübingen: Niemeyer.

Fodor, J. A. (1983). *The modularity of mind.* Cambridge, MA: MIT Press.

Fodor, J. A. (1985). Précis of *The Modularity of Mind. Behavioral and Brain Sciences, 8,* 1–42.

Furth, H. G. (1961). The influence of language on the development of concept formation in deaf children. *Journal of Abnormal and Social Psychology, 63*(2), 386–389.

Furth, H. G. (1991). Thinking without language: A perspective and review of research with deaf people. In D. P. Keating & H. Rosen (Eds.), *Constructivist perspectives on developmental psychopathology and atypical development* (pp. 203–227). Hillsdale, NJ: Lawrence Erlbaum Associates.

Gale, E., deVilliers, P., deVilliers, J., & Pyers, J. (1996). Language and theory of mind in oral deaf children. In A. Stringfellow, D. Cahana-Amitay, E. Hughes, A. Zukowski (Eds.), *Proceedings of the 20th Annual Boston University Conference on Language Development* (Vol. 1, pp. 213–224). Somerville, MA: Cascadilla Press.

Hanson, V. L. (1982). Short-term recall by deaf signers of American Sign Language: Implications of encoding strategy for order recall. *Journal of Experimental Psychology: Learning, Memory, and Cognition, 8,* 572–583.

Hill, J. H. (1988). Language, culture, and world view. In F. J. Newmeyer (Ed.), *Linguistics: The Cambridge survey,* vol. 4, *Language: The socio-cultural context* (pp. 14–36). Cambridge: Cambridge University Press.

Hoemann, H. W. (1991). Piagetian perspectives on research with deaf subjects. In D. P. Keating & H. Rosen (Eds.), *Constructivist perspectives on developmental psychopathology and atypical development* (pp. 229–245). Hillsdale, NJ: Lawrence Erlbaum Associates.

Hornstein, N., & Lightfoot, D. (Eds.). (1981). *Explanations in linguistics: The logical problem of language acquisition.* London: Longman.

Hyman, L., & Comrie, B. (1981). Logophoric reference in Gokana. *Journal of African Languages and Linguistics, 3,* 19–37.

Klima, E. S., & Bellugi, U. (1979). *The signs of language.* Cambridge, MA: Harvard University Press.

Koopman, H., & Sportiche, D. (1989). Pronouns, logical variables, and logophoricity in Abe. *Linguistic Inquiry, 20,* 555–588.

Kusché, C. A., Greenberg, M. T., & Garfield, T. S. (1983). Nonverbal intelligence and verbal achievement in deaf adolescents: An examination of heredity and environment. *American Annals of the Deaf, 128*(4), 458–466.

Lasnik, H. (1989). On certain substitutes for negative data. In R. J. Matthews & W. Demopoulos (Eds.), *Learnability and linguistic theory* (pp. 89–106). Dordrecht: Kluwer Academic Publishers.

Liberman, A. M., Cooper, F., Shankweiler, D., & Studdert-Kennedy, M. (1967). The perception of the speech code. *Psychological Review, 74,* 431–461.

Liddell, S. (1980). *American Sign Language syntax.* The Hague: Mouton.

Liddell, S. K. (1984a). THINK and BELIEVE: Sequentiality in American Sign Language signs. *Language, 60,* 372–399.

Liddell, S. K. (1984b). Unrealized-inceptive aspect in American Sign Language: Feature insertion in syllabic frames. In D. Testen, V. Mishra, & J. Drogo (Eds.), *Proceedings of the 20th Regional Meeting of the Chicago Linguistic Society* (pp. 257–270). Chicago: University of Chicago Press.

Liddell, S. K. (1990). Four functions of a locus: Reexamining the structure of space in ASL. In C. Lucas (Ed.), *Sign language research: Theoretical issues* (pp. 176–198). Washington, DC: Gallaudet University Press.

Liddell, S. K. (1995). Real, surrogate, and token space: Grammatical consequences in ASL. In K. Emmorey & J. Reilly (Eds.), *Language, gesture, and space* (pp. 19–41). Hillsdale, NJ: Lawrence Erlbaum Associates.

Liddell, S. K., & Johnson, R. E. (1986). American Sign Language compound formation processes, lexicalization, and lexical phonological remnants. *Natural Language and Linguistic Theory, 4,* 445–513.

Liddell, S. K., & Johnson, R. E. (1989). American Sign Language: The phonological base. *Sign Language Studies, 64,* 195–278.

Lillo-Martin, D. (1986). Two kinds of null arguments in American Sign Language. *Natural Language and Linguistic Theory, 4,* 415–444.

Lillo-Martin, D. (1991). *Universal Grammar and American Sign Language: Setting the null argument parameters.* Dordrecht: Kluwer Academic Publishers.

Lillo-Martin, D. (1995). The point of view predicate in American Sign Language. In K. Emmorey & J. Reilly (Eds.), *Language, gesture, and space* (pp. 155–170). Hillsdale, NJ: Lawrence Erlbaum Associates.

Lillo-Martin, D. (forthcoming). Modality effects and modularity in language acquisition: The acquisition of American Sign Language. In T. K. Bhatia & W. C. Ritchie (Eds.), *Handbook of Language Acquisition.* New York: Academic Press.

Lillo-Martin, D., & Fischer, S. (1992). Overt and covert wh-questions in American Sign Language. Paper presented at the International Conference on Sign Language Research, Salamanca, Spain, May 1992.

Lillo-Martin, D., & Klima, E. S. (1990). Pointing out differences: ASL pronouns in syntactic theory. In S. D. Fischer & P. Siple (Eds.), *Theoretical issues in sign language research,* vol. 1, *Linguistics* (pp. 191–210). Chicago: University of Chicago Press.

Lisker, L., & Abramson, A. S. (1964). A cross-language study of voicing in initial stops: Acoustical measurements. *Word, 20,* 384–422.

Lisker, L., & Abramson, A. S. (1970). The voicing dimension: Some experiments in comparative phonetics. In B. Hála, M. Romportl, & P. Janota (Eds.), *Proceedings of the 6th International Congress of Phonetic Sciences* (pp. 563–567). Prague: Academia.

Mann, V. A., & Liberman, A. A. (1983). Some differences between phonetic and auditory modes of perception. *Cognition, 14,* 211–235.

Marschark, M. (1993). *Psychological development of deaf children.* Oxford: Oxford University Press.

Marslen-Wilson, W., & Tyler, L. (1981). Central processes in speech understanding. *Philosophical Transactions of the Royal Society, 295,* 317–322.

Mattingly, I. G., & Liberman, A. M. (1985). Verticality unparalleled [commentary on "Précis of the Modularity of Mind" by J. A. Fodor]. *Behavioral and Brain Sciences, 8,* 24–26.

Mattingly, I. G., & Studdert-Kennedy, M. (Eds.). (1991). *Modularity and the motor theory of speech perception.* Hillsdale, NJ: Lawrence Erlbaum Associates.

Mayberry, R., Wodlinger-Cohen, R., & Goldin-Meadow, S. (1987). Symbolic development in deaf children. In D. Cicchetti & M. Beeghly (Eds.), *Symbolic development in atypical children* (pp. 109–126). San Francisco: Jossey-Bass.

Meadow, K. P. (1967). The effect of early manual communication and family climate on the deaf child's development. Ph.D. dissertation, University of California, Berkeley.

Meier, R. P. (1982). Icons, analogues, and morphemes: The acquisition of verb agreement in ASL. Ph.D. dissertation, University of California, San Diego.

Meier, R. P. (1990). Person deixis in American Sign Language. In S. D. Fischer & P. Siple (Eds.), *Theoretical issues in sign language research* (pp. 175–190). Chicago: University of Chicago Press.

Miyawaki, K., Strange, W., Verbrugge, R. R., Liberman, A. M., Jenkins, J. J., & Fujimura, O. (1975). An effect of linguistic experience: The discrimination of (r) and (l) by native speakers of Japanese and English. *Perception & Psychophysics, 18,* 331–340.

Morgan, J. L., & Travis, L. L. (1989). Limits on negative information in language input. *Journal of Child Language, 16,* 531–552.

Neville, H. J. (1991). Whence the specialization of the language hemisphere? In I. G. Mattingly & M. Studdert-Kennedy (Eds.), *Modularity and the motor theory of speech perception* (pp. 269–294). Hillsdale, NJ: Lawrence Erlbaum Associates.

Newport, E., & Meier, R. (1985). The acquisition of American Sign Language. In D. Slobin (Ed.), *The cross-linguistic study of language acquisition* (pp. 881–938). Hillsdale, NJ: Lawrence Erlbaum Associates.

Padden, C. A. (1983). Interaction of morphology and syntax in American Sign Language. Ph.D. dissertation, University of California, San Diego.

Padden, C. A., & Perlmutter, D. (1987). American Sign Language and the architecture of phonological theory. *Natural Language and Linguistic Theory, 5,* 335–375.

Perlmutter, D. (1992). Sonority and syllable structure in American Sign Language. *Linguistic Inquiry, 23,* 407–442.

Petitto, L. A. (1983). From gesture to symbol: The relationship between form and meaning in the acquisition of personal pronouns in American Sign Language. Ph.D. dissertation, Harvard University.

Petronio, K. M. (1993). Clause structure in American Sign Language. Ph.D. dissertation, University of Washington.

Petronio, K., & Lillo-Martin, D. (1997). Wh-movement and the position of Spec CP: Evidence from American Sign Language. *Language, 73,* 18–57.

Pisoni, D., & Tash, J. (1974). Reaction times to comparisons within and across phonetic categories. *Perception and Psychophysics, 15,* 285–290.

Poizner, H. (1983). Perception of movement in American Sign Language: Effects of linguistic structure and linguistic experience. *Perception & Psychophysics, 33,* 215–231.

Poizner, H., Fok, A., & Bellugi, U. (1989). The interplay between perception of language and perception of motion. *Language Sciences, 11,* 267–287.

Poizner, H., Klima, E. S., & Bellugi, U. (1987). *What the hands reveal about the brain.* Cambridge, MA: MIT Press.

Poulin, C., & Miller, C. (1995). On narrative discourse and point of view in Quebec Sign Language. In K. Emmorey & J. Reilly (Eds.), *Language, gesture, and space* (pp. 117–131). Hillsdale, NJ: Lawrence Erlbaum Associates.

Rodda, M., & Grove, C. (1987). *Language, cognition, and deafness.* Hillsdale, NJ: Lawrence Erlbaum Associates.

Ross, J. R. (1967). Constraints on variables in syntax. Ph.D. dissertation, Massachusetts Institute of Technology.

Sachs, J. (1967). Recognition memory for syntactic and semantic aspects of connected discourse. *Perception and Psychophysics, 2,* 437–442.

Sandler, W. (1989). *Phonological representation of the sign: Linearity and nonlinearity in ASL phonology.* Dordrecht: Foris.

Sandler, W. (1992). Sign language and modularity. *Lingua, 89,* 315–351.

Sandler, W. (1993). Sign language phonology. Special issue of *Phonology, 10.*

Sandler, W. (1995). Markedness in the handshapes of sign language: A componential analysis. In Harry van der Hulst and Jeroen van de Weijer (Eds.), *Leiden in Last: HIL Phonology Papers I* (pp. 369–399). The Hague: Holland Academic Graphics.

Sandler, W. (1996). Representing handshapes. *International Review of Sign Linguistics, 1,* 115–158.

Sandler, W., & Lillo-Martin, D. (forthcoming). *True language universals.* Cambridge: Cambridge University Press.

Sapir, E. (1933). The psychological reality of phonemes. In E. Sapir (Ed.), *Selected writings of Edward Sapir.* Berkeley: University of California Press.

Sapir, E. (1949). *Selected writings of Edward Sapir.* Berkeley: University of California Press.

Sisco, F. H., & Anderson, R. J. (1980). Deaf children's performance on the WISC-R relative to hearing status of parents and childrearing experiences. *American Annals of the Deaf, 125,* 923–930.

Spencer, P., & Delk, L. (1989). Hearing-impaired students' performance on tests of visual processing: Relationships with reading performance. *American Annals of the Deaf, 134,* 333–337.

Stokoe, W. C. (1960). Sign language structure: An outline of the visual communication systems of the American deaf. In *Studies in Linguistics: Occasional Papers* (vol. 8). Buffalo: University of Buffalo.

Stokoe, W. C., Casterline, D., & Croneberg, C. (1965). *Dictionary of American Sign Language.* Washington, DC: Gallaudet College Press.

Supalla, T. (1986). The classifier system in American Sign Language. In C. Craig (Ed.), *Noun classes and categorization* (pp. 181–214). Philadelphia: John Benjamins.

Werker, J. (1991). The ontogeny of speech perception. In I. G. Mattingly & M. Studdert-Kennedy (Eds.), *Modularity and the motor theory of speech perception* (pp. 91–109). Hillsdale, NJ: Lawrence Erlbaum Associates.

Whorf, B. L. (1956). *Language, thought, and reality.* Cambridge, MA: MIT Press.

Wilbur, R. B. (1987). *American Sign Language: Linguistic and applied dimensions.* Boston, MA: College-Hill Press.

Wood, D. (1991). Communication and cognition. *American Annals of the Deaf, 136,* 247–251.

Zwiebel, A. (1987). More on the effects of early manual communication on the cognitive development of deaf children. *American Annals of the Deaf, 132,* 16–20.

CHAPTER 4

Read the Lips: Speculations on the Nature and Role of Lipreading in Cognitive Development of Deaf Children

Ruth Campbell

The education of children born deaf is essentially a war against cognitive poverty.

—R. CONRAD, *The Deaf School Child* (1979)

CONFESSION

I came at studies of deafness sideways and backward, and a description of this trajectory will form the first part of this chapter. This concerns studies of lipreading conducted mainly but not exclusively with hearing children and adults. In a further willful twist, however, I will break off this particular story and consider some aspects of the acquisition of language and thought in people born without useful hearing, only to regain the track of the original story at a much later stage. Then, in a further loop (taking a shaggy dog for a walk?), I consider some aspects of the cerebral bases for understanding seen speech and attempt to relate them to what is known about the brain bases for understanding language in deaf people. I also consider some ways in which the acquisition of seen speech may and may not be optimized for people born with no effective hearing.

My main aim, overall, is to try to put some aspects of research on lipreading into the context of deafness and examine a number of claims concerning cognition and language from this perspective.

This may seem an "oralist" perspective that rejects all of the advances made in the last 30 years in research on sign language and in the advancement of sign language as a first or second language. This is not what I intend, and I hope it will become clear that this is not what I mean. In the course of these arguments, I will refer to some single case studies and to studies of language in anomalous groups other than the congenitally deaf. I will also refer to experimental psychological and neuropsychological studies and studies of the development of cognitive skills in children. This promiscuity is intentional. Evidence from all sources must be considered in order to gain a proper understanding of the issues and to glean some hints of solutions. The "war against cognitive poverty" that concerned Conrad cannot be fought by polemics in favor of one or other approach. Facts, as well as opinions related to them, are required, and I hope that some of those offered here will further the fight necessary for deaf people to achieve their full potential.

PLAN

The themes and claims that I explore in this chapter are the following:

1. Lipreading is a natural cognitive skill that informs cognitive performance in hearing people and also in many born-deaf people with no useful hearing from birth.
2. Lipreading does not afford a generally useful route into language acquisition in the deaf but nevertheless leaves its mark on some aspects of their cognitive performance (especially schooled skills, such as reading or writing).
3. Some aspects of how deafness affects the acquisition of cognition and language are sketched out in order to delineate a few of the complexities of the effect of the lack of sound on a range of early cognitive skills.
4. Maturational hypotheses of language learning are explored in relation to some special groups of children, with a view to determining whether the critical period for language acquisition may be extended.
5. Literacy and working memory are highlighted as functions of special relevance to understanding how reading speech from lips may play a particular role—in both deaf and hearing people. In deaf children, this is im-

portant in relation to the complete acquisition of a first language such as sign language and incomplete acquisition of a speech-based language.

6. I sketch out an information-processing scheme for analyzing lipreading, drawing on experimental and neuropsychological findings, and relate these to neurophysiological findings concerning lipreading and deafness.

NOMENCLATURE

Throughout this chapter, I will use the term *lipreading* to refer to studies of the functional properties of seeing speech. While *speechreading* is a term that is becoming more favored, its uses are not yet synonymous with those of lipreading, and since the older term has been used in all of the works that I cite, it is the one I will use here. Similarly, I will use the terms *oralism* and *oral* to indicate that immersion in speech has been used as the sole or primary means of inducing language. While *speech-based* is becoming more widely used as a synonym, this more recent term may not indicate reliably whether hearing or deaf people are referred to and sidesteps some of the opprobrium into which the older term has fallen. I would rather that the change in language use not do all of this work for me.

WHERE I COME FROM

In 1979, in the last stages of completing a Ph.D. on cerebral asymmetries in looking at faces and facial expressiveness, I was discussing research with my friend Barbara Dodd. At that time she was investigating deaf children with Neil O'Connor and Beate Hermelin at the Medical Research Council Child Development Unit at London University. Her work with these children, most of whom were reared within the heavily oralist (speech-based) British tradition of the time, was starting to convince her that even without any useful residual hearing, these profoundly deaf children were able to make some use of the phonological structures of spoken English *from lipreading alone.* Nor did this appear to be a skill that was particularly closely linked to degree of hearing loss or to the ease with which these children could make themselves understood by speaking.

In some ways this was an uncomfortable insight because it appeared to contradict some robust and systematic findings. The message that most people read from Conrad's classic experimental study of deaf children in Britain, *The Deaf School Child* (1979), is that speech coding from lipreading can only be useful in youngsters whose hearing loss is not at the most pro-found level (90–120 decibels in the worse ear). However, Conrad was actu-ally more precise, yet open, about the relationship between the uses of speech-based coding and degree of hearing loss. Some children in his large-scale study (he tested more than 600 youngsters) showed evidence of the use of speech coding in some cognitive tasks despite profound hearing loss ("We now know that internal speech is far from perfectly correlated with deafness" [Conrad, 1979, p. 119]).

Be that as it may, as Dodd (1980) then reported, born-deaf children with profound hearing loss were able to write from dictation phonological strings to which they had never been exposed (nonsense words). She also showed that in *hearing* children, lipreading played an interesting part in the child's cognitive development. Babies shown videotapes of their mother's face go-ing in and out of sound synchrony were visibly distressed as synchrony was lost and were contentedly attentive to the synchronized match (Dodd, 1979). Later, it became clear (Kuhl & Meltzoff, 1984) that this sensitivity was spe-cific to the perceived speech sound. Babies habituated to the correct seen vowel shape accompanying a spoken soundtrack rather than to simple offset and onset of pure tones synthesized to mouth opening. So, despite the clearly demonstrable failure of lipreading to deliver useful speech in most contexts where we require it (you cannot follow the TV news with the sound turned off; even the skilled deaf user of English requires captions or sign language translation), it seems to play a subtle role in cognition, which may be ob-served for hearing and for deaf people. Sensitivity to it develops early in hearing people, and in the profoundly deaf, lipreading can be sufficiently informative to carry some phonological information "by eye."

CLARIFICATION OF THE ROLE OF LIPREADING IN RELATION TO DEAFNESS

At this point I would stress that I am not suggesting that born-deaf individu-als compensate for their lack of hearing by developing special lipreading skills. With some very specific exceptions (both of individuals and of some constrained functions) that will be discussed at a later point in this essay, there is emphatically no reason to believe this is so. Studies with deafened and born-deaf people (see Gailey, 1987, and Rönnberg, 1996) show that the deaf are at least as disadvantaged as hearing people in trying to understand speech by following mouth movements alone. Even in oral England, this has been recognized, although those that have pointed this out have not always been heeded (see Evans, 1981, and Rodda & Grove, 1987).

IMMEDIATE MEMORY AND OTHER MATTERS

In 1979, then, Barbara Dodd had started some studies with hearing people, investigating some effects of desynchronizing vision (lipspeech) from hearing speech in noise. Seeing the speaker improves the intelligibility of heard speech in white noise, and the gain in comprehension from seeing the speaker under these conditions was the dependent variable in these tasks. She was investigating just how much of this lipreading advantage persisted when the seen and heard speech stream slipped out of synchrony. She found that even when the seen speech led the noisy heard tape by up to two seconds, subjects seemed to benefit from it. "They must be remembering what they have lipread," she said. "Now—how can we find out how they do this?" We decided to do some studies of immediate memory for silent lipread material. It was pretty easy, after all, to lipread number lists. (Just try mouthing numbers at someone. As long as the context "I am going to say numbers" is given, the task is trivial. This is a simple and convenient fact that has allowed us to perform a large number of studies on number recall.) After we had done these first studies of immediate serial ordered recall, we thought about it some more and realized that current theorizing in experimental psychology was fairly dogmatic about immediate memory processes in relation to hearing and to vision. The orthodox view was that hearing speech leaves an "echo," a precategorical trace in the auditory perceptual system, while seeing a speech event (such as a written number or letter) does not. This insight captured the fact that the last item in a heard list is better recalled than the last item in a list where the items are presented in graphic form (recency effect). We found that silently lipread lists seemed to leave an "echo" too. It seemed not only that the echo was not in any sense acoustic but also that silent lipspeech and auditory speech in immediate memory were intimately connected—that people essentially behave as if they have heard material they have lipread (Campbell & Dodd, 1980; De Gelder & Vroomen, 1994; Gathercole, 1987; Spoehr & Corin, 1978). This insight was to have some interesting consequences for us, as well as for theorists of immediate memory who started to find other situations that suggest speech leaves the echo and that this speech may be either heard or seen to be spoken or silently articulated. It looked as if the confluence of lipreading and hearing was a natural and effective one, at least in hearing people.

And what of the deaf? At least for the primarily oral-trained youngsters we were investigating, they seemed to remember lipread lists just as hearing people do. While immediate memory span is almost always shorter in deaf than in hearing people (MacSweeney, Campbell, & Donlan, 1996), the qualitative pattern of the serial recall curve and the types of errors they make seem very similar to those of hearing people: they too seem to make use of an echo in lipread recall, and this is not present for the recall of written material (Dodd, Hobson, Brasher, & Campbell, 1983). So in spelling and in immediate memory, Barbara Dodd and I found strong evidence for phonological structure in deaf immediate recall. As far as we could tell, it was lipreading that delivered this structure.

PHONOLOGICAL SKILLS IN SPELLING AND READING IN DEAF CHILDREN

In a series of studies of reading and spelling in British deaf teenagers, this basic insight—of phonological structures informing reading, writing, and remembering in the deaf—has been confirmed and extended (see, e.g., Burden & Campbell, 1994, and Campbell, 1992b). Moreover, it can be observed in other literate deaf youngsters, whether academic high achievers at Gallaudet University (Hanson, 1986; Hanson & Fowler, 1987) or in other scholastic groups (see, e.g., Waters & Doehring, 1990). While not all details of performance tally across all of these studies, the general picture that emerges is quite convincing. The deaf are not necessarily living in a world in which the phonological structure of speech plays no part. Their reading, writing, and remembering can bear traces of speech structuring, just as do those of hearing people.

Why is this important? Surely it is possible—even desirable—for reading, writing, and remembering in the deaf to be *good* rather than "speech based." As has been sadly confirmed many times since Pintner and Patterson's (1917) classic finding of reduced digit memory span in the deaf, the great majority of deaf 16–18-year-olds not only have the memory span of 10-year-old hearing children but also have reading skills of about the same level and may even be functionally illiterate despite many years of schooling. This seems to be unconnected in any simple way to mode of communication or native language, although deaf children of deaf parents (however reared) tend to be better scholars than deaf children of hearing parents. This unfortunate majority fail to reach their academic potential in many ways (see Marschark, 1993, for summaries), but one of the most telling failures is in literacy, where *all* component skills (word decoding, inference, use of syntax, vocabulary, pragmatic knowledge) are affected.

In most hearing people who are exposed and reared with an alphabetic or syllabic orthography such as English, Turkish, Italian, or Japanese kana, acquisition of reading and writing skills is intimately linked with speech-related abilities, including immediate verbal memory. Opinions differ over which is the key correlative variable, but all agree that the ability explicitly to reflect on and perform segmentation and blending tasks on the speech sounds of one's native tongue has a crucial role to play in gaining a hold on the task of decoding written words, remembering them, and using them in writing. Where orthographies do not deliver the speech-structure transparently (for example, in Mandarin), the acquisition of a reading vocabulary is more drawn out and fails to deliver phonological awareness (Bertelson, 1987). Having stated this, however, it should also be noted that exceptions to the rule exist. Indeed, Baron (1979) pointed out that school-age readers in the United States fell into two groups: those who broke written words up into parts and sounded them out—"Phoenicians"—and those who took a run at the whole word—"Chinese." These differences persisted through the lower grades and colored the children's performance on a range of tasks.

The important thing, though, is that Chinese-style reading need not always and invariably mean poor reading. To drive the point home, an English university student, RE (Butterworth, Campbell, & Howard, 1986; Campbell & Butterworth, 1985), was a fast and fluent reader and writer but was quite unable to perform any phonological task such as generating spoonerisms or subtracting initial or final phonemes from words (Me: "What is left when I take the last sound from the word 'comb'?"; RE [after nearly a minute of effort]: "komm"). RE had a shortened memory span for written and spoken material and was better at remembering written material with her eyes closed (suggesting she used a visually based code). She learned new written words by proxy: she would ask a colleague how such a word was pronounced and apparently had little difficulty committing it to memory despite her poor explicit phonological skills.

Since RE reads and writes this way, with no apparent support from the sound structure of the language, why don't the deaf? While the question may appear naive, many researchers, from Gates and Chase (1927) onward, have suggested that this is indeed how the deaf do it. And, in fact, there are traces of Chinese-style reading in some aspects of deaf literacy under some testing conditions. Many researchers (see Waters & Doehring, 1990, for one review) find that the deaf are less sensitive to speech-sound structure in some aspects of their word spellings and written word recognition than are hearing controls. The pattern is by no means universal, however, and I have been powerfully struck by the opposite pattern—the reliability of *some* sensitivity to speech-sound regularity in written word spelling and reading in many profoundly deaf youngsters (Burden & Campbell, 1994; Marschark & Harris, 1996) with relatively poor speech and no useful hearing. This seems counterintuitive. Does it offer any hope for the development of literacy in deaf people?

To answer this question, it is necessary to backtrack and to outline some of the characteristics of the acquisition of language in the congenitally deaf and in other groups. It is now time to nest a different set of stories within this main frame. We will return to this question eventually and hopefully will be able to attempt an answer.

DETOUR: SOME WAYS IN WHICH BEING DEAF IS BAD FOR LANGUAGE ACQUISITION

The claim that speech-based decoding in reading, writing, and remembering may be used by and be useful to the deaf seems paradoxical. First, they don't have ready access through hearing to the speech sound structure of the language. Moreover, despite our work on lipreading, we would not claim that lipreading alone, unaided and available as the sole speech medium *ab initio,* can readily deliver sufficient phonological contrasts for understanding speech. Most of the articulators used in speaking are invisible; they are behind the lips. Second, among the deaf youngsters we have investigated, it was unusual for there to be any special or additional early language support—support that is essential for normal language development, whether this is sign language or speech based. Most of these deaf youngsters (like deaf children everywhere) were born to hearing parents, and their deafness was not confirmed until their second or third year. By this time, the active conceptual and perceptual skills of the child are becoming engaged with linguistic regularities (Gleitman, 1994; Mandler, 1994), and the developing child starts to impose his or her own cognitive and linguistic constraints on the world that he or she is interpreting (Bowerman, 1994; Newport, 1990). There is even evidence that prenatal exposure "tunes" the child before birth to heard rhythmic and some segmental structures of the native language (Mehler & Christophe, 1994). For hearing infants, the many clues to the segmental structure of heard speech are available at the outset: speech-based distinctions can be sensed and perceived easily at every age. The hearing baby lives in a nourishing broth of human speech, one from which the relevant critical phonological contrasts and distinctions that indicate word meanings and utterance structures can be spooned out as required. Deaf children may be deprived of language-related input *in utero* and certainly during the crucially important first year or so. They can have only partial access to speech by viewing the speaker—partial in that it is available only when viewing the speaker and in that few of the relevant phonological contrasts are available by vision alone. This is thin gruel for language nourishment.

Taking this further, there may be some quite specific additional ways in which deafness is a particular handicap due to lack of *acoustic* as well as linguistic inputs. For example, one of the roots of referential communication may be lost. When a glass drops in the kitchen, the crash makes the mother turn toward the unexpected event. The hearing child must become sensitive both to the coincidence of the crash with the visual events—the glass dropping—and the mother's attention being drawn to it. Multimodal events have a strong effect in orienting the child to regularities in the world that are important for the development of cognitive and linguistic capabilities. The seeds for joint attention (Scaife & Bruner, 1975) may be sown in this way and, with them, the development of referential pointing and precursors of ostensive naming. Many such sound-and-vision events are likely to signal a range of important regularities in the world that can both trigger protolinguistic, communicative behavior in the infant and extend the child's perceptions beyond those in the immediate visual field.

In one important study, moreover, Baldwin and Markman (1989), investigating hearing toddlers, used an experimenter to point at objects in the child's environment or to point and name objects. Pointing effectively directed children's attention during testing, but only when objects were also labeled (named) did this have any effect on the child's behavior after the adult experimenter had left the lab. Children continued to look at objects that had been named and pointed at more than at objects that had just been pointed at.

Thus, the deaf child may be doubly disadvantaged in terms of language development: congenital hearing loss, through acoustic deprivation, can maroon the deaf child of hearing parents in a relatively unstable, potentially difficult social and communicative environment that, additionally, gives limited access to a prime language medium—speech (Marschark, 1993).

A FURTHER DETOUR?: MATURATION AND LANGUAGE LEARNING

This was just one example of how difficult language acquisition might be for the congenitally deaf child. Does this mean that profound prelingual deafness, incurred under these "usual conditions" of communication, might slam the door shut on language acquisition?

The answer is not entirely clear. While Chomsky has repeatedly insisted that language, just like an arm or a leg, is essentially preformed, requiring only an enabling environment to mature, theorists of a more psychological bent (see Chapter 3 and Pinker, 1994) point to the moderating, modulating influence of the child's developing conceptual and intellectual abilities and the specific environmental inputs at different ages—all of which follow a language-intertwined path through childhood. These studies, however, are more concerned with the "how" of language acquisition in the first few years than the "whether" or "why."

On a purely Chomskian view (see also Lenneberg, 1967), if language has not "caught" in the first 8 or so years, it never will. There is a critical period for language acquisition—most marked for, but not confined to, morpho-syntactic maturation, and this cannot be extended.

Congruent with this notion are studies of "wild children" (Curtiss, 1977) whose language never "catches up" if their social isolation lasted for their first 10 years. Furthermore, a few children have been identified with a familial genetic disorder coincident with a very specific problem in morpho-syntactic aspects of language (Gopnik, 1992). A simple interpretation of these findings is that under these conditions the language module fails to develop because of an inappropriate (social) environment or was never present because of a genetic anomaly.

However, this may be too simplistic. Newport (1990) makes a convincing theoretical case from the study of language in different groups that the mechanism for language acquisition in childhood is determined by the child's initial sampling strategy, itself constrained by memorial and perceptual limitations of childhood. She suggests that the componential structure of language can be processed only in its parts by young children because of their perceptual and memorial shortcomings. This part-sampling strategy allows the development of sensitivity to regularities in language (to phonotactic and morpho-syntactic rules). A similar claim was put forward by Pettito and Seidenberg (1979) in the context of monkeys and language. They argued that monkeys were too smart at too young an age to develop language.

An implication of this may be that in those who are language-deprived and in late second-language learners (but not young second-language learners), rather different mechanisms are used. More mature perceptual and memorial systems lead to a different processing mode: language acquired this way may be relatively rich in vocabulary but yet lack fully realized syntactic and phonological structures.

The story is convenient and elegant. It would also seem to account quite well for the fact that some children with poor intellectual capacities can nevertheless acquire language apparently normally. Yet it may not yet be sufficiently well formulated to cope with special groups. For example, it is often claimed that children with Williams Syndrome (WS), who have extremely low IQs and are unable to comprehend the world in any effective way, nevertheless have excellent language. This would betoken an especially important role for social, emotional, and pragmatic communication abilities as precursors and molders of normally acquired first language, as well as underlining Newport's point concerning restricted cognitive capacities as optimal for language learning. The speech of children with WS is certainly fluent, pragmatically correct, and rich in vocabulary, although their speech is typically poor in content, contradictory in meaning, and narratively unstructured. However, it seems that their syntax is not particularly secure. Karmiloff-Smith (see Karmiloff-Smith, Grant, & Berthoud, forthcoming; Karmiloff-Smith, Klima, Bellugi, Grant, & Baron-Cohen, 1995) has shown a number of shortcomings in the grasp of syntactic relations that would be trivial in normal young language users and that do not seem to be related to the intellectual deficits in the WS children (for example, they were not tested using formal, explicit tests that disadvantage the child with learning difficulties). In some ways, their mistakes, which were particularly clear in their poor use of prepositions and syntactic agreement, resemble those of the late language learner. Generally, it would be premature to conclude that intellectual endowment can be completely independent of language attainment— that poor intellectual endowment sets no lower limit on language acquisition. While the language abilities of these children are notable, their language is not normally structured.

Williams syndrome children enjoy good emotional and social relationships and have no difficulty understanding human intentionality (they have intact theory of mind; see Baron-Cohen, Campbell, Karmiloff-Smith, Grant, & Walker, 1995, and Karmiloff-Smith et al., 1995). By contrast, children with autism show impaired abilities in this field, as well as poor intelligence, especially on verbal testing. Nevertheless, to the extent that particular children with autism develop language, it seems to be syntactically well formed. The most obvious language deficits in autism reflect a failure to be sensitive to appropriate semantic, lexical, or inferential contexts (Frith & Happe, 1994) but not a failure to be sensitive to morpho-syntactic or phono-syntactic variables (Frith & Snowling, 1983).

The coherence failure in language use in people with autism—a failure to use context appropriately—might suggest that they should resemble early language learners in their language style; unable to see the whole for the parts, their cognitive effort is spent detecting local rules and regularities. This may, in some sense, account for the relatively good grasp of language structure in those people with autism who are able to communicate verbally. It is noteworthy that even the most noncommunicative autistic savant—say, a calendrical calculator—responds effectively to a relatively complex syntactic utterance (e.g., "In which year since 1987 did 5 March fall on a Thursday?"). However, at least one such person has been described who has acquired several languages after acquiring his native English (Smith & Tsimpli, 1991). He showed typical patterns of (later) second-language learning for these languages. His phonology and syntax remained resolutely those of his first language.

From the evidence to date, it would seem that when the cognitive potential of the learner is restricted and is comparable to that of a younger child, this does not mean that the delivery of a first language in all of its specific componential richness can occur over a more extended period. Even when the cognitive deficit appears to favor the use of a piecemeal sampling strategy, language does not come right. One way to accommodate these findings is to stress the multiple bases of language development: that language cannot develop normally without the appropriate communicative (social and emotional) and conceptual (intellectual, referential) components developing in a coherent way. In this sort of view, the consideration of WS children and children with autism offers no useful clue to the development of language in normal children or in children deprived of acoustic input but with otherwise intact mental equipment. But one cannot have everything. If language is to be considered a modular process, a specific mental organ, then the consideration of groups that show discrepant language and cognitive development *is* germane *and* Lenneberg appears to have been right. Language acquisition cannot be delayed. One interpretation of Newport's theoretical approach might have suggested otherwise. "Squeezed" cognitive potential (reduced intellectual, memorial, and perceptual capacities) cannot extend the critical period. Even an autistic intelligence, tuned to components rather than to wholes, can succeed only partially in acquiring language.

COMPOUNDING THE LOSS: CAN ACOUSTIC DEPRIVATION AFFECT THE DEVELOPMENT OF SOCIAL AND INTENTIONAL COGNITION?

I have already mentioned that deprivation of sound may set up a number of possible barriers to effective communicative development. The importance of bimodal inputs for the development of social cognition, specifically, requires further consideration. For a start, the coordination of face and voice, as shown by Dodd (1979) and by Spelke and Cortelyou (1981), is a powerful social attractor and quickly becomes well tuned, so that hearing babies can put facial and vocal emotion together correctly by the seventh month

(Walker-Andrews, 1986). I have also already mentioned that multimodal events may be important in setting up the conditions for ostensive reference in the development of early language. They can serve another purpose in the infants' world too. When the glass drops in the kitchen, the mother will turn to look at it. Observing her, the child can start to associate the unexpected distal event with the proximal one of her momentary change of attention; he can start to see what makes people tick, that they are responsive to events in the world that may be close or distant—or even to internal events that cannot be observed at all. Unlike a hammer hitting a nail or the cutting of paper by scissors, there is no immediate relationship between the fall of the glass in the kitchen and the mother's turned head: one causes the other not by direct physical action but by affecting the intention of the (observed) human being.

There may be glimmers of awareness of human intentionality in infants' behavior from the first months: in teasing (Reddy, 1991; Trevarthen, 1979); in eye-direction changes following interruptions of dyadic games (Phillips, Baron-Cohen, & Rutter, 1992); and in joint attention and social referencing behavior, the term for the way the infant in the second half of the first year checks out the social scene. Typically social referencing involves the child attending to the mother's (or other's) focus of attention and her expression, and pitching his own actions responsively—for example, by moving toward her or by pointing. Integrating the expressive (e.g., mother's face and voice) and attentional components of the event is increasingly seen to be crucial (Mundy, Kasari, & Sigman, 1992).

There has always been interest in uncovering the roots of children's awareness of these matters (Flavell, 1974). More recently, the specific mechanisms that allow mind reading to develop are under particular scrutiny.

Sound allows distal events to play into such social and socio-affective referencing and social interaction in a large number of ways; the mother's head turns when the doorbell rings and a minute later the father comes into the room. How can a deaf child "know" what informs the hearing mind under these circumstances? At the very least, a scotoma, a "blind spot," must be present in the infant's cognitive map—a puzzle to be resolved at a later time. Could such cognitive scotomas caused directly by a lack of acoustic input be sufficient to delay social cognitive development or set it on a deviant course? As it happens, there are indications that the development of social cognition is not straightforward for most deaf children (although some current theorizing suggests that sight, rather than sound, may be even more important for developing an understanding of intentionality in others [Baron-Cohen, 1994]).

Thus, it has been reported that the deaf child of hearing parents tends to be socially immature and impulsive, less able to take the emotional perspective of others and insensitive to others' needs, and less morally mature than age-mates (see Marschark, 1993, pp. 67–71, for a review). While there are a host of reasons why this might be so, it is possible that some of the roots of these problems may lie in the specific lack of acoustic input in infancy, which, through a slowing of the ability to infer intentional behavior in others (and also, possibly critically, in the self), would ramify into a range of social and emotional skills.

Interestingly, there is at least one study (Cates & Shontz, 1990) cited by Marschark (1993) that suggests *dissociated* social skills in young deaf children. Thus while deaf children's role-taking abilities in social games was reliably related to their social adjustment, self-image, and communication abilities, these children's ability to take the perspective of the other was *not* so related. The latter could be an indicator of social reflexive skills, the sort of skills that are required to understand what someone is thinking or planning.

Systematic studies of the deaf child's understanding of "mind" (use of and sensitivity to mental-state terms, sensitivity to false-belief tasks, social referencing skills) have not been undertaken, and the fragments obtained so far tell an ambivalent story. A number of researchers have investigated this relatively casually and failed to find deficits in such tasks in deaf children. Since their concern was not with the issues raised here, these negative results have not been reported. However, one recent published report does find that deaf youngsters cannot perform a simple first-order false-belief task (Peterson & Siegal, 1995). These authors suggest that "lack of conversation" in these children, who were deaf children of hearing parents, was the crucial factor. But, as indicated above, such tests may be sensitive to a range of factors that, taken together, may lead to suboptimal development in this area. Tager-Flusberg (1993) claims that, under some circumstances, linguistic, syntactic skills can deliver an understanding of intentionality (for example, in youngsters with autism, tests of syntactic ability tend to correlate closely with performance on theory of mind tasks such as the apprehension of false belief). And some studies suggest that social cognition in deaf children improves with their language mastery (Kusché & Greenberg, 1983).

I am not suggesting that the ability to take the "cold" perceptual perspective of the other (for example, to calculate line of sight or to perform Piaget's "mountains" task) is necessarily disturbed in deaf children. Indeed, deaf children with sign language as a first language are quite likely to have a perspective-taking *advantage* over hearing children in interpreting movements in space. Pettito (1987), for example, has elegantly shown that deictic reference (pointing gestures) is interpreted by deaf children in relation to the speaker, not the receiver (and that this use develops in a very similar manner to hearing children's use of the similar shifting reference pronouns "me" and "you"). Lateral inversion of gestures, too, is correctly performed by early signers. Space for a young signer is managed effectively and flexibly in relation to the speaker and the receiver. One recent study (Masataka, 1995) suggests that deaf children with sign language as a first language are *better* than age-matched young controls at reporting the "correct" (i.e., producer viewpoint) orientation of tactile forms like letters "drawn" on the perceiver's forehead. (Most recipients perceive these as mirror-reversed [Corcoran, 1977].) The question I have raised here is this: Are deaf children disadvantaged in relation to hearing and seeing children in developing the bases for understanding human minds?

RETURNING: CONGENITAL DEAFNESS AND LANGUAGE ACQUISITION

The point of the preceeding detour should now be clear. It was to try to glean some clues from other investigated groups and from other aspects of development concerning the likely course of language acquisition in the sound-deprived child. In fact, Newport's observations concerning the specifics of cognitive maturation in relation to language acquisition were made first on deaf people. Where the first language, whatever its form, was not acquired early, she found that it followed the pattern of second-language learning—a relatively weak grasp of syntactic regularities (and allied structures) that was independent of other language skills (such as vocabulary or communicative competence). Early-acquired sign language in deaf users did not show this pattern, but it was better formed, with more flexibility and generativity in the use of morpho-syntactic structures.

For children reared in an oral, speech-based environment, the same constraints are likely to hold. Many of those children have only a weak hold on language, with most of the indicators of language acquired in a manner similar to the second language for first-language learners.

However, a number of profoundly deaf children who have not been exposed to sign language but reared in a totally speech-based world can acquire excellent receptive language and sometimes can make themselves understood by speech too. The most likely possibility that distinguishes these children from the majority whose language develops more slowly and ineffectively is that lipreading "plus something" has served as an effective input from the child's earliest months.

Just what that magic something could be is still a mystery. From some comparative studies, such as those of Dodd and Murphy (1992), it is not anything obvious in a child's background. These children are not necessarily more intelligent, better adjusted, or more communication oriented than their less language-skilled deaf matched-controls. The magic ingredient is very likely to be a combination of things. There may be a little residual hearing in the early months that is later lost but yet serves to orient the child to speech and affords some early speech forms; there may be additional skills in swift visual analysis of lipshape. Possibly the use of some additional non-sound cues, such as tactile or visual ones, have a role to play. Furthermore, the social, emotional, and general communicative early environment of these deaf children may be optimized through early diagnosis and appropriate in-tervention. Once some language is functional, from whatever source, *boot-strapping*—making use of known forms to infer and process new ones, which is much in evidence in hearing children's acquisition of new forms (see, e.g., Gleitman, 1994)—will magnify the early achievement. Thus, magic ingredients may function as catalysts rather than as components in the chemical experiment.

LITERACY: MAKING THE MOST OF A SECOND LANGUAGE

Before making this foray into the acquisition of cognition and language, I asked, Why do deaf people use speech sound structures *at all* in their reading, spelling, and remembering? I pointed out that hearing children do not necessarily use such structures, though mastery tends to be achieved more quickly and fully if they do. One point of my detour was to indicate that most deaf children's grasp of language cannot simply be equated with that of a hearing child or the (rare) deaf child who responds effectively to seen speech. First steps in literacy for a child with a native language and for a child still struggling to achieve one may be very different. Few deaf children find themselves in the position of hearing children, who, when faced with the cryptogram of the first written word, have a specific task to perform: to make this fit a form he or she already knows from three to five years of experience with language by ear—that is, to decode the new written symbol to fit a known acoustic linguistic form. For most deaf children without sign language as a first language, learning to read and write cannot be grounded in detailed knowledge of acquired speech forms; it cannot be *just* a mapping problem that requires a solution.

A CHINESE ROOM (BUT NOT JOHN SEARLE'S)

The deaf child with sign language as a first language may have a problem when faced with written words. The situation is akin to hearing as English or French child who is faced with Mandarin as a written language: the unfamiliar written form does not map onto the native language but maps onto an entirely different one. The written word thus has to be translated back into the native language to be represented and communicated (i.e., to read Mandarin "in English" or "in French," not in Chinese). It is not too surprising that when tested in written English, children with sign language as a first language do relatively poorly (see Marschark & Harris, 1996), their literacy achievements being at marked variance with their expressive and receptive sign language abilities. To test such children in written English is the formal equivalent of testing the English child exposed to Chinese characters in Mandarin. While some may do relatively well, testing in "the second language" will bear all of the signs of *its* late acquisition and will show very marked variability among users, contrasting with their abilities in sign language.

READING AND WRITING TO THE RESCUE?: LITERACY ENABLES

If sign language as a first language cannot give an immediate purchase on reading and writing (Mayer & Wells, 1996) since the translation problem is a major one, perhaps the child who uses speech may be *relatively* less disadvantaged in this domain, however "unnatural," ill-formed, and ill-acquired his or her spoken language may be.

Most deaf children, whatever their upbringing, acquire some knowledge of the language of the spoken community in which they live. As we have seen, it is rare for deaf children to be fully functional in spoken language, and there are good developmental reasons to believe that difficult, possibly intractable, problems exist in the normal acquisition of speech by people born without hearing. Syntax may be poor, vocabulary limited. Reference skills may be incomplete with numerous cognitive scotomata, and these can compound the problem. Through lipreading alone, much speech remains ambiguous. Nevertheless, it may form a basis on which further knowledge of the spoken language can be built. One natural extension of spoken language is reading and writing. On the printed page, distinctions that may be unheard can be seen. This is true not just for deaf people but also for hearing people. In cultures with established traditions of literacy, the written language can continue to illuminate "lost" spoken distinctions that offer valuable clues to morphology. The "g," pronounced in "signal" but not in "signed," betokens its origin in the root morpheme "sign" (Chomsky, 1970). In languages where the orthography is based, however convolutedly, on the sound structure of the language, literacy can uncover important *linguistic* regularities not immediately available to deaf children by ear.

Vivien Burden and I struggled to find an analogy that might clarify how this could work with the deaf child. In Campbell and Burden (1995), after describing a number of ways in which the deaf were sensitive to phonological regularities in their spellings and written word recognition, we wrote:

> Even though the deaf may have good phonological *awareness,* in the sense that they are often drilled extensively in phonemic tasks as they approach the school years, this cannot make contact with properly specified phonological representations, for (by definition) these do not exist for the deaf. Only when they are confronted with an alphabetic orthography will some of the phonetic contrasts they cannot "hear," and which will thus be perceived as homophones in interpreting speech, become clear. Such clarifications may become instantiated both as orthographic *and* phonological realities. That they might develop in this way might be illustrated by analogy. Several years ago I wondered why it was that the Indian Independence leader and the two prime-ministers who shared his name had that name so consistently misspelled by English people. They spell it GHANDI (Campbell & Coltheart, 1984). It was because that particular letter string more closely fitted the orthographic constraints of English than the correct spelling, GANDHI. For English speaker/hearers the spellings are homophonous. A speaker of Indian languages explained to me that written GH and DH represent distinct phonemes than G and D and she showed me the differences by speaking words with the different phonemes in them. I could neither reliably pronounce nor (quite) hear them. Yet the distinction is a phonological fact and one which is I know as such, despite my poor production and perception of it. Because of this I know that other apparently homophonous Indian words may be distinguished in this way. Even if this knowledge is realized in a partial fashion (by unreliable discrimination or production), it will still be of specific use. I am suggesting that, in the deaf people we have studied, exposure to English written language enlightens in this way, but through covert sensitivity rather than overt instruction.

LITERACY SUPPORTS COGNITION OF LANGUAGE

One important aspect of the illumination that literacy can offer on speech structures is that it does not seem to be constrained by the critical period for the acquisition of a first language. Literacy itself is acquired relatively late in childhood, sometimes with difficulty, in most cultures by most people. People learn second languages both orally and in their written forms. A Western European classical education consisted in great part of the delivery of dead languages through their written forms (Latin, Greek, Hebrew) to boys aged 10 to 20 years. Paradoxically, literacy also can offer some hope for communication with other groups with apparent developmental communication difficulties; for example, anarthric individuals who have difficulty in planning and executing appropriate speech gestures use the written word ably and effectively to communicate. Moreover, their reading, writing, and remembering is structured by speech-based coding (Bishop & Robson, 1989). Some children with Down's Syndrome can make great progress in reading and writing. These children tend to have anatomical and physiological malformations affecting both the articulators and auditory reception to some extent. Reading and writing afford a second medium for expressing and mastering language.

In all of these cases, it appears that the written medium is acquired not in implicit, automatic fashion but carefully, explicitly, and attentively. It has, in the first place, to be taught. Unlike spoken language for hearing speakers, written language for most users demands metalinguistic skills: awareness of the components of the language and the ability to muster them appropriately. This usually occurs in the classroom; in any case, dialogue between teacher and pupil seems to be necessary for writing to be acquired. Even early reader/writers (Read, 1971; Treiman, 1992) who can read before coming to school do not pick it up by themselves; writing has to be shown to the child and practiced and commented upon in order for it to be learned. However, once it has been learned, there is no reason to believe that aspects of analysis cannot be automated, as in any other skill. This particular learning pattern suggests that the acquisition of literacy has the potential to do a number of things for the deaf child:

1. To enjoin the child, through appropriate instruction, in a shared cultural linguistic venture
2. To clarify aspects of language that may not be acquired by exposure to lipreading alone
3. To sensitize the learner to ortho-phonological regularities
4. To instill a range of problem-solving strategies and skills of interpretation of language

LITERACY AS A WORKSPACE

One reason why literacy can be taught and why it works is that, unlike speech, it leaves a permanent trace in the world. When language is uttered and when it is perceived, it is evasive and fugitive, requiring specifically tuned, fast-working mechanisms to "grab" its form before it disappears. Another discomfiting aspect of spoken language from the perceiver's standpoint is that it is subject to the many vagaries of complex muscular production systems: spoken words "smear" into each other because of the mechanical production and recovery characteristics of the articulators. The pervasive phenomena of anticipatory and retrograde co-articulation make the solution of the invariance problem (that a particular phoneme can be identified as that phoneme independently of its articulatory environment) nontrivial.

Literacy sidesteps this, too, except for the reading of handwriting, itself an interesting problem. The *perceptual* demands of reading are not great in comparison to the perceptual demands of understanding speech. *Mnestic* demands, also, are reduced for reading compared with listening; one can reinspect and pace one's encoding of the written word. Little wonder that, in hearing people, the written word-form can infiltrate the processing of heard material (see Seidenberg & Tanenhaus, 1979): it affords extra support for speech memory and understanding. In deaf people we might expect to find that such effects of orthography dominating phonology are even more pronounced; for instance, does the concept of rhyme for a deaf child lean more heavily on the look than the sound of the word? The answer is that in some ways it does, in some ways it does not. What seems to characterize deaf children's use of speech-related concepts is greater cross-task variability than in children with normal hearing.

Thus, for example, Helen Wright and I (Campbell & Wright, 1989) asked deaf children to judge rhyme on the basis of picture presentations. They were first given practice on an odd-man-out task to ensure that their grasp of the concept was similar to that of hearing youngsters, matched for reading age. We found that the deaf teenagers, like their young controls, matched pictures on the basis of rhyme pretty well and were no more or no less confused by orthography ("bear" and "snare" rhyme although their spellings differ; "fear" and "wear" do not, although their spellings are similar) than their controls. Both showed *some* false positives in this task. On this basis, their grasp of the notion of rhyme seems rather secure; it must have been derived by mapping the known spelling patterns onto the lip patterns that the words make. But this does not seem to insulate them from some orthographic "leakage" in these decisions. However, in contrast to these findings, when deaf children were expected to use rhyme *implicitly* as a cue to paired associate learning (Campbell & Wright, 1990), they did not do so. They were better than matched hearing controls at remembering picture-word pairs that were randomly associated (blue-fork) but showed no sign of using rhyme as a cue when it was available in the list (blue-shoe), although even young hearing children did use this.

Similarly, Leybaert and her colleagues (e.g., Leybaert & Alégria, 1993) found that deaf readers are prone to Stroop color-word interference when the letter string is a color word homophone (like "Bloo"). This is very similar to the pattern in hearing youngsters. However, in deaf readers, unlike hearing controls, this sensitivity to the speech structure of the color carrier word disappears when a child makes a manual rather than a spoken response.

It seems that deaf children have some aspects of inner speech available, but their mental lives need not be dominated by them to the same extent as are the mental lives of hearing children. Thus, it is possible for some researchers to find less phonological dominance in reading than we have found (Waters & Doehring, 1990) but, more important, for deaf children to show more flexibility in coding than hearing children.

VERBAL WORKING MEMORY: A WORKHORSE?

I would like to underline here that the use of inner speech, for hearing and for deaf people, is of value for a range of cognitive tasks. It extends the available workspace for linguistic task solving (this is what working memory, in Baddeley's formulation, delivers). For example, it enables people to resolve syntactically complex spoken utterances and to acquire new vocabulary through practice, as well as setting up and testing interpretive hypotheses for written language (see, e.g., Vallar & Shallice, 1990, for indications of how acquired working memory loss can impair a range of language-based tasks). I do not think it would be particularly fanciful to reinspect Vygotsky's insights into the relationship between cognition and language in young children in this light. An inner voice can be your own or the internalized voice of a significant other; in any case, it has a role in planning and guiding self-initiated behavior—it allows the action component of speech to be embedded in representational processes.

Speaking to oneself and other forms of memory in explicit rehearsal are modes of self-possession and controlled action. These constitute one of the ways in which human thought and language interpose themselves between the twin imperatives of input (sensation) and output (action). Just as syntax allows all imaginable worlds to be constructed by virtue of its componentiality and symbolic reference functions, so working memory can give us a respite from the online demands of the world, allowing us to impose some control over our surroundings—control in selection and in action. Inner speech (for hearing people) is one of the most effective ways in which this can occur; that it shows signs of being present in the deaf, too, should be a cause for optimism. Nor would I restrict consideration of verbal working memory to phonological working memory; there is no reason whatever to believe that sign language does not function in a very similar way, offering, as a rehearsal code, an "offline" medium for analysis and planning.

THE NATURE OF THE PHONOLOGICAL CODE
IN DEAF READERS

One interesting question concerning speech coding is, "Is it the same in deaf and hearing people?" The answer to this must be yes and no. Yes, in the sense that inner speech delivers phonology, and phonology is abstract: phonological distinctions deliver linguistic meaning directly. (It is also in this sense that the *orthographic* distinction between "gh" and "g" could be said to be phonological, at least for a distant apprehension of an Indian phonology, as in the "Ghandi" illusion). Similarly, to the extent that phonological distinctions for deaf and for hearing people map onto each other, they are the same—they deliver the same information. However, the experience of inner speech may well be different for hearing than for deaf people. In one study (Campbell & Wright, 1990), we found that immediate recall of *written* lists of monosyllables ("pa," "va," "tha") was different in hearing and deaf groups. In the deaf group, and in that group alone, letter strings that could be discriminated by lipreading were better recalled than those that could not, although the material was presented in written form throughout. This dimension of lipreadability had no effect whatever on hearing subjects. Further studies are required to explore these qualitative differences in detail (see Marschark & Harris, 1996); meanwhile one group of subjects offers a particularly privileged view of this question.

CUED SPEECH: THE BRUSSELS EXPERIENCE

A team of researchers based at the Free University of Brussels has been investigating a group of 20 or so profoundly deaf children who, under the direction of Olivier Perier, have been exposed to cued speech from a very early age (within the first year) and 24 others who were exposed to it on starting school. Cued speech (Cornett, 1967), or CS, uses lipreading as the basic system of communication, but words that may be ambiguous in lipreading are disambiguated through synchronized hand gestures. Unlike some other lipreading support systems (e.g., tactile speech), the missing information is not replaced by delivery of the invisible components of lipspeech (primarily the *phonetic* manner of articulation—for instance, vocal cord vibration or voicing). Instead, and depending closely on the spoken language, the hands could be said to deliver systematic distinctive information at a *phonological* level.

> The principle that determines the attribution of consonants and vowels to hand-shapes and hand-positions respectively is that items sharing the same handshape or hand position must be easy to discriminate by lipreading. Conversely items difficult to discriminate must belong to different groups. For example a particular hand shape is shared by /p, d, zh/ which are easily discriminated from each other by lipreading. . . . Consonants that are difficult to discriminate by lipreading like the bilabials /b, p, m/ have different handshapes. The same principle has been used for vowels: a particular hand position is shared by items presenting high discriminability like /i/o~, a~/ . . . , and vowels that present similar lipshapes, i.e., the rounded French vowels /y, u, o, o~/ have different hand positions. (Alégria, Charlier, & Mattys, 1994).

Note that syllabic structure in cued speech is indicated systematically; hand position (in space) always indicates a vowel (or diphthong), while hand form indicates a consonant. Thus, one single gesture indicates a CV (consonant-vowel) (while VC forms require two actions).

Both as an early and a later-acquired system, cued speech seems to be an effective induction into speech as long as it is consistently used. That is, it improves speech understanding in children (see, e.g., Charlier, 1992), with early use giving the greatest advantages. Some very considerable achievements in reading, writing, and immediate memory in these children have also been reported, and these literacy-based skills seem to use phonological support in ways very similar to those of hearing children (Alégria, Leybaert, Charlier, & Hage, 1992, Leybaert, 1993; Leybaert & Charlier, 1996). It would not be an exaggeration to say that, when it comes to understanding the written word, deaf children with early cued speech and normally hearing children are closely compatible.

But does this mean that a child with CS "hears speech in his or her head" the way a hearing child does? Studies are currently under way to establish what happens when the cued speech child is given different forms of utterance to repeat and to write down under lipreading alone and cued speech conditions. Cued speech improved repetition (and writing) over lipreading alone. This was achieved mainly by improving repetition of lipreading-ambiguous phonological segments. Furthermore, there was some evidence that specific syllabic structure of CS leaves a trace: utterances that required several handshape changes (e.g., VCVC forms requiring three or four changes rather than CVCV forms requiring only two) were somewhat more error prone in CS than for lipreading alone; errors were in the expected direction given the syllabic structuring of CS.

Did the cued speech users make "slips of the hand" in repetition? Elicitation studies to date suggest that their errors did *not* show hand-specific errors—that is, that (for early-CS users at least) hand and lip forms are closely integrated and occur "without introducing spurious segmental effects" (Alégria et al., 1994). It would seem that these children, like deaf infants acquiring sign language as a first language, attend to both face and hands in an *integrated* way to arrive at the linguistic representation (Snitzer-Reilly, McIntire, & Bellugi, 1990).

Clearly a great number of interesting and important observations are still to be made concerning users of cued speech. For example, their receptive speech skills—thanks to CS—are generally very good, but their productive speech can lag. There may be sufficient redundancy in the handshapes for cued speech users to communicate with each other without using lip patterns consistently. Some preliminary evidence from Alégria's laboratory suggests that early-CS users may sometimes ignore the lipspeech pattern in favor of a (conflicting) handshape gesture. This suggests that a language learned orally may be transmuting into sign language—an interesting development indeed!

FUNCTIONAL AND CORTICAL ASPECTS OF LIPREADING

I now turn to an examination of lipreading as a functional skill. What is it that people do when they lipread? For a start, they do look at the lips—that is, at the lower part of the face. Moreover, it is the changing shape of the lips that delivers most of the useful information for lipreading (Summerfield, 1979), with some important additional support from the visibility of the teeth and tongue (Summerfield, McLeod, McGrath, & Brooke, 1989). While some recent studies (e.g., Rosenblum & Saldana, 1996) suggest that perceived biological movement rather than lip shape can affect phonological percepts, these data are not conclusive, and at the moment it seems safer to conclude that both lip shape and lip movement are more important in delivering speech (Campbell, 1996; Cathiard, 1994).

What are perceivers using this information for? What are they computing? This is a provocative and unresolved question with a number of possible answers. According to one theoretical standpoint, the seen mouth is no more and no less privileged for the perception of speech than any other potential source of information for a multimodal event (Massaro, 1988). To the extent that a seen mouth will allow for a range of phonological outcomes, it will be integrated with other information to produce a specific response (fuzzy logical model of integration). Yet another notion is that it is the *gesture* of mouth movement that is privileged for understanding speech. In this view, it does not matter how this is delivered, but it is acknowledged that the gestural properties of the articulators can be derived more readily from well-specified heard speech than from vision alone. A range of other theoretical standpoints can also be held (Green, in press).

In my view, lipreading is best understood as a staged visuo-perceptual function that maps onto phonetic analyzers. The visual image undergoes some quite specific processing in order to derive mouth shape and views of the articulators, and this information maps speedily, possibly interactively, onto phonetic processors that themselves deliver information to phonological recognition systems. It is not necessary for categorical, identificatory information to be serially and completely extracted at each stage; lipreading probably works in cascade, with "final" identification of the lipread utterance depending on a range of contextual and perceptual factors.

EVIDENCE FOR LOCALIZED, FUNCTIONALLY DISTINCT ANALYSIS OF LIPSHAPE AND LIPREADING

Evidence for localized, functionally distinct analysis of lipreading comes from two sources: experimental and neuropsychological. In studies recently completed (Campbell, Brooks, De Haan, & Roberts, 1996), we have shown that categorization of lipspeech and of facial identity from face photographs proceeds independently. Reaction time studies of face matching showed that while same-different matches for identity ("Are these pictures of one person or two different people?") were faster for personally familiar than for unfamiliar faces, matching for lipshape ("Are these faces both saying 'oo' or 'ee'?") was not sensitive to familiarity. Perceiving what someone says occurs quite independently from perceiving who they are. Similar evidence has been used to boost claims that expression and identity are processed in separate streams from the facial image (Bruce & Young, 1986; Ellis, Young, & Flude, 1990; Young, McWeeny, Hay, & Ellis, 1986).

The neuropsychological evidence for functionally distinct analyses of lipshapes is twofold: from patients and from studies of lateralized lip presentations. Studies of patients indicate that lipreading dissociates from a range of other abilities in its pattern of sparing and impairing following acquired brain damage. From studies of lateralization we can start to gain an understanding of the interplay between homologous areas in the two cerebral hemispheres.

With patients, the story started simply and then became complex. Several years ago we showed that two patients with lesions to the right and the left medio-occipito-temporal regions (following posterior cerebral artery stroke) had doubly dissociated patterns of impairment in perceiving faces (Campbell, Landis, & Regard, 1986). The patient who had a right-side stroke (Frau D) was unable to recognize familiar faces but was unimpaired on a range of lipreading tasks. By contrast, Frau T (left-hemisphere stroke) was impaired at lipreading but not at face recognition. This indicates very clearly that homologous areas in the two hemispheres may be specialized for different skills. I am not necessarily suggesting that there is a "lipreading" site in the left hemisphere, only that there may be particularly useful visual processing mechanisms or pathways in that hemisphere that can subserve lipreading if need be.

It was informative that Frau T was also alexic—perhaps the sites that were damaged were those required to map *any* visual input onto language forms (Geschwind, 1965). In any case, lipreading appeared to have a (preferential) left-hemisphere site.

Then the story became more complex. First, several patients were identified by Marianne Regard who were alexic but could lipread and vice versa. Then, a patient with receptive auditory word deafness (patient DRB, who had left-hemisphere temporal damage following a stroke) was found to be helped in identifying words by lipreading. A woman with assumed developmental right-hemisphere disorder was impaired both at face recognition *and* lipreading (AB; see Campbell et al., 1990).

We accommodate these facts as follows. First, it is important to conceive of multiple stages of information processing in lipreading. In patient DRB, whose brain damage was anterior (lateral parts of the temporal lobe) to that of the two women, Frau D and Frau T, there was no difficulty in seeing lipshapes and interpreting them. Posterior regions that support vision and spatial understanding were intact. Lipreading was therefore able to help by providing additional information about phonological structure, information that hearing no longer provided accurately because of damage to the left-temporal sites close to the primary auditory reception areas. In patient AB, we believe that (posterior) right-hemisphere dysfunction has left her with a generalized face-processing disorder. Lipreading, facial identification, and facial expression skills were all poor in AB. So, too, were some visual object identification abilities. But visual skills, especially reading, which are thought to make more use of left-hemisphere processes, are excellent (see Campbell, 1992a). AB's generalized face-processing disorder suggests that a relatively early stage of visual information processing has been affected (yet not so early that letters are affected).

A further complication is provided by considering lipreading in patients with callosal sections—split-brain patients. In these patients, by delivering material selectively to one or the other hemisphere (for visual material, this means controlled unilateral visual presentation), one can directly infer the capabilities of each separate hemisphere. Baynes, Funnell, and Fowler (1995) reported that patient JW, who underwent complete commisurotomy in 1979, was sensitive to lipreading no matter which hemisphere was tested. They used the McGurk fusion illusion to test the patient. A face saying "night" synchronized to a voice saying "might" was shown and the patient was asked to point to one or the other written word to indicate what he had perceived (was it "might" or "night"?). Under these conditions, similar (high) levels of visually influenced responses were obtained, whether the speaking face was seen in the left visual field (projecting to the right hemisphere) or the right visual field (left hemisphere). Similarly, in unpublished experiments with Dahlia Zaidel and Eran Zaidel (see Campbell, 1992a, for a brief report), we established that patient NB, who underwent complete callosal section in 1960, managed lipreading with either hemisphere. The task we used was matching a centrally viewed mouthed number between 1 and 10 to an aftercoming unilaterally presented digit. Under these circumstances, matches were equally speedy with either hemisphere.

This suggests that there is, potentially at least, more equipotentiality for lipreading across the two hemispheres than for other tasks, such as face identification or reading, which tend to lateralize more clearly in split-brain patients. However, it should not be overlooked that temporal lobe epilepsy, which is the precipitating condition for callosal section, may be *specifically* implicated in disturbed cross-modal processing (Campbell, 1994). These patients may have had anomalous brain organization in respect to this prior to surgery.

RIGHT-HEMISPHERE LIPREADING

A further indication that lipreading should not be viewed solely as a left-hemisphere function, like reading or listening to speech, is that there are clear suggestions of a useful right-hemisphere component in lipspeech analysis. In studies of normal hearing, right-handed people, Campbell (1986) found marked right-hemisphere advantages in speed of identifying lipshape and Baynes et al. (1995) found a similar right-hemisphere advantage in the McGurk task outlined above. (Poor lipreading in AB, who we assume has a developmental right-hemisphere anomaly, converges on this suggestion.)

The way that I currently conceive of these disparate findings is as follows. Occipito-parietal systems analyze the visual face pattern and extract lipshape. It is well established that in humans, right-hemisphere occipito-parietal areas are faster than corresponding areas on the left in the analysis of shape, especially shapes of naturally occurring three-dimensional events and objects (Warrington & James, 1967; Warrington & Taylor, 1973). Similarly, it is well established that lateral temporal structures in the human left hemisphere are better at analyzing speech sounds than analogous right-hemisphere areas. In speeded identification of lipshapes alone, there may well be a right-hemisphere advantage. In obtaining influences of lipread vision on audition, the "best" combination should be of a right-posterior input to a left-anterior system (and this fits well with Baynes, Funnell, and Fowler's [1995] findings on sensitivity to visual speech in normal subjects).

Frau T's lipreading failure can be ascribed to a combination of weaker left-hemisphere inputs from seen lips to the phonetic processor *and* blocked right-hemisphere inputs to that site, due to the medial site of lesion damage. This is analogous to the classical (Déjerine, 1914) explanation for impaired reading following posterior damage to the left hemisphere.

Lipreading dissociates quite cleanly from a range of other cognitive skills. Lipspeech analysis occurs independently of face identification. It does not seem to use the same functional base as reading; developmentally and experimentally there is little sign of cross-talk. Lipspeech analysis can be separate from auditory phonetic processing, though it maps onto a phonetic processor.

VISUAL EVOKED POTENTIALS AND ALLIED EFFECTS

A series of studies by Samar and colleagues (e.g., Samar & Sims, 1983, 1984) followed up a finding by Shepherd, DeLavergne, Frueh, and Clobridge (1977) that suggested that there is a fast-occurring component of the human visual evoked response that can be seen more reliably in (hearing) good lipreaders than in poor ones. Because it occurs to a visual flash, not to a structured display, it may be related to early visual processing. Does this mean that good lipreaders have better (speedier, more efficient) abilities to detect visual environmental changes? It could, but unfortunately the Shepherd et al. study has not stood the test of replication well (see Rönnberg, Arlinger, Lyxell, & Kinnefors, 1989). While there do seem to be some correlations between lipreading skill and the presence of a component of the visual evoked response (VN130/P200), it is not at all clear how these are functionally related.

Neville and Lawson (1987) studied evoked brain potentials for the detection of simple visual targets in deaf people with sign language as a first language. One of their major findings is that the deaf show more marked potentials for peripheral visual events than do hearing people, and they speculate that this is directly due to auditory sensory loss—a form of neural compensation. They also found laterality differences between deaf and hearing groups: whereas hearing subjects showed greater amplitude differences and more activity in the right hemisphere for this task, the advantage switched to the left hemisphere in the deaf group. This appears to be due to the acquisition of left-hemispheric specialization for sign language (Poizner, Battison, & Lane, 1979), because a similar asymmetry was found in hearing children of signing deaf parents (see Marschark, 1993, for a review).

DEAFNESS AND LIPREADING: IMPLICATIONS OF STUDIES WITH NORMALLY HEARING PEOPLE

What are the implications of these patterns of localization and specialization of function for considering the role of lipreading in people born deaf? It might be considered that when hearing is absent, the functional and cerebral basis for the development of phonetic processing cannot be realized. Certainly, studies of the lateralization of reading and writing in deaf groups give a rather different picture than those in hearing groups, generally with less distinct patterns of left-hemisphere lateralization for language-related tasks (see, e.g., Neville, Kutas, & Schmidt, 1982, and Vargha-Khadem, 1983). However, this need not mean that speech and speech-related processes do not become localized effectively in deaf people. I have emphasized that it is possible for seen speech to map onto phonological systems, although these may be underspecified. In someone who has an inadequate grasp of speech due to hearing loss but has sign language competence, lipshape could still play an important role; we might expect to see, in the deaf as in hearing groups, different patterns of lateralization depending on which aspect of the process is most salient (e.g., right-hemisphere advantage for lipshape discrimination, left for phonetic identification).

To my knowledge, no studies analogous to those of Neville on deaf people with American Sign Language as a first language have been performed on the "oral" deaf or on deaf people with first-language deprivation (the majority of young deaf Britons). These claims, therefore, await direct experimental testing.

CONCLUSIONS

When I started writing this chapter, I did not know where it would lead. (The plan outlined at the outset was inserted at a later stage.) I was trying to gather my disparate thoughts about deafness; language acquisition; some aspects of academic skills in remembering, reading, and writing; and lipreading.

This may seem a perverse enterprise. I have admitted that lipreading can deliver spoken language reliably in only a few cases of prelingual deafness and, further, that we do not yet know how this happens. I have emphasized that the delivery of language through seeing the speaker is part of natural spoken language, and while it certainly is not particularly efficient in delivering the required phonetic contrasts for a fully specified language, it may yet serve some useful purposes for inducting the person without hearing into some aspects of the speech structure of the hearing community, which will include, like as not, the deaf child's own parents. Cued speech, if it is systematically used and available early, may offer hope for the acquisition of good receptive language and good literacy. There is certainly evidence that speech structures can inform literacy in deaf children, and I have also suggested that literacy may afford an important way into spoken language through clarifying distinctions that may not be grasped by lipreading alone. I have advocated a fairly relaxed stance with respect to the time course of language learning by underlining how literacy develops somewhat independently of the time span over which a first language is learned, while acknowledging that early language learning offers great advantages in syntactic, phonological, and lexical power.

It seems that in deaf and hearing people alike, lipreading is a natural and interesting function, delivering some limited but nevertheless useful information about speech to the viewer. In the context of the perception and processing of other facial information, it offers the possibility of dissecting a range of functions emanating from the seen face and this, itself, offers a privileged view of neuropsychological function: a neat potential separation between visual functions on the one hand and linguistic ones on the other.

It would seem sensible, at least, to bear these findings in mind in considering how cognition and language may develop in people with congenital or early-onset hearing losses. Moreover, the traces of speech acquired through lipreading in the cognitive skills of people born deaf—traces that look quite similar to those in hearing people—suggest that deaf and hearing people alike may share some common linguistic structures—structures based on speech. How these may interact with sign language acquired as a first or second language is a question that future research will answer.

ACKNOWLEDGMENTS

Much of the work referred to here was supported by project grants from the Economic and Social Research Council of Great Britain (ESRC), the Medical Research Council (MRC), and Oxford University. The Leverhulme Foundation supported the fellowship that provided the time and funds to write this piece.

The following individuals have all helped directly in the studies cited, and I thank them for their friendship and collaboration: Simon Baron-Cohen, Barbara Brooks, Vivian Burden, Barbara Dodd, Sue Franklin, Jeanette Garwood, Edward De Haan, Thedi Landis, Marianne Regard, Rebekah Smith, Jane Wilson, Helen Wright, Dahlia Zaidel, and Eran Zaidel. Mairead MacSweeney helped me find some of the references and puzzled over several of the findings with me. The participants in the ESRC cognition and deafness seminar series contributed to the ideas proposed here.

REFERENCES

Alégria, J., Charlier, B., & Mattys, S. (1994). The role of lipreading and cued speech on the processing of phonological information in deaf children. Unpublished manuscript, Lab de Psychologie Experimentale, ULB, Brussels, Belgium.

Alégria, J., Leybaert, J., Charlier, B., & Hage, C. (1992). On the origin of phonological representations in the deaf: Hearing lips and hands. In J. Alégria, D. Holender, J. Morais, & M. Radeau (Eds.) *Analytic approaches to human cognition* (pp. 107–132). Amsterdam: North-Holland.

Baldwin, D. A., & Markman, E. M. (1989). Establishing word-object relations: A first step. *Child Development 60,* 381–398.

Baron, J. (1979). Orthographic and word-specific mechanisms in children's reading of words. *Child Development, 50,* 60–72.

Baron-Cohen, S. (1994). How to build a baby that can read minds: cognitive mechanisms in mindreading. *Cahiers de Psychologie Cognitive/Current Psychology of Cognition, 13,* 513–553 (and commentaries).

Baron-Cohen, S., Campbell, R., Karmiloff-Smith, A., Grant, J., & Walker, J. (1995). Are children with autism blind to the mentalistic significance of the eyes? *British Journal of Developmental Psychology, 13,* 379–398.

Baynes, K., Funnell, M. G., & Fowler, C. A. (1995). Hemispheric contributions to the integration of visual and auditory information in speech perception. *Perception and Psychophysics.*

Bertelson, P. (1987). *The onset of literacy: Cognitive processes in reading acquisition.* Cambridge, MA: MIT Press.

Bishop, D. V. M., & Robson, J. (1989). Unimpaired short-term memory and rhyme judgement in congenitally speechless individuals: implications for the notion of "Articulatory Coding." *Quarterly Journal of Experimental Psychology, 41,* 123–141.

Bowerman, M. (1994). Early grammatical development. *Philosophical Transactions of the Royal Society of London, B, 346,* 37–46.

Bruce, V., & Young, A. W. (1986). Understanding face recognition. *British Journal of Psychology, 77,* 305–327.

Burden, V., & Campbell, R. (1994). The development of word coding skills in the born-deaf. *British Journal of Developmental Psychology, 12,* 331–349.

Butterworth, B. L., Campbell, R., & Howard, D. (1986). The uses of short-term memory: A case study. *Quarterly Journal of Experimental Psychology, 38A,* 705–737.

Campbell, R. (1986). The lateralisation of lipreading: A first look. *Brain and Cognition, 5,* 1–21.

Campbell, R. (1992a). The neuropsychology of lipreading. *Philosophical Transactions of the Royal Society of London, B, 335,* 39–45.

Campbell, R. (1992b). Speech in the head?: Rhyme skill, reading, and immediate memory in the deaf. In D. Reisberg (Ed.), *Auditory imagery* (pp. 73–95). Hillsdale, NJ: Lawrence Erlbaum Associates.

Campbell, R. (1994). Audiovisual integration of speech: Who, when, where, how? *Cahiers de Psychologie Cognitive, 13,* 76–80.

Campbell, R. (1996). Seeing speech in space and time: Psychological and neurological findings. In *Proceedings of the 4th International Conference on Spoken Language Processing* (1493–1496). Wilmington: University of Delaware and Alfred I. duPont Institute.

Campbell, R., Brooks, B., De Haan, E. H. F., & Roberts, A. (1996). *The view from the mouth: Dissociated processes in face identification, lipreading, and expression judgement from personally familiar faces. Quarterly Journal of Experimental Psychology 49,* 295–314.

Campbell, R., & Burden, V. (1995). Phonological awareness, reading, and spelling in the profoundly deaf. In B. de Gelder & J. Morais (Ed.), *Speech and reading: Comparative approaches* (pp. 109–123). Hove, UK: Lawrence Erlbaum Associates.

Campbell, R., & Butterworth, B. (1985). Phonological dyslexia in a highly literate subject. *Quarterly Journal of Experimental Psychology, 37A,* 435–475.

Campbell, R., & Dodd, B. (1980). Hearing by eye. *Quarterly Journal of Experimental Psychology, 32,* 85–89.

Campbell, R., Garwood, J., Franklin, S., Howard, D., Landis, T., & Regard, M. (1990). Neuropsychological studies of auditory-visual fusion illusions. *Neuropsychologia, 28,* 787–802.

Campbell, R., Landis, T., & Regard, M. (1986). Face recognition and lipreading. *Brain, 109,* 509–521.

Campbell, R., & Wright, H. (1989). Immediate memory in the orally-trained deaf: Effects of "lipreadability" in the recall of written syllables. *British Journal of Psychology, 80,* 299–312.

Campbell, R., & Wright, H. (1990). Deafness and immediate memory for pictures: Dissociations between inner speech and the inner ear? *Journal of Experimental Child Psychology, 50,* 259–286.

Cates, D. F., & Shontz, F. C. (1990). Role taking ability and social behavior in deaf school children. *American Annals of the Deaf, 135,* 217–221.

Cathiard, M. A. (1994). La perception visuelle de l'anticipation des gestes vocal-iques: Coherence des evenements audibles et visibles dans la flux de la parole. Ph.D. dissertation, University of Grenoble, Pierre Mendes, France.

Charlier, B. (1992). Complete signed and cued French. *American Annals of the Deaf, 137,* 331–337.

Chomsky, C. (1970). Reading, writing, and phonology. *Harvard Educational Review, 40,* 287–311.

Conrad, R. (1979). *The deaf school child.* London: Harper Row.

Corcoran, D. W. J. (1977). The phenomenon of the disembodied eye (or is it a matter of personal geography?). *Perception, 6,* 247–253.

Cornett, O. (1967). Cued speech. *American Annals of the Deaf, 112,* 3–13.

Curtiss, S. (1977). Genie: A psycholinguistic study of a modern-day "wild child." New York: Academic Press.

De Gelder, B., & Vroomen, J. (1994). Memory for consonants versus vowels in heard and lipread speech. *Journal of Memory and Language, 33,* 737–756.

Déjerine, J. (1914). *Semiologie des affections du système nerveux.* Paris: Masson.

Dodd, B. (1979). Lipreading in infants: Attention to speech presented in and out of synchrony. *Cognitive Psychology, 11,* 478–484.

Dodd, B. (1980). The spelling abilities of profoundly deaf children. In U. Frith (Ed.), *Cognitive processes in spelling* (pp. 423–442). London: Academic Press.

Dodd, B., & Murphy, J. (1992). Visual thoughts. In R. Campbell (Ed.), *Mental lives: Case studies in cognition* (pp. 47–60). Oxford: Blackwell.

Ellis, A. W., Young, A. W. & Flude, B. M. (1990). Repetition priming and face processing: Priming occurs in the system that responds to the identity of the face. *Quarterly Journal of Experimental Psychology, 42A,* 495–513.

Evans, L. (1981). Psycholinguistic perspectives on visual communication. In B. Woll, J. Kyle, & M. Deuchar (Eds.), *Perspectives on British Sign Language and deafness.* London: Croom Helm.

Flavell, J. (1974). The development of inferences about others. In T. Mitchell (Ed.), *Understanding other persons* (pp. 66–116). Oxford: Blackwell.

Frith, U., & Happe, F. (1994). Autism: Beyond theory of mind. *Cognition, 50,* 115–132.

Frith, U., & Snowling, S. (1983). Reading for meaning and reading for sound in autistic and dyslexic children. *British Journal of Developmental Psychology, 1,* 329–342.

Gailey, L. (1987). Psychological parameters of lipreading skill. In B. Dodd & R. Campbell (Eds.), *Hearing by eye* (pp. 115–142). Hove, UK: Lawrence Erlbaum Associates.

Gates, A. I., & Chase, E. H. (1927). Methods and theories of learning how to spell tested by studies of deaf children. *Journal of Educational Psychology, 17,* 289–300.

Gathercole, S. (1987). Lipreading: Implications for theories of short-term memory. In B. Dodd & R. Campbell (Eds.), *Hearing by eye: The psychology of lipreading* (pp. 227–242). Hove, UK: Lawrence Erlbaum Associates.

Green, K. (forthcoming). The use of auditory and visual information during phonetic processing. In R. Campbell, B. Dodd, and D. Burnham (Eds.), *Hearing by eye II: The psychology of speechreading and auditory-visual speech.* Hove, UK: Psychology Press.

Geschwind, N. (1965). Disconnection syndromes in animals and man. *Brain, 88,* 237–294, 585–644.

Gleitman, L. (1994). Words, words, words. *Philosophical Transactions of the Royal Society of London, B, 346,* 71–78.

Gopnik, M. (1992). When language is a problem. In R. Campbell (Ed.), *Mental lives: Case studies in cognition* (pp. 66–84). Oxford: Blackwell.

Gray, C. S., & Hosie, J. (1996). Deafness, story understanding, and theory of mind. *Journal of Deaf Studies and Deaf Education, 1,* 217–233.

Hanson, V. (1986). Access to spoken language and the acquisition of orthographic structure: Evidence from deaf readers. *Quarterly Journal of Experimental Psychology, 38A,* 193–212.

Hanson, V., & Fowler, C. (1987). Phonological coding in word reading: Evidence from hearing and deaf readers. *Memory and Cognition, 15,* 199–207.

Karmiloff-Smith, A., Grant, J., & Berhoud, I. (forthcoming). *Within domain dissociations in Williams Syndrome: The case of language.* Buenos Aires: FEPI.

Karmiloff-Smith, A., Klima, E., Bellugi, U., Grant, J., & Baron-Cohen, S. (1995). Is there a social module?: Language, face-processing, and theory of mind in subjects with Williams Syndrome. *Journal of Cognitive Neuroscience, 7,* 196–208.

Kuhl, P., & Meltzoff, A. (1984). The intermodal representation of speech in infancy. *Science,* 218, 1138–1141.

Kusché, C. A., & Greenberg, M. T. (1983). Evaluative understanding and role-playing ability: A comparison of deaf and hearing children. *Child Development, 54,* 141–147.

Lenneberg, E. (1967). *Biological foundations of language.* New York: John Wiley.

Leybaert, J. (1993). Reading ability in the deaf. In M. Marschark & D. Clark (Eds.), *Psychological perspectives in deafness.* Hillsdale, NJ: Lawrence Erlbaum Associates.

Leybaert, J., & Alégria, J. (1993). Is word processing involuntary in deaf children? *British Journal of Developmental Psychology, 11,* 1–29.

Leybaert, J., & Charlier, B. (1996). Visual speech in the head: The effect of cued speech on rhyming, remembering, and spelling. *Journal of Deaf Studies and Deaf Education, 1,* 234–249.

MacSweeney, M., Campbell, R., & Donlan, C. (1996). Varieties of short-term memory coding in deaf teenagers. *Journal of Deaf Studies and Deaf Education, 1,* 249–262.

Mandler, J. M. (1994). Precursors of linguistic knowledge. *Philosophical Transactions of the Royal Society of London, B, 346,* 63–69.

Marschark, M. (1993). *Psychological development of deaf children.* New York: Oxford University Press.

Marschark, M., & Harris, M. (1996). Success and failure in learning to read: The special case (?) of deaf children. In J. Oakhill & C. Cornoldi (Eds.), *Reading comprehension disabilities* (pp. 279–300). Hillsdale, NJ: Lawrence Erlbaum Associates.

Masataka, N. (1995). Decentralization and absence of mirror reversal tendency in cutaneous pattern perception of deaf children. *British Journal of Developmental Psychology, 13,* 379–398.

Massaro, D. (1988). *Speech perception by ear and by eye.* Hillsdale, NJ: Lawrence Erlbaum Associates.

Mayer, C., & Wells, G. (1996). Can the linguistic interdependence theory support a bilingual-bicultural model of literacy education for deaf students? *Journal of Deaf Studies and Deaf Education, 1,* 93–107.

Mehler, J., & Christophe, A. (1994). Language in the infant's mind. *Philosophical Transactions of the Royal Society of London, B, 346,* 13–20.

Mundy, P., Kasari, C., & Sigman, M. (1992). Nonverbal communication, affect sharing, and intersubjectivity. *Infant Behavior and Development, 15,* 377–381.

Neville, H. J., Kutas, M. & Schmidt, A. (1982). ERP studies of cerebral specialization during reading II—congenitally deaf adults. *Brain and Language, 16,* 316–337.

Neville, H., & Lawson, D. (1987). Attention to central and peripheral visual space in a movement detection task: An event-related potential and behavioral study—I: Hearing subjects; II: Congenitally deaf adults. *Brain Research, 405,* 253–267, 268–283.

Newport, E. (1990). Maturational constraints on language learning. *Cognitive Science, 14,* 11–28.

Peterson, C., and Siegal, M. (1995). Deafness, conversation, and theory of mind. *Journal of Child Psychology and Psychiatry, 36,* 459–474.

Pettito, L. A. (1987). On the autonomy of language and gesture: Evidence from the acquisition of personal pronouns in American Sign Language. *Cognition, 27,* 1–52.

Pettito, L. A., & Seidenberg, M. (1979). On the evidence for linguistic abilities in signing apes. *Brain and Language, 8,* 162–183.

Phillips, W., Baron-Cohen, S., & Rutter, M. (1992). The role of eye-contact in the detection of goals: Evidence from normal toddlers and children with autism or mental handicap. *Developmental Psychopathology, 4,* 375–383.

Pinker, S. (1994). *The language instinct.* New York: Penguin/Viking.

Pintner, R., & Patterson, D. (1917). Comparison of deaf and hearing children in visual memory for digits. *Journal of Experimental Psychology, 2,* 76–88.

Poizner, H., Battison, R., & Lane, H. (1979). Cerebral asymmetries for American Sign Language: The effects of moving stimuli. *Brain and Language, 7,* 351–362.

Read, C. (1971). Preschool children's knowledge of English phonology. *Harvard Educational Review, 41,* 1–31.

Reddy, V. (1991). Playing with others' expectations: Teasing and mucking about in the first year. In A. Whiten (Ed.), *Natural theories of mind.* Oxford: Blackwell.

Rodda, M., & Grove, C. (1987). *Language, cognition and deafness.* Hillsdale, NJ: Lawrence Erlbaum Associates.

Rönnberg, J. (1996). Compensation in sensory and skill domains. In R. A. Dixon & L. Backman (Eds.), *Compensating for psychological deficits.* Hillsdale, NJ: Lawrence Erlbaum Associates.

Rönnberg, J., Arlinger, B., Lyxell, B., & Kinnefors, C. (1989). Visual evoked potentials: Relation to adult speechreading and cognitive function. *Journal of Speech and Hearing Research, 32,* 725–735.

Rosenblum, L. D., & Saldana, H. M. (1996). Visual primitives for audiovisual speech integration. *Journal of Experimental Psychology: Human Perception and Performance.*

Samar, V. J., & Sims, D. C. (1983). Visual evoked correlates of speechreading performance in normal adults: A replication and factor-analytic extension. *Journal of Speech and Hearing Research, 26,* 2–9.

Samar, V. J., & Sims, D. C. (1984). Visual evoked response components related to speechreading and spatial skills in hearing and hearing-impaired adults. *Journal of Speech and Hearing Research, 27,* 162–172.

Scaife, M., & Bruner, J. (1975). The capacity for joint visual attention in the infant. *Nature, 253,* 265–266.

Seidenberg, M. S., & Tanenhaus, M. K (1979). Orthographic effects in rhyming. *Journal of Experimental Psychology: Human Learning and Memory, 5,* 546–554.

Seidenberg, M. S., Waters, G. S., Barnes, M. A., & Tanenhaus, M.K. (1984). When does irregular spelling or pronunciation influence word recognition? *Journal of Verbal Learning and Verbal Behavior, 23,* 383–404.

Shepherd, D. C., DeLavergne, R. W., Frueh, F. X., & Clobridge, C. (1977). Visual-neural correlate of speechreading ability in normal hearing adults. *Journal of Speech and Hearing Research, 20,* 752–765.

Smith, N., & Tsimpli, I. M. (1991). Linguistic modularity?: A case of a savant-linguist. *Lingua, 84,* 315–351.

Snitzer-Reilly, J., McIntire, M. L., & Bellugi, U. (1990). Faces: The relationship between language and affect. In V. Volterra & C. J. Erting (Eds.), *From gesture to language in hearing and deaf children* (pp. 128–145). Berlin: Springer.

Spelke, E., & Cortelyou, A. (1981). Perceptual aspects of social knowing: Looking and listening in infancy. In M. E. Lamb & L. R. Sherrod (Eds.), *Infant social cognition: Empirical and theoretical considerations* (pp. 61–84). Hillsdale, NJ: Lawrence Erlbaum Associates.

Spoehr, K., & Corin, W. J. (1978). The stimulus suffix effect as a memory coding phenomenon. *Memory and Cognition, 6,* 583–589.

Summerfield, A. Q. (1979). Use of visual information for phonetic processing. *Phonetica, 36,* 314–331.

Summerfield, A. Q. (1991). The visual perception of phonetic gestures. In I. G. Mattingley & M. Studdert-Kennedy (Eds.), *Modularity and the motor theory of speech perception: Proceedings of a conference to honor Alvin M. Liberman.* Hillsdale, NJ: Lawrence Erlbaum Associates.

Summerfield, A. Q., McLeod, A., McGrath, M., & Brooke, M. (1989). Lips, teeth, and the benefits of lipreading. In A. W. Young & H. D. Ellis (Eds.), *Handbook of research in face processing* (pp. 218–223). Amsterdam: North-Holland.

Tager-Flusberg, H. (1993). What language reveals about the understanding of minds in children with autism. In S. Baron-Cohen, H. Tager-Flusberg, & D. Cohen (Eds.), *Understanding other minds: Perspectives from autism.* Oxford: Oxford University Press.

Treiman, R. (1992). *Beginning to spell: A study of first grade children.* New York: Oxford University Press.

Trevarthen, C. (1979). Communication and cooperation in early infancy: A description of primary intersubjectivity. In M. Bullow (Ed.), *Before speech: The beginnings of interpersonal communication.* Cambridge, MA: Cambridge University Press.

Vallar, G., & Shallice, T. (Eds.) (1990). *Neuropsychological impairments of short term memory.* Cambridge, MA: Cambridge University Press.

Vargha-Khadem, F. (1983). Visual field asymmetries in congenitally deaf and hearing children. *British Journal of Developmental Psychology, 1,* 375–387.

Walker-Andrews, A. S. (1986). Intermodal perception of expressive behaviors: Relation of eye and voice? *Developmental Psychology, 22,* 373–377.

Warrington, E. K., & James, M. (1967). Disorders of visual perception in patients with unilateral cerebral lesions. *Neuropsychologia, 5,* 253–266.

Warrington, E. K., & Taylor, A. (1973). The contribution of the right parietal lobe to object recognition. *Cortex, 9,* 152–164.

Waters, G. S., & Doehring, D. (1990). The nature and role of phonological information in reading acquisition: Insights from congenitally deaf children who communicate orally. In T. Carr & B. A. Levy (Eds.), *Reading and its development: Component skills approaches* (pp. 323–373). New York: Academic Press.

Young, A. W., McWeeny, K. H., Hay, D. C., & Ellis, A. W. (1986). Matching familiar and unfamiliar faces on identity and expression. *Psychological Research, 48,* 63–68.

CHAPTER 5

Making Faces:
Coextant Domains for
Language and Visual Cognition

Ruth Campbell

My original impulse in studying speechreading (I now enter the modern era) was that it gave an interesting perspective on the interface between language—usually construed in terms based on auditory/articulatory processing—and visual processes that are nonlinguistic, especially those concerned with face processing. This perspective does not place special emphasis on hearing impairment. This is still the impulse that motivates me, but thanks to the work of researchers in American Sign Language (ASL) psycholinguistics, such as Siple and Lillo-Martin, the study of speechreading may be placed in a fuller context.

In this response, I will consider just one aspect of this enlarged context: the uses of the face in signed languages.

THE FACE IN SIGN LANGUAGE

One point elegantly clarified by the contributions of Lillo-Martin and Siple is that the underlying structural constraints and parameters of language have become clearer in recent years. To a large extent this is due to the work of theoretical linguists taking into account not only signed languages but structural aspects of *all* human languages. In this newer context, as Lillo-Martin makes clear, typical syntactic forms in signed languages can be seen to have similar underlying principles to those of some spoken languages— commonalities that were not apparent when sign language was compared with the more familiar European languages.

In this broader context, the uses of the face in sign language can offer interesting challenges to research. Although evident to people who use sign language, and described by sign linguists such as Liddell (1978), the nonsign community hardly appreciates that sign languages are *never* purely manual: the face is also an important input source. Moreover, obligatory facial actions contribute to sign language at every linguistic level: some lexemes are distinguished by facial actions, indicating their significance at the phonemic/cheremic level; others function adverbially; while yet others carry grammatical function, including conditionals, relative clause marking, and question type (see Reilly, McIntire, & Bellugi, 1991, for a brief overview of ASL). In addition, very many face actions, while not obligatory, nevertheless are optional.

Mouth actions have specific significance in sign language; for example, facial adverbials in ASL are, more often than not, mouth patterns like "smiling mmm" (with pleasure) or "th" (carelessly).

How are these actions used by the sign language system? Reilly and colleagues (1990, 1991) have pioneered studies of the development of the use of the face in sign language in children acquiring ASL as a first language. Perhaps the most important point is that the infant at first uses the face correctly with manual signs—that is, he or she shows integrated manual/facial production. But at a slightly later stage, manual signs may be accompanied by inconsistent face actions. Later still, the reconfiguring of language production is indicated by the correct recombination of the elements. This pattern—of an initial gestalt-based production form followed by a partial decomposition and only later by skilled recombination— has been observed for other production patterns in speech and sign language (Pettito, 1987) but has not been considered across what might be thought to be different input channels.

Reilly's work with children underlines the idea that, although sign's ancestry is in gesture—a nonlinguistic system of display and interaction—as soon as language takes hold, any apparent link is broken and remade; for example, while the canonical lexeme for "sad" should include the appropriate facial display, the child acquiring this form may produce the manual form without the appropriate face action at an intermediate stage. A similar point can be gleaned from recent work in sign neurolinguistics. Kegl and Poizner (1996) have studied a patient with agrammatism consequent to cortical trauma to areas of the brain that include Broca's area. His (sign) productions are typically telegraphic, using simplified syntactic forms. The authors point out that, while this patient's facial expressions are appropriate in communication, they are very circumscribed when used in sign, especially when they should be used syntactically. Thus, both developmental and neuropsychological studies to date suggest that sign language can *appropriate* facial actions.

EMOTION AND INTENTION IN THE FACE

Reilly's work, as well as that of Lillo-Martin and Siple, also recognizes a crucial theme: that the origins of sign and the uses of gesture (nonlinguistic) have common elements and that the developmental intertwining of one with the other must be significant. For Reilly, the important aspect is that of affect: displays of emotion (sadness, happiness, etc.) are often echoed in the sign forms as facial actions. But emotion—narrowly described in terms of either the six universal expressions or dimensionally as gradations of pleasure, pain, flight, or fear—cannot constitute the full language of the face.

In Chapter 4 I indicated that the development of knowledge about other people's thoughts and wishes (theory of mind) might be at risk in some deaf children because they may not share the same referential world that is delivered by multimodal inputs as do their hearing peers. But one world that the deaf child does share with his or her hearing peers is that of sensitivity to actions of the face. Our faces reveal to any human observer whether we are interested, amorous, bored, thoughtful, worried, curious, excited, jealous, or anxious. Interpretation of these human intentions may sometimes need to be contextualized but not always (see Baron-Cohen, 1995). Our faces give us away time and time again. But we can also control what we say with the face. Face actions are critical in turn taking in conversation (gaze and gaze aversion), in subverting a spoken message (the sly wink), in control (the imperious gaze, the polite smile). Very few of these important actions have been systematically explored, in or out of sign (see Ekman, 1992, for an exception).

We have recently embarked on some experimental studies in this area that we hope will cast light on how language-based and intention-reading-based systems may converge and separate (Campbell, Woll, Benson, & Wallace, 1996). The facial expression of surprise is one that indicates a mental rather than an emotional state. One is surprised when events do not turn out as one has predicted. Puzzlement is a similar state—here, more than one interpretation of events awaits resolution. The facial displays that signal surprise (raised brows, dropped jaw) and puzzlement (furrowed brow, pursed mouth) are easily distinguished. Using photographic morphing techniques to produce images containing systematically different amounts of these actions, we have shown that people perceive the distinction between a puzzled and a surprised face categorically and that hearing status and sign experience do not moderate this.

A similar distinction is used very systematically in British Sign Language (BSL)—the wh-question ("Where are we meeting?") must be produced with furrowed brows and a "puzzled" face; the yes-no question ("Are we meeting at the bookshop?") requires a surprised look with raised brows and direct engagement of the viewer. However, this grammatical distinction does not generate categorical perception in native sign users, who were nevertheless accurate at classifying the faces. It seems, therefore, that different perceptual modes characterize the way the face is perceived in and out of sign language.

But these findings raise more questions. Why is a surprise face obligatory in so many sign languages for yes-no questions, and why does it contrast with the puzzled face used for people asking wh- questions? These seem the appropriate facial displays for people asking these questions in English too (although possibly not to naïve subjects: those without sign language were unable to categorize the question faces correctly). Could the formal sign distinction have developed from a gestural, behavioral regularity in the way people ask questions? If so, it seems likely that it is in the realm of referential pragmatics—in the mutual understanding of what is being requested (requiring empathic communication)—that this develops and may later become codified as a syntactic distinction.

PROCESS AND STRUCTURE IN SPEECH AND SIGN

This study generated an interesting paradox. Categorical perception—the perception and classification of similar events as identical, suggesting the use of a categorical prototype—characterizes the processing of speech, especially consonantal phonemes. Spoken language uses categorical perception to a marked extent. By contrast, other acoustic discriminations tend to show less categoricity. But in our study, categorical perception characterized non-linguistic face reading, while linguistic face reading (syntactic disambiguation) was dimensionally processed. It seems that, in considering face actions, the conditions for categoricity reverse.

Once more, considering language from the perspective of sign language offers new and surprising insights. Newport (1987) has reported that manual shape and position do not appear to be perceived categorically. She concluded that the issues of categoricity and language were orthogonal. But our findings force us further to ask why similar face actions can be perceived categorically in the nonlinguistic context and noncategorically in a linguistic one. Why have the processing systems taken on these distinct characteristics? These questions have been asked before in the acoustic domain but have tended to generate modality-limited answers (speedy classification required for stop- consonants, for instance). Such explanations must be, at best, incomplete.

DIRECTIONS FOR FUTURE RESEARCH

Speechreading accompanies the perception of spoken language and also plays a part in the language of the face that is used in sign language. This latter area is almost entirely unexplored. We know from sign linguists that a variety of mouth actions can carry a range of linguistically significant pieces of information—adverbs or initialization, for example. In addition, when deaf and hearing people communicate in sign language, they often use (silent) speech as another channel. All of these will form a fascinating topic for further research. Once again, I expect this interface to reveal important insights concerning face and language processing. Some of these actions are mandatory; others are optional. Could the issue of categorical processing map onto this distinction? If so, how? Only further research will help us to answer these questions.

Although the use of the face in sign language may not be categorical, what of the face in speech? Finally, taking a cue from sign research, might *spoken* languages incorporate face actions systematically? Can they form part of language itself rather than be an accompaniment to it? It could well be that our easy distinction between linguistic and paralinguistic gestures—whether visual or vocal—may have been drawn prematurely. These studies will help to provide the start of an answer.

ACKNOWLEDGMENT

This response was prepared using insights gained from discussion with Bencie Woll.

REFERENCES

Baron-Cohen, S. (1995). *Mindblindness: An essay on autism.* Cambridge, MA: MIT Press.

Campbell, R., Woll, B., Benson, P. J., & Wallace, S. B. (1996). Categoricity in facial actions. Paper presented at ESRC Meeting on Language from the Face, Bristol, 26 March.

Ekman, P. (1992). Facial expressions of emotion: An old controversy and new findings. *Philosophical Transactions of the Royal Society of London, B 335,* 63–69.

Kegl, J., & Poizner, H. (1996). Crosslinguistic/crossmodal syntactic consequence of left hemisphere damage: Evidence from an aphasic signer and his identical twin. *Aphasiology.*

Liddell, S. (1978). Nonmanual signals and relative clauses in American Sign language. In P. Siple (Ed.), *Understanding language through sign language research* (pp. 59–90). New York: Academic Press.

Newport, E. L. (1987). Task specificity in language learning?: Evidence from speech perception and American Sign Language In E. Wanner & L. Gleitman, (Eds.), *Language Acquisition: The state of the art* (pp. 450–486). Cambridge, MA: Cambridge University Press.

Petitto, L. (1987). On the autonomy of language and gesture: Evidence from the acquisition of personal pronouns in American Sign Language. *Cognition, 27,* 1–52.

Reilly, J. S., McIntire, M. L., & Bellugi, U. (1990). In V. Volterra & C. J. Erting (Eds.), *From gesture to language in hearing and deaf children* (pp. 128–145). Berlin: Springer.

Reilly, J. S., McIntire, M. L., & Bellugi, U. (1991). Baby face: A new perspective on universals in language acquisition. In P. Siple & S. D. Fischer (Eds.), *Theoretical issues in sign language research* (pp. 9–23). Chicago: University of Chicago Press.

CHAPTER 6

In Support of the Language Acquisition Device

Diane Lillo-Martin

I hope that Chapter 3 and my comments here strongly support my position that deafness does not result in "cognitive poverty" (Conrad, 1979, cited by Campbell in Chapter 4). Rather, what I hope to have shown is that a child born deaf is essentially no different from a child born hearing—more specifically, both have the benefit of a modular language acquisition device that guides language acquisition but leaves (most of) the rest of cognition essentially unaffected. Thus, *given the appropriate (visual) input,* the language acquisition device operates as usual: the deaf child acquires a native language, and the rest follows.

I would like to take this opportunity, however, to clarify my interpretation of the workings of this language acquisition device, especially as it applies in special circumstances, since both Campbell and Siple have argued against its existence. I find the evidence for it convincing, particularly in the area of complex syntax—the area that has received the bulk of the attention from linguists working within this approach. Furthermore, I find the model completely compatible with the evidence given for noncanonical situations. As Campbell points out, such cases are germane, but I do not think that they contradict the essence of the theory.

Second, I will add a bit to the discussion in Chapter 3 of phonological awareness in deaf readers' processing of English text. This is a complicated issue, but I find a variety of data consistently pointing to the possibility that profoundly deaf readers can be phonologically aware and that this can be helpful for reading English.

Finally, I would like to briefly respond to a few issues in cognition that the other chapters address.

EVIDENCE FOR A LANGUAGE ACQUISITION DEVICE

In *Aspects of the Theory of Syntax,* Noam Chomsky (1965) proposed that linguistic theory ought to strive for "explanatory adequacy"—that is, an account for linguistic structure that also takes into consideration the limitations in input with which a child is faced. His proposed Language Acquisition Device (LAD) is an innate mechanism that takes as input the primary linguistic data to which a child is exposed and produces a grammar that is consistent with these data; furthermore, it goes beyond the input to correctly generate certain structures that were not part of the input and to recognize the ungrammaticality of certain other structures that were also not part of the input. It is because the data underdetermine the output that such a device is needed—language cannot be learned by inductive generalization alone.

This point is so important to the argument for innate linguistic knowledge that it is worth repeating some of the discussion in Chapter 3. By assumption, the input consists of overt instances of grammatical utterances spoken in meaningful circumstances. Certainly, false starts, fragments, and mistakes will be present in the speech that the child hears, but it cannot be assumed that ungrammatical utterances identified as such (negative data) are available for all children, therefore the theory must be able to account for language acquisition on positive evidence alone. Under these assumptions, partial generalizations pose a hefty challenge to a theory without innate constraints. Let me use an example slightly different from the one I use in Chapter 3.

(1)   a. I think that UConn will beat Syracuse.
      b. I think UConn will beat Syracuse.
(2)   a. Who do you think that UConn will beat?
      b. Who do you think UConn will beat?
(3)   a. *Who do you think that will beat Syracuse?
      b. Who do you think will beat Syracuse?

Example (1) illustrates the fact that many embedded clauses in English declaratives can optionally be introduced by the overt complementizer "that." In example (2), we see the same is true for wh-questions formed on the object of the embedded clause. However, in example (3) we see that it is not true for wh-questions formed on the embedded subject—in these examples, the complementizer "that" cannot be present.

By assumption, the child learning English is exposed only to overt instances of grammatical utterances, so examples like (1a, b), (2a, b), and (3b) should be part of the input, but no information about the grammaticality or ungrammaticality of (3a) will be given. Based simply on the overt evidence, a learning theory without innate knowledge would almost certainly incorrectly predict that (3a) should be grammatical. An innate language acquisition device is needed to rule out examples like (3a). Clearly, the innate knowledge cannot be specific to English since there can be only one language acquisition device that must serve for all possible human languages. Thus, linguistic theory has for the last 30 years developed various accounts of the contrast in (1–3), comparing the phenomenon in English to similar phenomena in other languages, some of which do not show the same surface effects (see, e.g., Chomsky & Lasnik, 1977; Lasnik & Saito, 1992; and many others). To my knowledge, no proposed innate knowledge of a general cognitive sort (rather than linguistic knowledge per se) has been advanced to account for the contrast in (1–3), and it is difficult to see how any proposal that is not particular to language could do so.

Thus, the study of knowledge in the absence of experience provides one of the strongest kinds of evidence for innate linguistic knowledge. It is even possible to make some progress in linguistic analysis by the detailed study of one language or a group of related languages, even when making claims about Universal Grammar (UG) (part of the contents of the LAD), when the poverty of the stimulus is borne in mind. I agree with Siple (Chapter 2) that crosslinguistic work should support proposed universals. But even cross-modality studies using only one sign language are helpful tests of proposed universals, and generalizations and proposals about suspected universals can be profitably made from studying a limited number of languages.

In addition to knowledge in the absence of experience and crosslinguistic generalizations, a third type of evidence for the proposals of UG comes from studies of young children. Innate constraints guide language acquisition by preventing the child from making certain incorrect hypotheses. Thus, we expect to find evidence that children adhere to the principles of UG from a very young age. Of course, the examples in (1–3) are complex. Children do not produce (many, if any) such long-distance wh-questions before the age of 4 or so. But when they do produce such questions, they are not expected to violate the universal constraints that account for the ungrammaticality of (3a).

For further discussion of the issues raised here in support of the UG model of language acquisition, I recommend Stephen Crain's article in *Behavioral and Brain Sciences* (1991). Now I would like to turn to the predictions that this model makes about language acquisition in situations other than that of a young, mentally intact child acquiring a first language.

One of the clearest predictions of this model for noncanonical populations is the potential for dissociations between language and cognitive development. Since, according to this model, UG is modular (specific to language), language acquisition does not depend on cognitive development or social interaction. Of course, language acquisition requires input—a child exposed to English acquires English, after all—but the logical possibility exists for double dissociations between normal (or near-normal) language development in the face of severe cognitive or social deficits and vice versa.

For example, suppose some child (or children with a particular disorder) has a severe mental impairment across a range of cognitive tasks. If language acquisition were based on general cognitive principles, then impairment in cognition would be predicted to result in impairments to language. On the other hand, the UG model allows for the possibility that cognition will be impaired but language preserved. In particular, the model allows for the sparing of those aspects of language governed by UG, even if language-particular aspects (e.g., certain morphological idiosyncrasies) are affected. Children with Williams Syndrome (WS) exhibit just such a dissociation between language and cognition, as pointed out by Campbell. As Bellugi, Marks, Bihrle, and Sabo (1988) put it, in WS children, the

> expressive language is complex in terms of morphological and syntactic structures including full passives, embedded relative clauses, a range of conditionals and multiple embeddings. The children's sentences are complex and the syntax correct, although there are occasional "errors" of overgeneralization of morphology and pronoun usage. Despite these occasional weaknesses, it is interesting that the children spontaneously use specific linguistic structures (such as full reversible passives) in the absence of their purported cognitive prerequisites or concomitants. (p. 183)

Campbell notes that WS children make mistakes in prepositions and syntactic agreement. Depending on the particular errors, these too can probably be classified as language-particular matters of the sort that must be learned, not linguistic universals. If so, WS children provide an example of the dissociation between language and cognition that the UG model expects.

Similarly, autistic children often display a dissociation between advanced language and poor social skills (see Chapter 4). Using the same logic, we can see that a theory of language development dependent on social interaction would not expect to find language preserved in the face of such severe social deficits. On the other hand, this possibility is consistent with the UG model.

The dissociation may be double, at least in the case of language impairment, also cited by Campbell. An independent language module might be selectively impaired, despite normal intelligence and socialization. Gopnik (1990) argues that this occurs in some cases of developmental dysphasia.

What about the critical period hypothesis? Is UG available for second-language acquisition in adults? What about late first-language acquisition?

The UG model makes no particular prediction about the critical period hypothesis. That is, taken by itself the UG model does not lead to the expectation that there would be a critical period for first- or second-language acquisition. It is possible, as Lenneberg (1967) proposed, that due to neural changes the language acquisition device becomes unavailable to postpuberty learners, but there does not seem to be uniform support for this proposal. Other cognitive or social differences between adults and children could affect late second-language acquisition, as proposed by Newport (1990) (cf. Chapter 4). But Newport herself acknowledges that her proposal could be taken together with the continued existence of a language acquisition device: "Note that such an explanation might be agnostic on whether innate constraints particular to language also exist; it would merely hypothesize that these language-particular constraints are not the locus of maturational decline in language learning" (p. 22).

A growing number of linguists, in fact, studying second-language acquisition with the benefit of the UG model, are finding that the poverty of the stimulus argument for UG in first-language acquisition also applies to second-language acquisition (e.g., Flynn & O'Neil, 1988; White, 1995). Thus, any differences between first- and second-language learners do not disprove the UG model for either situation.

Late first-language acquisition may be different. Few situations are available for study in which a child who is not otherwise deprived or impaired fails to receive input in time for normal first-language acquisition. According to the view defended here, deaf children of hearing parents are usually members of such a group. Deaf children of deaf, signing parents are not; their normal course of language acquisition, as outlined by Siple (cf. Lillo-Martin, forthcoming), indicates that being deaf is *not* bad for language acquisition (see Chapter 4). Not being exposed to an accessible language is.

In the case of late first-language acquisition of American Sign Language (ASL), studies by Galvan (1989), Mayberry (1993a, b), and Newport (1988, 1990) cited by Siple (Chapter 2) indicate that there is a long-lasting disadvantage. Again, the UG model does not specifically predict such an outcome. One important question is whether the linguistic deficits found in late first-language learners are constraint violations. If not, this would suggest the availability of UG, combined with additional factors that make using it less effective in these circumstances. This possibility is entirely consistent with both Newport's account of the disadvantage of language-learning in adulthood and the UG theory.

Thus, some of the evidence from special populations supports the UG model; the rest does not contradict it. One might then ask, as Siple does in a slightly different domain, why would a theory of language acquisition include both UG and aspects of learning? The answer, to me, is clear: both are needed. UG is necessary, especially in the cases of constraints, as illustrated in (1–3) above. But languages differ in lexicon, in morphology, in parameter settings, in the periphery. The Language Acquisition Device may well be used in acquisition in these areas, but where there is more linguistic variation, more learning in some sense is required. I find no conflict in having both. Learning is needed. Although Siple argues that "it is possible to account for some aspects of syntactic development with more general rules of cognitive processing," however, I am utterly unconvinced that it is possible to so account for all aspects, especially in the face of the poverty of the stimulus. Thus innate knowledge is needed as well.

PHONOLOGICAL AWARENESS AND READING

Numerous studies with hearing children have found that skilled reading is associated with phonological awareness, such as the ability to separate words into their component sounds and manipulate these sublexical elements (see, e.g., Liberman & Shankweiler, 1985). Studies with deaf readers have also found that skilled reading is associated with phonological awareness (see, e.g., Hanson, 1989). Why should this be so?

It has been proposed that for hearing individuals, working memory operates most effectively using phonological coding (Baddeley, 1979; Shankweiler & Crain, 1986). Whatever the reason for this, it clarifies the relationship between phonological awareness and reading: a more efficient working memory can be used more effectively in the service of higher levels of processing. A breakdown at the lower levels of reading (phonological analysis/working memory) will have implications for overall reading success.

Should phonological awareness be out of reach for individuals who cannot hear? Not at all. Phonology is an abstract notion, and phonological awareness might be derived through experiences other than sound. Experiences with orthography, speech training, and even explicit training in the phonological relationships among English words through pictures might be used for the development of phonological awareness in deaf individuals (on the latter, see Lillo-Martin, Hanson, & Romano, forthcoming).

Apparently, many deaf children do not succeed in developing phonological awareness. But this is not a necessary consequence of hearing loss, nor is it exclusive to deaf children; after all, some hearing children similarly do not succeed in developing phonological awareness (and become poor readers). Are alternative strategies available? Perhaps, as Campbell speculates, there is more flexibility in coding strategies for deaf readers (see also Treiman & Hirsh-Pasek, 1983), but so far the bulk of the evidence suggests that phonological coding is the most effective strategy for reading English, even for deaf readers.[1]

Does the connection between phonological coding and success in reading English put the signing deaf child at a disadvantage over the oral one? Of course, as Campbell points out, the child whose first language is ASL may show patterns of second-language acquisition in English (as found, for example, by Bochner, 1978, and Lillo-Martin, 1992). But I do not see why this means that "the child who uses speech may be *relatively* less disadvantaged in this domain," as Campbell states. Only if the orally trained deaf child succeeds in learning English through speech prior to learning to read will he or she be "less disadvantaged," for then the process of learning to read will be a process of mapping known forms onto new symbols, as it is for hearing children. If the orally trained deaf child has not acquired English prior to attempting to learn to read, then he or she will need to learn a linguistic system without any efficient language through which to teach it. The signing deaf child must master a second language, but at least the first is available for use in the education of the second.

In other words, only the orally trained deaf child who is blessed with the "magic ingredient," as described by Campbell, that enables some to succeed in acquiring language in a totally speech-based world will be relatively less disadvantaged. In the absence of prior knowledge of which children will be so blessed, I find the hope of magic to be an insufficient justification to deprive children of a first, accessible language.

DEAF CHILDREN AND SOCIAL COGNITION

Campbell worries that deaf children are disadvantaged in the development of social cognition because of their lack of auditory cues for various events. I would like to point out two types of studies in response to this, although I cannot do much more than point them out.

First, Erting, Prezioso, and O'Grady Hynes (1990) have studied the interactions of deaf mothers with their deaf children. They show that deaf mothers draw their babies' attention to events through visual cues, but hearing mothers of deaf children do so less often, perhaps because they are unaccustomed to the need for a visual cue. Perhaps parents can compensate for the potential problems Campbell poses by using visual cues to substitute for the missing auditory ones.

Second, Campbell asks, "Are deaf children disadvantaged in relation to hearing and seeing children in developing the bases for understanding about human minds?" A recent study by Gale, deVilliers, deVilliers, and Pyers (1996) argues that for both deaf and hearing children, a mature theory of mind is dependent on the development of the linguistic structures that are used in expressing cognition propositions. Thus, according to them, deaf children are not disadvantaged per se, but only if their language acquisition is delayed.

NOTE

1. In fact, contrary to Campbell's claim, some researchers have found evidence for phonological awareness in readers of Mandarin (Ren & Mattingly, 1990). This finding suggests the importance of phonological coding as the most effective strategy for reading in general.

REFERENCES

Baddeley, A. D. (1979). Working memory and reading. In P. A. Kolers, M. E. Wrolstad, & H. Bouma (Eds.), *The Proceedings of the Conference on the Processing of Visible Language* (Vol. 1, pp. 355–370). New York: Plenum.

Bellugi, U., Marks, S., Bihrle, A., & Sabo, H. (1988). Dissociation between language and cognitive functions in Williams Syndrome. In D. Bishop & K. Mogford (Eds.), *Language development in exceptional circumstances* (pp. 177–189). Edinburgh: Churchill Livingstone.

Bochner, J. (1978). Error, anomaly, and variation in the English of deaf individuals. *Language and Speech, 21,* 174–189.

Chomsky, N. (1965). *Aspects of the theory of syntax.* Cambridge, MA: MIT Press.

Chomsky, N., & Lasnik, H. (1977). Filters and control. *Linguistic Inquiry, 8,* 425–504.

Crain, S. (1991). Language acquisition in the absence of experience. *Behavioral and Brain Sciences, 14,* 597–650.

Erting, C. J., Prezioso, C., & O'Grady Hynes, M. (1990). The interactional context of deaf mother-infant communication. In V. Volterra & C. J. Erting (Eds.), *From gesture to language in hearing and deaf children* (pp. 97–106). New York: Springer-Verlag.

Flynn, S., & O'Neil, W. (Eds.) (1988). *Linguistic theory in second language acquisition.* Dordrecht: Kluwer Academic Publishers.

Gale, E., deVilliers, P., deVilliers, J., & Pyers, J. (1996). Language and theory of mind in oral deaf children. In A. Stringfellow, D. Cahana-Amitay, E. Hughes, & A. Zukowski (Eds.), *Proceedings of the 20th Annual Boston University Conference on Language Development* (vol. 1, pp. 213–224). Somerville, MA: Cascadilla Press.

Galvan, D. (1989). A sensitive period for the acquisition of complex morphology: Evidence from American Sign Language. *Papers and Reports on Child Language Development, 28,* 107–114.

Gopnik, M. (1990). Feature blindness: A case study. *Language Acquisition, 1,* 139–164.

Hanson, V. L. (1989). Phonology and reading: Evidence from profoundly deaf readers. In D. Shankweiler & I. Y. Liberman (Eds.), *Phonology and reading disability: Solving the reading puzzle* (pp. 69–89). Ann Arbor: University of Michigan Press.

Lasnik, H., & Saito, M. (1992). *Move α: Conditions on its application and output.* Cambridge, MA: MIT Press.

Lenneberg, E. (1967). *Biological foundations of language.* New York: John Wiley.

Liberman, I. Y., & Shankweiler, D. (1985). Phonology and the problems of learning to read and write. *Remedial and Special Education, 6,* 8–17.

Lillo-Martin, D. (1992). Deaf readers and Universal Grammar. In M. Marschark and D. Clark (Eds.), *Psychological perspectives on deafness* (pp. 311–337). Hillsdale, NJ: Lawrence Erlbaum Associates.

Lillo-Martin, D. (forthcoming). Modality effects and modularity in language acquisition: The acquisition of American Sign Language. In T. Bhatia & W. Ritchie (Eds.), *Handbook of language acquisition.* San Diego: Academic Press.

Lillo-Martin, D., Hanson, V. L., & Romano, C. (forthcoming). *Effects of phonological awareness training on deaf children's reading and segmentation ability.*

Mayberry, R. (1993a). First-language acquisition after childhood differs from second-language acquisition: The case of American Sign Language. *Journal of Speech and Hearing Research, 36,* 1258–1270.

Mayberry, R. (1993b). The first language timing hypothesis as demonstrated by American Sign Language. *Child Language Research Forum, 25,* 76–85.

Newport, E. (1988). Constraints on learning and their role in language acquisition: Studies of the acquisition of American Sign Language. *Language Science, 10,* 147–172.

Newport, E. (1990). Maturational constraints on language learning. *Cognitive Science, 14,* 11–28.

Ren, N., & Mattingly, I. G. (1990). Serial recall performance by goood and poor readers of Chinese. Haskins Laboratories Status Report on Speech Research, SR-103-104 (pp. 153–164).

Shankweiler, D., & Crain, S. (1986). Language mechanisms and reading disorder: A modular approach. *Cognition, 24,* 139–168.

Treiman, R., & Hirsh-Pasek, K. (1983). Silent reading: Insights from second-generation deaf readers. *Cognitive Psychology, 15,* 39–65.

White, L. (1996). The tale of the Ugly Duckling (or the coming of age of second language acquisition research). In A. Stringfellow, D. Cahana-Amitay, E. Hughes, & A. Zukowski (Eds.), *Proceedings of the 20th Annual Boston University Conference on Language Development,* (vol. 1, pp. 1–17). Somerville, MA: Cascadilla Press.

CHAPTER 7

Modules and the Informational Encapsulation of Language Processes

Patricia Siple

It is nearly impossible to discuss the relation between language and cognition without talking about modularity. The currently dominant view of modularity is that of Fodor (1983). In Fodor's account, the language processor is one of several input systems, and input systems are, by and large, modular. The primary characteristic of modular systems is that they access limited information when analyzing input, or, as Fodor puts it, "informational encapsulation of the input systems is . . . the essence of their modularity" (p. 71). It is not surprising, then, that each of the chapters in this volume makes reference, implicitly or explicitly, to modularity, and when we do discuss modularity, we generally take a view akin to that of Fodor.

Fodor argues that information encapsulation gives rise to a host of other features of modules. These include domain specificity, innate specification, and hardwiring in fixed neural structure. Modules are not assembled from more primitive processes. In addition, modular processes are fast and mandatory, and their outputs are "shallow." Central, cognitive processes have limited access to the information encapsulated within modules. Finally, modules show characteristic and specific breakdown patterns, and their development exhibits a characteristic pace and sequencing. If, as Fodor suggests, language processing is modular, the relation between language and cognition is one of independence.

Lillo-Martin makes modularity the focus of her argument. She begins by laying out the Sapir-Whorf hypothesis. While agreeing that it has been generally discredited, she points out that it is possible that learning a particular language may influence perception of speech in general and even more general aspects of perception and cognition. It has been impossible to test this latter possibility for spoken language, she argues, because there is no way to set the necessary conditions—hearing children growing up in an otherwise cognitively and socially stimulating environment but without language. Lillo-Martin argues that one can, however, address the question for signed language because one can compare children, hearing or deaf, growing up with or without signed language.

To address the Sapir-Whorf hypothesis rather than the issue of language modality difference, it is necessary first to demonstrate that there are no substantive differences between signed and spoken languages. Lillo-Martin does this masterfully. Then, based on the arguments of Fodor (1983) and Chomsky (1981), she assumes a modularity hypothesis for language processing that posits that language is processed through a module, Universal Grammar (UG), that receives perceptual input from the environment and sends output to the general cognitive processing system. After demonstrating that "essentially the same language mechanisms" underlie signed and spoken language structure and processing and that purported violations of modularity are limited to the translation of perceptual input to the language module, she concludes that the language module is amodal, serving both signed and spoken language, and that language acquisition, whether signed or spoken, does not influence cognition. That is, there is no foundation for the Sapir-Whorf hypothesis.

The processing system with which Lillo-Martin ends differs somewhat from that with which she began. The Fodor-Chomsky processing system originally assumed by Lillo-Martin includes a processing module specific to the domain of language. The language module consists of submodules for phonology, morphology, syntax, and semantics. Lillo-Martin differs with Sandler's (1993) interpretation of Fodor, arguing that the language module is amodal rather than specific to spoken language. To support this, Lillo-Martin argues that sign language processing is similar to spoken language processing in that it is mandatory and fast acting. It is associated with similar neural structures that, when damaged, produce similar breakdown patterns. Acquisition of signed language occurs at a similar pace, and the sequence of acquisition is similar to that of spoken language. Most important, she argues that the analyses of signed language syntax, morphology, and phonology are consistent with UG described for spoken language.

Lillo-Martin's system differs from that of Fodor in at least two ways. First, it seems that each of the separate subsystems of the language module display domain specificity and informational encapsulation; information flows one way, from phonology to logical form. Fodor, I believe, is silent on the issue of whether the output of a module can serve as input to another module. One reading of the concept of vertical structure would suggest that each input system receives perceptual information and produces output that is available to the nonmodular cognitive system. Is the output of each submodule also available to the cognitive system or only to a specified language submodule? Second, Lillo-Martin proposes separate auditory and visual phonetic processing modules for spoken and signed language, respectively. These clearly provide input to the amodal language module. Do they also provide input to the cognitive system? Lillo-Martin argues that there is some interaction between these systems and general perception and cognition, at least early in language acquisition. Is the implication that these modules are somehow "learned"? Or is there an interleaving of modular and nonmodular systems within the overall processing system? However these questions are answered, the nature of the overall system has gotten more complex.

Campbell, in Chapter 4, sets out to explore the potential contributions of lipreading to spoken language and literacy acquisition in deaf persons. In doing this, Campbell considers the system that mediates spoken language acquisition in hearing persons. While she considers alternatives, Campbell appears to support a language processing system for spoken language acquisition and processing in hearing persons similar to that described by Lillo-Martin. Following arguments of Newport (1990), she also accepts that the language module guides language acquisition only during a critical period of development, and it is only during this early period that language in all of its complexity can be acquired. Late language learners cannot fully acquire language, though they can, with the aid of the cognitive system, perform adequately in some language tasks. One of these, she argues, is literacy.

In order for spoken language acquisition to occur, the child must first develop the ability to map specific spoken language input onto appropriate phonetic categories. Liberman and Mattingly (1985) propose that this analysis is carried out by an innate phonetic processing module with characteristics like those proposed by Fodor (1983). According to Liberman and Mattingly, both acoustic and visual (optical) information serve as input to the module and "relevant optical information combines with relevant acoustic information to produce a coherent phonetic percept in which . . . the bimodal nature of the stimulation is not detectable" (p. 28). In this account, lipreading is a part of the activity carried out by the phonetic module for hearing persons and possibly the only activity carried out by the module for profoundly, congenitally deaf persons. Though Campbell does not specifically assume a phonetic module, her description of lipreading as a natural function that delivers "some limited but nevertheless useful information about speech to the viewer" seems to presuppose such a system. She provides evidence that processes associated with lipreading are informationally encapsulated and mediated by fixed neural structure (after initial visual analysis) similar to that for phonetic processing. Both experimental and neuropsychological data, she argues, show a dissociation of lipreading from other skills like face recognition.

Campbell, like Lillo-Martin, uses similarities between hearing and deaf persons to argue that language processing is carried out by similar processing systems in the two populations. At least for some deaf persons, spelling and immediate recall of lipread lists are similar to that for hearing persons, and reading and writing show evidence of the use of phonological representations similar to those used by hearing persons. In addition, some deaf persons can make rhyme judgments that are not represented in orthography; immediate memory for words shows the use of abstract phonological codes, though deaf persons show more reliance on lipread information than hearing persons. Furthermore, deaf persons demonstrate early language learner patterns similar to those of hearing persons if enough information is present so that spoken language acquisition can occur early (e.g., through cued speech). Otherwise, lipread information engages the phonetic module but is insufficient to produce fully developed spoken language acquisition, and late language-learner patterns pertain. Most deaf children, she argues, acquire some knowledge of spoken language through lipreading, and this can provide a basis for further acquisition of spoken language through reading and writing. Late learning of spoken language through reading builds on the language knowledge already acquired through lipreading. Language knowledge achieved through lipreading is covert, however, or informationally encapsulated and unavailable to the general cognitive system.

The system proposed by Campbell to process lipread information operates at the same level as the two (auditory and visual) phonetic modules proposed by Lillo-Martin. Lillo-Martin added a visual phonetic system, though, to process signed language, not lipread information. She likens the auditory phonetic module to one proposed by Liberman and Mattingly (1985). Does this module, then, also process lipread information? To avoid duplication it should, since otherwise information about the phonetic structure of spoken language must be represented in each module. Is it more appropriate, then, to describe these two modules as language specific? Or as specialized for spoken versus signed language?

In Chapter 2, I discuss the issue of universals of language processing in general and, more specifically, for different aspects of language acquisition. Universals of language acquisition and processing are taken to be the information encapsulated in the Fodor-Chomsky language module; they constitute UG. I argue that the universality of purported universals may not yet have been adequately tested; in many cases, more crosslinguistic, especially signed, language data are needed. In addition, I suggest that universality alone does not determine *language* modularity; universals can arise from "innately determined, abstract cognitive constraints."

Lillo-Martin proposed that the language module consists of submodules that are specialized for phonology, morphology, syntax, and semantics. I have argued that these and other aspects of language acquisition and processing must be considered separately when assessing modularity. It is possible that some aspects of language processing are modular and others are not. While arguing that the data are inadequate to draw firm conclusions, I have argued that at least some aspects of language acquisition are the result of or are guided by cognitive abilities that may be universal. Is the development of specific cognitive abilities necessary before the language module or its submodules are activated? Or is language acquisition the result of cognitive modules whose domains are specific types of processing (e.g., analysis of perceptual representations of objects)?

QUESTIONS ABOUT MODULES FOR LANGUAGE PROCESSING

Consideration of Chapters 2–4 has produced several questions about modules proposed to carry out language acquisition and processing. One of the most important questions concerns the nature of the domain of a module. How large is the domain of a module, or, stated differently, what constitutes the class of processes assigned to each module? If language processing is carried out by a set of modules, as these authors appear to believe, how are these modules organized within the processing system? Finally, Fodor argues that modules are innate. Need they be? Each of these questions will be addressed in turn.

What defines a domain? Modules are domain specific, but what constitutes a domain? Fodor (1983) does not provide criteria for a domain. Instead, he discusses the question of how many domain-specific input systems there are and puts forward possible candidates with which we can compare others by analogy. Fodor specifically rules out former interpretations that the five traditional sensory/perceptual systems plus language are the input modules. Instead, he says that "within (and, quite possibly, across) the traditional modes, there are highly specialized computational mechanisms in the business of generating hypotheses about the distal sources of proximal stimulations" (p. 47). Examples provided include mechanisms for color perception, analysis of shape, detection of melodic structure, and assignment of grammatical description. In discussion of the modularity of the mechanism underlying speech analysis, Liberman and Mattingly (1985) define the domain of speech perception handled by their proposed phonetic system as "an ecologically significant natural class" (p. 28).

The domains of proposed modules seem to get smaller as they are more deeply studied. The language module is believed to consist of submodules that are themselves treated as informationally encapsulated; for example, the syntactic processor is not believed to have access to knowledge encapsulated in the phonological processor. The phonetic system proposed by Liberman and Mattingly (1985) would appear to be on a par with the (other?) submodules of the language module with respect to the "level of grain" of modularity, to use Fodor's term. Summerfield (1991) has proposed, however, that lipreading may constitute a submodule of the phonetic processor, and Campbell appears to agree with him. Campbell also suggests, however, that other types of visual input, the gestures of cued speech, may come to be analyzed by this module. Lillo-Martin proposes two phonetic modules, one for auditory/speech processing and the other for visual/sign processing. Are these meant to be modality specific? I think not, given Lillo-Martin's discussion of them. But asking the question again, are these two systems specialized for English versus American Sign Language or for spoken versus signed language? Furthermore, if the speech processing module consists of submodules, does the sign processing module also?

Anderson (1990; Neves & Anderson, 1981) has proposed informationally encapsulated processing units consisting of even smaller domains that have many characteristics of modules. These units, called productions, consist of if-then rules that carry out the "then" part of the rule when the conditions specified in the "if" part are found to exist in the general cognitive system. Productions are informationally encapsulated, mandatory, and fast. Anderson (1990) has suggested that language parsing may be carried out by a set of productions that relate word patterns of sentence constituents to meaning structures that are realized as propositions in memory. It seems possible that the "phonetic module" could also consist of a set of productions mapping language input onto phonetic gestures or a similar form of representation. As the size of submodules becomes smaller and smaller, they increasingly resemble productions.

How are modules organized? While modules need not be modality specific, according to Fodor (1983), they do have vertical structure. Fodor suggests that modularity is limited to input systems whose function is input analysis. These systems complete their analyses before passing their output to the cognitive system whose function is to integrate this output with knowledge possessed by the individual to "fix belief." This description is consistent with the proposal of a language module with vertically organized submodules that pass on output from one submodule to the next, until processing is completed. In this way, the higher order modular process of assigning grammatical structure is a step in the processing carried out by the vertically organized language module.

Other organizations of modules are possible, however. The phonetic modules suggested by Lillo-Martin appear not to be a part of the amodal language module. As indicated above, it is unclear whether their output is available only to the language module or whether it is also available to the general cognitive system. When and how can general cognition have its influence?

Organization may be less constrained if sets of productions underlie language processing. When conditions specified for a particular production exist in the general cognitive system, the production carries out its work and sends its output back to the general cognitive system. While all of the productions that act on language input may be encapsulated together in a language processing module, they need not be. Anderson divides memory into declarative and procedural components, where declarative memory represents knowledge about facts and experiences and procedural memory represents encapsulated knowledge units that carry out specific cognitive activities. Procedural memory may not need further organizational structure.

If one allows the possibility that modular language processes are loosely organized in procedural memory, several questions about the nature of that processing arise. If different aspects of language processing (e.g., phonological analysis and grammatical description) are carried out by different productions, then it is possible for general cognition to have an effect at their interface since characteristics of memory determine which productions are initiated. Carrying this further, modules that are productions need not only be input systems. It is also possible that cognitive activities other than language input might set the conditions for productions that also typically process language input. That is, the domain of these productions may not be specific to language.

Must modules be innate? Proposals of the modularity of language processing nearly always come with assumptions of innateness. One exception to this is the set of productions proposed to reside in procedural memory. Anderson (e.g., Neves & Anderson, 1981) argues that reflexlike cognitive activity can be learned and stored as productions. In this proposal, productions are formed through a process called *proceduralization,* and larger productions are formed by combining productions through the process of composition. In the words of Neves and Anderson (1981), "The knowledge underlying procedures starts out as propositions in a network. Knowledge in this form can be changed and analyzed by the cognitive system. As one applies knowledge, the proceduralization process turns it into faster production rules automatically. Then composition forms larger units out of the individual proceduralized productions, in a gradual manner" (p. 82). Thus, in this account, it is possible to learn the rules of language processing. In this kind of system, what may be innate are the abstract processes that build and combine productions.

QUESTIONING MODULARITY

Up to this point, we have examined proposals that include some notion of modularity. It might be argued that an account based on loosely organized sets of productions kills the spirit of modularity as it is generally conceived, but this account preserves the notion of information encapsulation and domain specificity. Other, more recent proposals question whether any aspects of language processing are modular in nature. These proposals leave open the possibility of interaction of language and cognition at all levels of language processing.

Interactive activation and connectionist models have been proposed for many aspects of language acquisition and processing. In these models, language and cognitive processing have the potential of being completely interrelated. McClelland (1987), for example, makes the case that all of language processing is completely interactive. Information from the highest, cognitive levels flows downward and has the potential of influencing the processing of incoming language information at any level. Arguments have also been presented within the connectionist framework that some aspects of language acquisition can take place in an initially equipotential environment with the types of input normally experienced by children (e.g., McClelland & Rumelhart, 1986). Inclusion of a chapter on connectionist models of acquisition in Fletcher and MacWhinney's recently published *Handbook of Child Language* (Plunkett, 1995) attests to the growing influence of these models.

CONCLUSION

One's view of the relation between language and cognition is shaped to a great extent by one's view of the modularity of language processes. While both Lillo-Martin and Campbell accept some or all of the aspects of the dominant view of modularity described by Fodor (1983), the debate is hardly over. Lillo-Martin expands and clarifies one modularity hypothesis for language processing through an examination of cognition and sign language processing in deaf individuals. Campbell does much the same thing for a modularity hypothesis applied to the phonetic analysis of speech.

Lillo-Martin concludes, however, that her analysis provides only indirect support for a modularity hypothesis. While the data she reviews are consistent with the language modularity hypothesis she proposes, she concedes that other explanations have not been ruled out. The purpose of this discussion has been to explore some of these other explanations. As suggested by Lillo-Martin, the various positions must be contrasted with each other, and that is a tall order. A review of the chapters in this volume makes it clear, however, that studies of deafness and the acquisition and processing of signed language will play an important role in both identifying and sorting out answers to questions related to modularity and the relation between language and cognition.

REFERENCES

Anderson, J. R. (1990). *Cognitive psychology and its implications* (3rd ed.). New York: Freeman.

Chomsky, N. (1981). *Lectures on government and binding.* Dordrecht: Foris.

Fodor, J. A. (1983). *The modularity of mind.* Cambridge, MA: MIT Press.

Liberman, A. M., & Mattingly, I. G. (1985). The motor theory of speech perception revisited. *Cognition, 21,* 1–36.

McClelland, J. L. (1987). The case for interactionism in language processing. In M. Coltheart (Ed.), *Attention and performance XII: The psychology of reading* (pp. 3–36). Hillsdale, NJ: Lawrence Erlbaum Associates.

McClelland, J. L., & Rumelhart, D. E. (1986). On learning the past tenses of English verbs. In J. L. McClelland, D. E. Rumelhart, & PDP Research Group, *Parallel distributed processing: Explorations in the microstructure of cognition,* Vol. 2, *Psychological and biological models* (pp. 216–271). Cambridge, MA: MIT Press.

Neves, D. M., & Anderson, J. R. (1981). Knowledge compilation: Mechanisms for the automatization of cognitive skills. In J. R. Anderson (Ed.), *Cognitive skills and their acquisition* (pp. 57–84). Hillsdale, NJ: Lawrence Erlbaum Associates.

Newport, E. L. (1990). Maturational constraints on language learning. *Cognitive Science, 14,* 11–28.

Plunkett, K. (1995). Connectionist approaches to language acquisition. In P. Fletcher & B. MacWhinney (Eds.), *The handbook of child language* (pp. 36–72). Oxford: Blackwell.

Sandler, W. (1993). Sign language and modularity. *Lingua, 89,* 315–351.

Summerfield, Q. (1991). Visual perception of phonetic gestures. In I. G. Mattingly & M. Studdert-Kennedy (Eds.), *Modularity and the motor theory of speech perception* (pp. 117–137). Hillsdale, NJ: Lawrence Erlbaum Associates.

CHAPTER 8

Models, Modules, and Modality

Victoria S. Everhart and Marc Marschark

We mentioned in the preface that we initiated this project in an attempt to better understand whether or not being deaf or growing up with a sign language as a first language might influence the course of cognitive development differently from growing up hearing and learning a spoken language. Necessarily, this is a discussion about the relations of language and cognition and how such relations might be affected by developmental histories, age, and the particular language of interest. However, determining the extent to which modality-specific language effects appear in cognitive development or the extent to which particular cognitive processes differentially affect the acquisition of signed versus spoken languages requires some basic agreement on the language or cognitive mechanisms that underlie observable (or inferable) behaviors. It also requires some agreement on what qualifies as a purely linguistic process as opposed to a more general process that happens to be operating on linguistic information. To the extent that assumptions about these two issues differ, conclusions about possible interactions of language and cognition in development or in any given situation will vary considerably. Therefore, in this chapter, we review the primary issues surrounding possible links between language development and cognitive development and consider what arguments our three contributors find most compelling.

In Chapter 1, we suggested several alternative models for the relation of language and thought. In addition to an identity position and an independence position, there were several forms of an interactionist position. Our expectation was that Lillo-Martin, Siple, and Campbell all would come down in favor of different positions, with empirical and theoretical evidence to support their cases. If that expectation included clear demarcations among their perspectives, we erred. The contributors staked their claims well and provided a host of support for their positions, even while acknowledging their own needs for further investigation. The difficulty appears to be that the question "What is the relation of language and thought?" is too simplistic. The issues confronting us are somewhat more complex than just the ways in which a signed language might affect cognitive development differently from a spoken language. From the outset, two natural confoundings make the question problematic: (1) most children who grow up with sign language as their first language are deaf; and (2) most deaf children have hearing parents who are less than fluent in their sign language skills, if they have any sign skills at all. Although it means breaking with the mechanistic and reductionistic North American tradition in psychology and linguistics, this situation suggests that we need to consider the child from a more organismic, whole-child perspective. In this case, the broader perspective serves us well.

The preceding chapters have identified a variety of similarities and differences related to language modality and to deaf versus hearing children. Discussions have included considerations related to differing levels of cognition (from perception to problem solving) and differing levels of language (from phonology to conversation). Let us first consider briefly whether the observed differences between deaf and hearing children, growing up with signed and spoken language, respectively, are seen as having any real significance. Then, we will return to those alternative models for language and thought relations that still appear to be viable.

DIFFERENCES BETWEEN DEAF AND HEARING CHILDREN: WHAT DO THEY MEAN?

In attempting to examine possible influences of language on cognition, and vice versa, Siple, Lillo-Martin, and Campbell discuss a variety of obvious (or suggested) differences between deaf and hearing children. For Lillo-Martin and Campbell, however, those differences do not appear either to reflect the influence of learning a specific language or to entail any implications for higher cognitive functioning. Ruth Campbell, for example, suggests that deaf children's social cognition may differ from hearing children's due to deaf children's possible difficulties in maintaining joint attention and inferring others' intentions. However, for her, these possible difficulties would be caused by being deaf (lack of access to auditory cues) rather than by the language deaf children might use. She also argues that many of the differ-

ences observed between language development in deaf and hearing children
may be due to the tendency of most deaf children to have later first-language
acquisition than hearing peers (or deaf peers with deaf parents) rather than
being related to modality of their language per se. She notes that some of
the characteristics of deaf children's later language learning resemble characteristics of hearing individuals learning a second language, thus suggesting
that some processing mechanisms or strategies may be involved in later
rather than earlier language learning.

In a related context, Campbell raises the issue of children's theory of
mind (i.e., the awareness that they and others are thinking beings with emotions, memories, wishes, etc.). Depending on one's theoretical preference,
the development of children's theories of mind relies heavily on linguistic
interactions, observations of others, intrinsic maturational (biological and
cognitive) changes, or interpersonal episodes with adults and other children.
Campbell suggests that deaf children's theory of mind may be different from
hearing children's (Gray & Hosie, 1996). Once again, she attributes this
difference to more generic consequences of childhood deafness—experiential variability resulting from communicative and social isolation—rather
than to anything directly related to language. In either case, she clearly suggests that deaf children are lacking something that hearing children have,
whether it is impoverished environments or insufficient linguistic and cognitive tools.

Diane Lillo-Martin reviews the results from several studies examining the
differences in various cognitive tasks between deaf and hearing individuals,
as well as between deaf children of deaf parents and deaf children of hearing
parents (presumably the former group is exposed to sign language earlier
than the latter group). She concludes that the dissimilarities that are observed
between deaf and hearing individuals (in both directions) result from differences at lower levels of cognitive processing (e.g., image generation, visual
perception, and recognition). Lillo-Martin concedes that "exposure to a sign
language in childhood may have as a consequence differences in certain
areas of cognitive processing," but she makes the case that these processing
differences "do not directly affect the central systems" or higher cognitive
functioning.

Pat Siple describes differences between the development of hearing children and deaf children who are exposed primarily to sign language via their
deaf parents. Pragmatics is a particularly rich area for investigation in this
regard because it straddles the line between cognitive and linguistic functioning, normally involving social functioning as well. In this case, Siple
notes that deaf children tend to show delays in the use of pragmatic devices
to get the attention of others and initiate conversations with others. She

stresses that attention getting is more complex in a visual-manual language than in an aural-oral language and that the learning of that behavior therefore may require greater metacognitive awareness (see also Chapter 4). Consistent with proposals of Slobin (1973) and others, such differences in deaf and hearing children's development of pragmatics lead Siple to propose cognitive prerequisites for language development. In proposing this direct relation between cognition and language at a relatively high level of functioning, she sets herself apart from Campbell and Lillo-Martin.

SIMILARITIES BETWEEN DEAF AND HEARING CHILDREN: WHAT DO THEY MEAN?

Chapters 2–4 discuss similarities existing in deaf and hearing children's language development. Lillo-Martin and Siple describe in detail the striking similarities that exist between deaf children acquiring American Sign Language (ASL) from their deaf parents and hearing children acquiring spoken language from their hearing parents—similarities in the sequence and time course of acquisition in the areas of phonology, morphology, and semantics. Campbell, meanwhile, describes some common linguistic structures based on speech that at least some deaf individuals share with those who can hear. She notes, for example, that both deaf and hearing individuals acquiring spoken language utilize similar underlying neurological processing. These are evidenced in both groups, insofar as they exhibit similar phonological structure in immediate recall, reflecting "echoes" in lipreading and similar traces of speech structuring in reading, writing, and remembering. In Chapter 4, she describes how at least some deaf children develop phonological awareness comparable to hearing peers, even if it emerges later and may be less reliable (Marschark & Harris, 1996). This ability to analyze words into their component parts serves a common function during reading for the two populations, contributing to the recognition of vocabulary and supporting meaning to the extent that common morphemes are perceived across different words and contexts.

For Lillo-Martin, the similarity of language acquisition across modalities implies that the same computational system underlies both signed and spoken languages at some level. For her, this argues for the existence of an amodal language module, or Universal Grammar (UG), available to essentially all language learners. For Siple, in contrast, the fact that the process of language acquisition generalizes across language modality implies the existence of innate cognitive universals guiding language development. Both investigators describe the processes whereby, regardless of the modality of their language, children analyze linguistic information by breaking strings down into their component parts and learning the rules for acceptable combination at different levels. For Lillo-Martin, the mechanism that best explains the ease and success with which young children can accomplish these feats is an innate language acquisition device like UG. In her modular view, language and cognitive development are thus essentially independent (cf. Bates, Bretherton, & Snyder, 1988).

Siple, in contrast, argues that the mechanisms allowing for language development are not necessarily language specific but are guided by cognitive as well as biological constraints. She suggests that young children utilize the language analyses described above, not because they are preprogrammed into a language acquisition device but because of cognitive limitations in attention and memory that demand their use. Noticing the component parts of language is the easiest if not the only way a young child has to acquire language, and it does not matter if the children are hearing (Slobin, 1973) or deaf (Marschark, 1993, chap. 12), learning a spoken language or a sign language. Siple thus invokes cognitive universals to explain observed similarities between deaf children learning sign language and hearing children learning spoken language in the domains of gesture, phonology, morphology, and semantics. In a response to Lillo-Martin (see Chapter 7), she proposes a language-learning scenario in which the rules of language processing can be learned through a process of combining lower level, "reflex-like" cognitive activities into higher level, more complex operations that serve to support perception, comprehension, and production. For Siple, if there are any innately determined, abstract constraints involved, they surely must be cognitive.

REPRISE: ARE LANGUAGE AND THOUGHT INDEPENDENT?

In our initial description of the language-and-thought-are-independent model, we emphasized the historical roots of such a position within linguistic theory (e.g., Chomsky, 1965; see Chapter 3). Lillo-Martin embraces and Campbell is clearly comfortable with the linguistic notion of a language-specific module, and thus they view language and cognitive development as fundamentally independent paths. Such preferences should not be surprising given their backgrounds in linguistics and neuropsychology, respectively—domains in which the compartmentalizing of function makes the most sense. Accordingly, Campbell and Lillo-Martin see similarities in language acquisition by deaf and hearing individuals as indicating that language processing is carried out by similar processing systems in the two populations. Campbell, for example, suggests that there is a specialized mechanism for lipreading that functions in a way comparable to mechanisms that process phonology. Similarly, for native users of sign language, the processing of certain nongrammatical facial expressions is different from the processing of grammatical facial expressions because they involve different neurological structures (see Chapter 5). If Lillo-Martin does not have to be concerned with differences in neurological structures, her modularity position nonetheless leads her to argue that the modality of language learning will not influence the development of higher cognitive processes even if she acknowledges some interactions in limited domains (e.g., morphological development). Further, in her view, the kinds of research described by Siple (Chapter 2) need not indicate a direct link between language modality and higher cognition (see Chapter 7).

REPRISE: DOES THOUGHT DETERMINE LANGUAGE?

Most current cognitive views of development (but not all views of cognitive development) suggest that the child maps language onto the world, a position that requires the preeminence of cognitive over linguistic processes. In accepting this perspective, Pat Siple suggests that cognitive universals (i.e., general rules of cognitive processing) are sufficient to account for essentially all aspects of language learning. In her view, this theoretical approach provides a more coherent account of development than the assumption of separate language-specific and cognitive-specific mechanisms in development. According to Siple, the necessity of encapsulating all of the procedural components required for language into a language processing module may seem parsimonious, but the parsimony is more apparent than real. She agrees with Lillo-Martin and Campbell that different aspects of language processing (e.g., phonological, grammatical) are clearly carried out by different processing components. However, Siple argues that it would be more efficient to make use of general processing components that operate on both linguistic and nonlinguistic information (Ceci, 1990). In this view, lower level, reflexlike cognitive activities become proceduralized as automatic components of more complex functioning. The essential task then becomes one of determining how such components are combined and how different languages map onto them.

Confronted with each other's positions and evidence, Siple, Lillo-Martin, and Campbell all acknowledge that their theoretical positions require additional research support. This does not indicate any weakness in their original formulations but only the need or desire to extend them into new domains. Whether or not such research will favor the language-development-and-cognitive-development-as-independent position or the cognitive-development-guides-language-development position remains to be determined. We find it unlikely, however, that one or the other will prove entirely satisfactory. Rather, we suspect that in different domains of language and cognition, the evidence will weigh more heavily in favor of one position or the other. This domain specificity is likely to be further complicated by those situations in which it is language that guides cognition rather than the other way around. Insofar as this latter relation will not be found to hold in any of its strongest forms (see Chapter 3), we will forgo consideration of our initial language-development-guides-cognitive-development model. Instead, at the risk of appearing to take advantage of having the last word, we consider what seems the most inclusive position in this debate.

ARE COGNITION AND LANGUAGE INTERDEPENDENT?

Considerable evidence has been presented thus far indicating that language does not *determine* cognition in the strong sense that implies that without language one cannot think. Nor do we think that the superficial characteristics of any individual's language use can be taken to reflect anything about the complexity or sophistication of the underlying cognition involved. Nevertheless, as we indicated in Chapter 1, it seems to us that in providing a systematic, arbitrary symbol system for communication and mental representation, language allows the individual to go beyond the here-and-now, beyond the concrete, and beyond the linear. It appears inescapable that the nature of cognition at this point in human evolution is such that it has a co-dependent relation with language that entails bidirectional influences. To deny a significant influence of language on cognition seems to throw the metaphorical baby out with the bath water. The empirical and theoretical problem for us is to define the depth of that influence—that is, the *penetrability* of higher and lower cognitive processes to different levels of language (e.g., grammatical, lexical).

Both Diane Lillo-Martin and Ruth Campbell have described findings showing that language can influence lower levels of cognition. In particular, early exposure to signed language versus spoken language can affect processes that subserve their perception, analysis, and comprehension. In Chapter 3, for example, Lillo-Martin describes several findings relating the modality of early language exposure to visual perception and recognition in adults (e.g., face recognition, detection of mirror reversals, image generation). Development in an environment where sign language is the primary mode of communication also affects the ability to perceive stimuli in the periphery of the visual field (Neville & Lawson, 1987). In the case of signs being easier to identify than print, the effect is an accident of the fact that signs tend to be larger than print and usually involve movement. Swisher (1993), however, has shown that perception of signs in peripheral vision also is affected by the meaningfulness of those stimuli, separate from effects related to components of the signs per se (e.g., handshape, position, movement). Swisher noted that "the evidence that native signers as a group are more sensitive to peripheral stimuli does not clarify exactly what aspects of sign language use bring about the sensitivity" (p. 215). It thus remains unclear whether the "tuning" of such processes is specifically a function of linguistic experience (see Chapter 3) or a more general consequence of the fact that children who have deaf parents are likely to encounter a variety of important signals in the visual periphery that are not redundant with (the perception of) auditory signals.

At a somewhat higher level, modality of language also can affect memory. In her chapter, Ruth Campbell describes some of her work with Barbara Dodd showing that memory for lipread material is essentially the same for deaf and hearing children. Two recent studies, however, have demonstrated that language modality can have significant effects on retention, at least at the level of working memory. MacSweeney, Campbell, and Donlan (1996) compared short-term recall of pictures by deaf (signing) and hearing adolescents under conditions that affected the modality of encoding and rehearsal. In one experiment, they presented the pictures to deaf and hearing subjects under five conditions: with (1) no interference, (2) while simultaneously mouthing a single word over and over, (3) while simultaneously making a single sign over and over, (4) while alternately tapping their hands on their knees, or (5) while alternately tapping their feet on the floor. The most important findings were that no difference was found in recall in the no-interference condition, recall in both groups was depressed by word repetition, and only the deaf students were affected by sign repetition.

Marschark (1996) also examined the effects of signed language versus spoken language coding in working memory. In two of his experiments, he used a digit span task in which deaf and hearing subjects saw digits presented on a computer screen or signed "live" by the experimenter under three different conditions: (1) while performing a concurrent task involving the mouth, (2) while performing a concurrent task involving the hands, or (3) with no interference. In contrast to the results reported by MacSweeney et al. (1996) with pictures (but see Chapter 4), Marschark found that deaf subjects showed significantly shorter digit spans than hearing subjects under all three conditions. However, when the data for each subject were corrected for differences in articulation time for digits (deaf subjects in sign language, hearing subjects in spoken language), the two groups showed *articulatory loops* of essentially equal length (about 2 seconds). The concurrent task that occupied the hands was found to produce articulatory suppression (i.e., reduced memory span) for deaf subjects but not hearing subjects, while the concurrent task that occupied the mouth produced articulatory suppression for both groups. These results indicate that although deaf and hearing individuals may have equivalent memory capacity, the use of sign language coding requires a greater amount of space than spoken language coding, thus resulting in less information being recalled. Moreover, deaf subjects clearly vary in the extent to which they make use of the two modalities in working memory, a variable that Marschark showed to be related to their fluencies and preferences within the two modalities.

Both the Marschark and MacSweeney et al. results indicate that deaf subjects but not hearing subjects make use of sign language coding in working memory, while both groups make use of speech-based coding to some extent. The reasons for the differing results relating to retention under no-interference conditions in the two groups are not immediately obvious, although two likely influences are the use of pictorial materials in the Mac Sweeney et al. study (which may have attenuated differences) and the use of a memory span task and relatively rapid stimulus presentation in the Marschark study (which may have increased differences). Meanwhile, the results of both studies and those of Marschark, Everhart, and Dempsey (1991) suggest that both language preference and hearing status contribute to observed differences in cognitive and psycholinguistic functioning. The latter study was our initial attempt to resolve our own differences of opinion (see Chapter 1) concerning the relative influences of language modality and other aspects of deafness (i.e., cognition, experience), so it is worth touching on here.

Several of our earlier studies with children had shown that although deaf children did not use figurative language in their story writing, they used just as many or more nonliteral and creative devices than their hearing peers when they signed (and hearing children spoke) their stories. Our primary conclusion was that previous English-based testing of deaf children's comprehension of figurative language had led to biased assessments of their language and cognitive flexibility (see Marschark, 1993, chap. 10, for a review of both sides of the issue). Those studies had claimed that deaf children's failure to understand nonliteral constructions in English indicated that they are concrete and literal in their cognitive functioning. Although our results suggested otherwise, we were unable to agree on the extent to which deaf children's observed use of nonliteral language was truly an indicator of their cognitive flexibility or a consequence of the potentially greater plasticity of sign language. In the Marschark et al. (1991) study, we therefore examined the use of nonliteral language by mothers who were either deaf or hearing, where half of the hearing women had learned ASL as their first language from their deaf parents and used sign language every day. The bilingual mothers signed and spoke different stories, while the monolingual hearing and deaf mothers spoke and signed their stories, respectively.

Our idea was that if our earlier findings with deaf children were a consequence of sign language per se, signed stories would show more nonliteral constructions than spoken stories, regardless of whether the mothers were deaf or hearing. In contrast, if something about being deaf made for the apparent superiority of deaf children in this domain, then the bilingual and monolingual hearing mothers would look much the same regardless of production modality. The results showed some interesting differences in the kinds of nonliteral constructions produced, but the deaf mothers produced significantly more differences than the signing bilingual mothers overall, and the bilingual mothers did not show any reliable differences in nonliteral production as a function of language modality. These findings clearly indicated that the more frequent use of nonliteral language by deaf adults and children is not solely the consequence of some greater flexibility within signed as opposed to spoken language. However, we were (and are) still faced with the problem of disentangling the subtle interplay between the characteristics of the language and of the language user. What is it about a deaf person's linguistic and nonlinguistic functioning that results in their greater use of nonliteral language forms?

Results like these and others described in Chapter 1 suggest that language may be differentially correlated with some higher level cognitive processes in deaf and hearing individuals even when there is no direct implication of language modality effects. Does language experience or some aspect of language other than modality per se still have a causal role? Both Ruth Campbell and Diane Lillo-Martin acknowledge evidence for interactions between language and cognition at lower levels. The nature of the language-cognition interplay at higher levels, in contrast, remains unclear; Pat Siple warns that those effects may differ for different language mechanisms (see also Gopnik & Meltzoff, 1993). Lillo-Martin argues in Chapter 3 that the amodal, modular character of both language and cognition should make them impenetrable to each other and to effects of language modality at higher levels. That lack of interaction follows naturally from models that assume modularity, but that is an assumption some are unwilling to make. Intons-Peterson (1996), for example, provides convincing evidence that both language and world knowledge have regular and consistent effects on allegedly impenetrable and amodal cognitive processes, suggesting either that the notion of modularity is in need of reconsideration or that some processes previously considered modular and amodal really are not.

Like Intons-Peterson (1996), Pat Siple argues in Chapter 7 that information from higher cognitive levels can flow downward and influence processing of incoming language information, a position that appears to rule out modularity. Both, however, appear to acknowledge that the influence can be bidirectional. One possible integration of these apparently divergent views is that there is a cumulative effect of lower level cognitive processes that results in strategy differences (e.g., Clark, 1993; Swisher, 1993). Strategic differences in memory and problem solving may well be related to language modality, and thus the result is that individuals with different language fluencies or preferences may reveal differences in cognitive performance even if the influence is somewhat indirect. In this view, bottom-up influences of both linguistic and nonlinguistic processes will affect more complex processes of which they are a part. Together with the clear top-down effects of linguistic and nonlinguistic knowledge, the result is a true interaction of language and cognition, both ontogenetically and within any particular task situation.

Where all of this leaves us is pretty much where the two of us started 10 years ago and where we still were at the beginning of this collaboration. In Chapters 2, 3, and 4, Pat Siple, Diane Lillo-Martin, and Ruth Campbell have shown us that the relations of language and thought both require and reflect some aspects of development that span the two domains and some that are specific to one domain or the other. The extent to which the relations observed at various levels are causal or merely correlational is yet to be resolved fully. It is clear (to us, anyway) that growing up with signed language versus spoken language as one's primary mode of communication has no lasting impact on the course of language development per se, assuming that all other factors are equal (shared language with parents, similar language environments, etc.). Summarizing a body of controversial and contradictory research, Meier and Newport (1990) have shown that there is a small but consistent *sign advantage* for both deaf and hearing children learning sign language as their first language (i.e., they show earlier emergence of individual signs and faster vocabulary development). That difference disappears by the two-word stage, however, and has not yet been shown to have longer term or "sleeper" effects.

Somewhat less clear are the ways in which growing up deaf with sign language as a primary mode of communication (cf. Chapter 4) results in

subtle and not-so-subtle cognitive differences. Are differences like those described in Chapter 1 the consequence of the atypical early environments and
inconsistent exposure to language experienced by most deaf children with
hearing parents? Are they linked to experiential and neuropsychological consequences of lacking auditory input (see Chapters 3 and 4) or to the consequences of relying more heavily on visuospatial processes in cognition (see
Chapter 3)? Do they involve both language-specific effects and cultural-
experiential effects that cannot be disentangled without "unnatural" control
groups? Both the absence of auditory input and the emphasis on visuospatial
information clearly affect some cognitive processes but not others. The direction of those effects are variable, however, and their sum total appears
neither more nor less than the sum total of the potential for children who
can hear.

The interactive effects of language and cognition clearly are not uniform
across development, nor is the direction of influence easily discernable even
in a snapshot of a particular child taken at a particular time. Nonetheless,
examination of the similarities and differences in development both among
deaf children and between them and their hearing peers has had a profound
effect on our understanding of language and cognition, as well as the development of both. For our part, we now feel better equipped to pursue research
that delves further into the commingling of the cognitive and language processes in various contexts. The results will bear on practical and educational
issues relevant to deaf children and will further sharpen the theoretical focus
on sign language, deafness, and the relations between language and thought.

REFERENCES

Bates, E., Bretherton, I., & Snyder, L. (1988). *From first words to grammar.* New
York: Cambridge University Press.

Ceci, S. J. (1990). *On intelligence—More or Less: A bio-ecological treatise on intellectual development.* Englewood Cliffs, NJ: Prentice-Hall.

Chomsky, N. (1965). *Aspects of the theory of syntax.* Cambridge, MA: MIT Press.

Clark, M. D. (1993). A contextualist/interactionist model and its relationship to deafness research. In M. Marschark & M. D. Clark (Eds.), *Psychological perspectives
on deafness* (pp. 353–362). Hillsdale, NJ: Lawrence Erlbaum Associates.

Gopnik, A., & Meltzoff, A. (1993). Words and thoughts in infancy: The specificity
hypothesis and the development of categorization and naming. *Advances in Infancy Research, 8,* 217–249.

Gray, C. S., & Hosie, J. (1996). Deafness, story understanding, and theory of mind.
Journal of Deaf Studies and Deaf Education, 1, 217–233.

Intons-Peterson, M. J. (1996). Integrating the components of imagery. In M. de Vega, M. J. Intons-Peterson, P. N. Johnson-Laird, M. Denis, & M. Marschark, *Models of visuospatial cognition* (pp. 20–89). New York: Oxford University Press.

MacSweeney, M., Campbell, R., & Donlan, C. (1996). Varieties of short-term memory coding in deaf teenagers. *Journal of Deaf Studies and Deaf Education, 1,* 249–262.

Marschark, M. (1993). *Psychological development of deaf children.* New York: Oxford University Press.

Marschark, M. (1996). Influences of signed and spoken language on memory span. Paper presented at annual meetings of Psychonomic Society, Chicago, November.

Marschark, M., Everhart, V. S., & Dempsey, P. R. (1991). Nonliteral content in language productions of deaf, hearing, and native-signing hearing mothers. *Merrill-Palmer Quarterly, 37,* 305–323.

Marschark, M. & Harris, M. (1996). Success and failure in learning to read: The special case (?) of deaf children. In J. Oakhill & C. Cornoldi (Eds.), *Reading comprehension disabilities: Processes and intervention* (pp. 279–300). Hillsdale, NJ: Lawrence Erlbaum Associates.

Meier, R. P., & Newport, E. L. (1990). Out of the hands of babes: On a possible sign advantage in language acquisition. *Language, 66,* 1–23.

Neville, H., & Lawson, D. (1987). Attention to central and peripheral visual space in a movement detection task: An event-related potential and behavioral study—II: Congenitally deaf adults. *Brain Research, 405,* 268–283.

Slobin, D. I. (1973). Cognitive prerequisites for the development of grammar. In C. A. Ferguson and D. I. Slobin (Eds.), *Studies of child language development* (pp. 175–208). New York: Holt, Rinehart, Winston.

Swisher, M. V. (1993). Perceptual and cognitive aspects of recognition of signs in peripheral vision. In M. Marschark & M. D. Clark (Eds.), *Psychological perspectives on deafness* (pp. 209–228). Hillsdale, NJ: Lawrence Erlbaum Associates.

Index